YOUR CHILD AND THE ZODIAC

YOUR CHILD AND THE ZODIAC

Teri King

ANGUS & ROBERTSON PUBLISHERS

ANGUS & ROBERTSON • PUBLISHERS
London • Sydney • Melbourne • Singapore • Manila

First published by Angus & Robertson (UK) Ltd 1980

ISBN 0 207 95857 2

Book and cover design Steve Hogwood

Printed in Hong Kong

To three wonderful kids —
Deborah (Cancer), Justin (Pisces)
and Lindsay (Virgo). And to all
parents who retained their sense
of humour through parenthood.

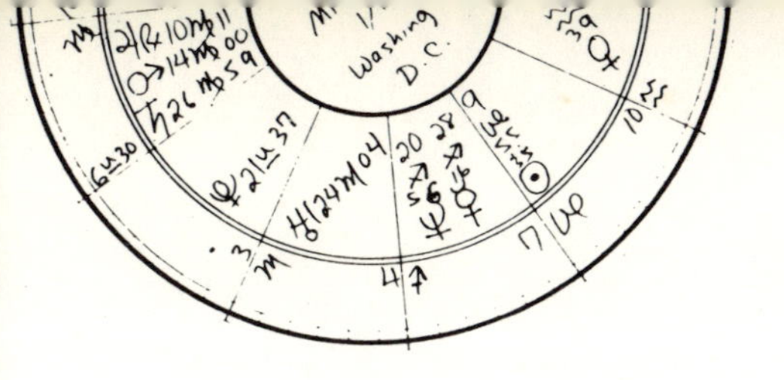

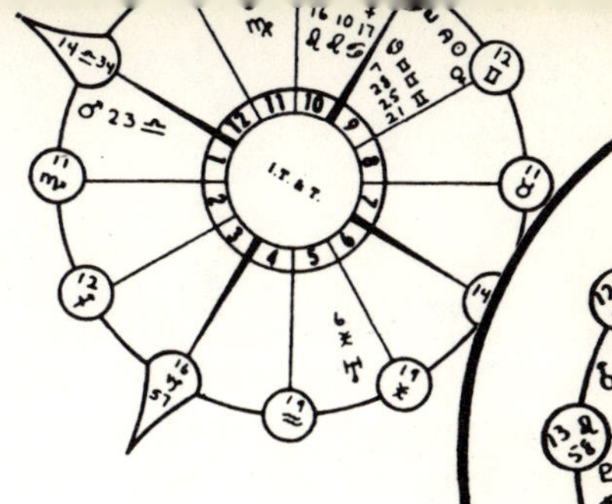

CONTENTS

INTRODUCTION

Astrology is a complex science that has of necessity been treated in a general way in the following pages. I should, however, like to discuss briefly the mechanics of the subject in an attempt to correct any misconceptions the reader may possess.

The cynic usually asks: 'How can a forecast for any zodiac sign be accurate for everyone born under that sign?' The obvious answer is of course that all horoscopes must be general unless the astrologer is able to work from specific details regarding hour, place and day of birth.

As an example, let us take a person born on 3 September. Broadly speaking he or she is a Virgoan, for the sun occupies that section of the sky known as Virgo between 24 August and 23 September, although this varies from year to year. We must also, however, account for the position of the moon, which enters a new sign approximately every forty-eight hours. It may have occupied Gemini on the day in question, and if so our subject would be a Virgoan/Geminian. (Here it must be explained that the sun rules will-power and feelings and the moon the subconscious, so our particular case will have the will-power of a Virgoan and the subconscious of a Geminian.)

Progressing further, we must consider the sign rising at the exact time of birth. This is an ever-changing process as it takes approximately two hours for each sign to pass over the horizon. It may be that Pisces was rising at the hour in question, in which case the subject's image would be Piscean. Now our example is a Virgoan/Geminian/Piscean. This procedure is carried on through all nine planets, each depicting a feature of the subject's make-up: their position, the signs they occupy and the aspects they form with one another all play an important part. Should an astrologer calculate and interpret these movements, then we would have what is known as a birth-chart. Due to the constant changes in the sky, persons sharing a chart are very rare, but it obviously happens when two babies are born in the same place and at exactly the same time. In this event, as both are given identical gifts, environment will be the deciding factor dictating which characteristics are used constructively and which destructively.

Returning to our example it will be noted that all three important sides to this personality are in differing signs, so our case is not a typical Virgoan. If, on the other hand, several planets had occupied Virgo, then our subject would have displayed all the true Virgoan traits.

Lastly, the quiz located under each sign will enable the readers to assess whether or not their particular child is typical of his or her sign. This is not as reliable as a birth-chart, but a considerable help to the parent.

Astrology should be used as a guide to character – its original and true purpose – and I believe no better form of character analysis exists.

It enables us to learn about ourselves, our friends and children, and once this information has been understood and digested it becomes easier for us to accept our limitations and those of others, leading inevitably to inner peace.

CAPRICORN

THE THIRD EARTH SIGN

Symbol The Goat

Colour Green

Metal Lead

Planet Saturn

Motivation To be a scholar, ambassador or scientist

Cautious; able to endure difficulty; responsible; melancholic; has a liking for solitude

GENERAL CHARACTERISTICS

Dr Jekyll: positive

The true Capricorn takes life seriously, is extremely ambitious and possesses the ability to adapt to almost any environment. These characteristics lead the Capricorn into *abnormal* industry. Objectives are rarely confused. He knows exactly where he is going. He can accept conventions and traditional customs more easily than any other sign, partly because historical values appeal and partly because he possesses an understanding of humanity – all its possibilities, its trials and its shortcomings. Therefore he is ready to admit a need for some kind of restraint.

The symbol of the sign – the Goat ascending the mountain – is a very appropriate one because it is always depicted as following the upward path. Every experienced climber knows that the beaten track is the safest road for those who desire to travel far, and that the attractive short-cut is generally an illusion. Capricorn will scarcely give the latter a glance. His reverence for those who have already preceded him and have already attained the heights to which his own soul is set is very great indeed. At times he may pause for a breathing-space and look backward, remembering with gratitude the resting-places and the guidance given in the earlier part of his journey. But he speedily resumes the climbing and continues until his goal is reached, after which his ambitions simply become more inclusive and embracing of the careers of others.

Capricorns like to remember special anniversaries and to make plenty of fuss about them. They are excellent hosts and hostesses. Appearance is all important: it is a real affliction for these types to appear anywhere in unbecoming or unsuitable garments. They rarely begrudge the time given to preparation for any great occasion. This tendency to give importance to externals affects friendships, as this inclines the Goat to cultivate people of superior social position, and to pay undue attention to those who are in the running. In short, one of the vices of this type is snobbery, which appears and reappears in many strange guises.

Happiness and achievement often come late to the Capricorn and a much longer and older prime is enjoyed than by any other sign. Many of them live until well over eighty, and for the most part remain hale and hearty. Perhaps instinctively, the Goat realizes this – hence that slow, slow climb.

Mr Hyde: negative

There is naturally another side to the coin and this character finds ambition a source of worry rather than happiness. It may be a splendid spur to activity but to onlookers it is only recognizable in the form of gloomy discontent and pessimism. Worldly success is often given a disproportionately large place in his life, and methods by which money and position are attained are not very closely scanned. Furthermore, when ambition is thwarted this induces discontent and gloom. There will be many occasions when friends and relatives will decide that here is the original manic depressive. In personal relationships this character has an intense desire to influence and manage, mother, direct, prod, wheedle or meddle in one way or another with the affairs of others. Naturally enough this tendency proves to be irritating to those around him. In his Mr Hyde form, the Goat can be summed up as an interfering manic depressive.

Is Your Child a Typical Capricorn?

Answer the questions honestly. Score three for every 'Yes', two for every 'Sometimes' and one for every 'No'. Turn to page 215 for the answers.

1 Is your child a pessimist?

2 Does he enjoy his own company?

3 Is your child careful to the point of being mean with his pocket-money?

4 Is your child overly serious?

5 Is concentration obsessive?

6 Is your child fussy with his wardrobe?

7 Was your child late in his physical developments – sitting, walking, etc . . .

8 Is your child a worrier?

9 Is your child patient?

10 Is your child obedient?

11 Does he take pleasure seriously?

12 Does he find it difficult to mix with other children?

13 Does he like a change in routine?

14 Is there an air of dignity about the child?

15 Is your child quite happy to go to bed?

16 Is your child self-pitying?

17 Did you have a particularly difficult time during teething?

18 Is your child determined?

19 Is it difficult to make the child laugh?

20 Does the child frown?

THE CAPRICORN BABY

Up to four years of age

If you are new to the parent game and have long ago decided that all babies look like the late Sir Winston Churchill, then under this particular sign you can enjoy the satisfaction of being absolutely right, for baby Goats look rather like senior citizens in their youth, but retain good looks when into old age.

There will be times when adoring parents are often made to feel uncomfortable with their Capricorn baby. It is extremely unlikely that they will be able to explain exactly why this is. Nevertheless, junior makes them feel rather ridiculous and stupid. If they are honest they will admit that their little angel makes them feel rather like children instead of parents.

For example, a well-meaning mother will say, 'Does my teeny weeny bubba want his nice wed twain?' And what happens? This bit of nonsense is greeted by a frown and a serious, thoughtful look. Mum won't be slow to get the message, for it is quite apparent that baby Goat is just beginning to wonder what kind of dummy he has for a mother! Because of this it shouldn't take long for parents to realize that this kind of baby-talk is strictly out.

The typical Capricorn child is self-willed and positive. But don't expect a big fuss when he starts transmitting his desires. There will be no temper tantrums or dramatic pounding of fists into your best cut-glass, but the little Goat will manage to communicate reactions quite clearly. This type is totally unlike the Libran and makes no attempt at charming anyone into helping him to reach a forbidden object. Just watch him. He crawls, drags and pulls himself with obvious purpose to the place he wants to reach. You could be forgiven for thinking that his manoeuvres had been planned, possibly while you were feeding him or changing his nappy. Now that the opportunity has arisen for him to fulfil his plans he is going to follow them through. Yes . . . this is an organizer, one who loves routine. Everything is kept in its own place and he will be quite disgusted if anything disturbs the system.

The best gift parents can bestow upon the Capricorn child is a sense of humour. For although the determination, serious attitude to life and a keen sense of responsibility are all to be applauded, your young Capricorn will be a lot happier if he can occasionally be made to see the funny side of life.

Health

Capricorn is ruled by Saturn, a planet whose effect is often felt health-wise in colds, falls and dental problems. It is important that the Goat be taught to clean his teeth as early as possible and this, together with a regular six-monthly trip to the dentist, should protect him from unnecessary dental problems.

As far as falls are concerned, prevention is the best cure and is, therefore, your responsibility. Safety precautions around the home must be observed, especially with regard to stairs. A toddler with a broken leg is a heart-rending sight and not very comfortable for the child. Try to do your best to avoid such unnecessary suffering.

Colds are always difficult to avoid, and again prevention is the wisest course. A visitor with a cold should be politely discouraged from going near your baby. If there is a cold in the family all should take extra care when approaching the infant. Wash your hands before feeding or handling him. Don't try to treat a new baby's cold by yourself; it is safer to first check with your doctor, who will make sure that the child's chest is not infected. Children often catch repeated colds when they first start at playgroups or school.

A child with a cold will breathe easier if propped up when going to sleep. Children should be taught to put their hands in front of their faces before sneezing, coughing, and so on. They should be able to take pride in doing this from about the age of two. Blowing the nose however is an ambitious skill that usually comes later.

Capricornians have highly sensitive tummies which are particularly upset by wind and flatulence. Never leave your little Goat crying for too long. He will swallow gallons of air and become even more distressed. Also, try your level best to bring up wind after feeding. Gripe-water may prove to be invaluable if your baby has difficulty in this direction. Many Capricorns suffer from a stream – nay, a torrent – of irritating illnesses, but they usually manage to avoid anything too serious.

Food

The Goat has the reputation for eating anything within reach and there is a certain amount of truth in this. However, this type does not consume mountains of food, he prefers a little of this and a little of that – a nibbler. Problems of nourishing this child are minimal, although parents are advised to discourage this individual from eating too quickly or from attempting to consume over-heated meals. Either will play havoc with that hypersensitive tummy. Furthermore, no matter how much pride you may take in your psychic abilities, reading this young character's mind will prove difficult. The Capricorn rarely shows his feelings on the surface. For example, he may frown at the meal placed in front of him, but does this mean that he is displeased? Not necessarily so, though you could be forgiven for thinking so. Life is a serious matter to the Goat and he is probably trying to decide whether to begin with the meat or the vegetables! This type must be organized. No haphazard attack for him. Therefore don't anticipate his actions with any kind of food; rather let the empty plate speak for itself.

Crying

The Capricorn infant is really a small adult and because of this he is extremely well behaved. He will tolerate an empty tummy or a wet nappy for hours longer than any other type. Regardless of how tiny he is, that little bundle seems to sense that you are doing your best and for this reason will be prepared to wait. However, don't take advantage of his good nature, for once the Goat decides that your are incompetent or untrustworthy he will yell fit to burst for simply everything.

Apart from the usual causes of upset – nappy, hunger, and so on – your young Goat can be a depressive character, and when under a black cloud he will positively wallow in self-pity. Try to make a point on these occasions of lifting his spirits and you will soon stem the flow of tears before they soak everything within a five-mile radius!

When eardrums are pierced by a high-pitched scream from those lips this indicates a windy tummy. A cuddle and a pat on the back should soon rectify the situation.

As previously stated, the Capricorn is a well-behaved child, so he is not undignified enough to show distress without a good reason, a fact to be borne in mind.

Teething

The Capricorn baby is far too methodical to cut his teeth in anything but the right order. Furthermore, the procedure is likely to be performed without as much as one sleepless night. But don't completely relax, for there are no happy mediums with the Goat. Either the teeth will pop through obediently and without pain, or he will suffer the full rigours of teething. It is quite common for this individual to develop tombstones instead of teeth and these through normal-sized gums. And there are unlikely to be any handy forewarning symptoms, such as a rash. The first time you will suspect that all is not well will be when your nerves are shattered at two in the morning. Unless you ask your doctor for help your Capricorn will scream himself hoarse until the procedure is over and done with. You will need to enlist as much help from the family as you can. A tired irritable mother can hardly give effective consolation to this little soul who believes his world is about to come to an end.

A green teething-ring may quieten him for a while but it can hardly be expected to work miracles. Only you and your doctor can relieve this infant – he certainly cannot help himself.

Bath-time

The Capricorn child will not splash and giggle with the same obvious glee as the Cancerian, or smile smugly like the Taurean, as the delicious smells and feelings of this ritual luxuriate around him. But do not be fooled, your little Goat is having the time of his life. Observe. Is not that characteristic frown threatening to disappear? And the flush. It is nothing to do with the heat. Yes . . . you've guessed it. This individual is tightly hugging his pleasure to himself. It is a misinformed parent who expects the Goat to behave in any way other than with impeccable dignity. Therefore, allow him to keep it intact. Never throw him into the bath with other youngsters. He won't be amused when subjected to witnessing their unbecoming antics. Always try to give him privacy and plenty of time. He may gradually allow you to share in his enjoyment, providing you can refrain from jollying him along into what you may consider to be a more relaxed and carefree attitude to life. It won't work. Concede to his individuality. This serious outlook on life may be difficult for you to understand but it is the only way to be when you are born under the sign of Capricorn.

Interests and Games

Once more the little Goat will be drawn to that which is undemanding physically and is above all else quiet. Yes . . . this infant is difficult to understand. There he will sit playing quietly with his bricks when Mum is clumsy enough to drop a saucepan. *Crash!* She mutters, not too politely, and bends down to retrieve the offending object. Suddenly she experiences a feeling of discomfort. She raises her eyes and they are met with a disapproving face. 'For Heavens sake, woman,' it seems to be saying. Before she can stop herself Mum mutters a guilty apology, only to immediately suspect that she is going mad. He couldn't have expressed his disgust in such an adult manner, surely? Yes, he could. After all, you won't catch your Goat creating unpleasant chaos so why, he thinks, should anyone else? Quiet games, then, that rely on patience, determination and imagination are the ones which will appeal. Bead-threading, brick-building, shapes to be fitted together into an object – all are ideal. Rag-books will fascinate, but don't expect him to enjoy a drum or to want to dress up in any way. The little Goat will be a good student later so any skill you wish to teach him will be easily learned if you begin early. Above all else try to spend as much time with him as possible.

Television can also be invaluable, providing it is not taken to excess and the volume is kept at a reasonable level. It is important that your Goat be shown how to appreciate the lighter side to life. Cartoons may bring a smile to his face, although the slapstick humour of Laurel and Hardy, for instance, will leave him cold. View with him and teach him to laugh with you and you will have taught this individual an important lesson: how to relax.

Walking and Talking

The Goat's progress is, wisely, always a step at a time. He will not attempt to walk while he is learning to talk. Therefore, do not betray your disappointment if he is still on his bottom at eighteen months. Instead take delight in the fact that his vocabulary is developing well. Encourage mental dexterity, while overlooking the physical lack of effort. You have a determined infant, and once walking becomes a priority there will be no holding him. But let your Goat decide just when that is going to be.

Toilet-training

In this area the Capricorn's sense of dignity works in the parents' favour. After all, he cannot remain cool and aloof with wet pants, or when he has just made a puddle on the floor! Therefore, you can be sure that as soon as it is humanly possible, or perhaps before, he will rectify what he considers to be this disgusting state of affairs! But do wait until he is at least eighteen months before introducing him to that strange plastic object known as a potty. Children can rarely control themselves before that age and you will only make him feel miserable if you try toilet-training too early. Privacy is a prerequisite in this particular instance. Don't plonk him on the potty in the presence of others. The less ceremony the better. A dazzling smile should reward success and indifference greet failure. These rules observed, he will amaze you with the speed at which he learns until he is completely toilet-trained.

Starting School

The casual, practical approach is the best when this all-important stage in life is reached.

'Mummy is going to buy a surprise present for you and do some shopping, but I'll be back later,' will be understood on the first day. Of course he cannot go along if you want to surprise him. Anyway, shopping is such a bore.

Steer well away from emotional scenes. Not that he will be perturbed, but he will be acutely embarrassed for *you*. How could you make such a display in front of strangers? Neither is there any point in telling him of the fun he will have with other children. This will not appeal until he has discovered it for himself. Besides, this little infant is likely to enjoy the activities on offer rather than the company, initially anyway.

On the following day you could tell him you are going shopping once more, or participating in some other activity which he dislikes. Then ask him whether he would prefer to come with you or go to school again. The chances are that he will choose the latter. If not, don't feel you are regressing if you allow him to skip school. It is wise to let your Goat feel that education is non-compulsory; the fact that it isn't will be accepted later. In the meantime he can be slow and he needs time to adjust. Gradually he will come to realize that you need time to perform various activities and he will be quite happy to go to school while he is waiting for you.

THE CAPRICORN CHILD
Four to twelve years of age

Health

Capricorn rules the knees. Injuries to this particular part of the anatomy can have repercussions later in life in the form of cartilage troubles. Therefore, if your Goat is a sporting type you will need to raise him to respect this particularly vulnerable part. When accidents do occur, obtain medical help instantly. Don't be embarrassed; better for your doctor to think you are being over-protective than your child to be crippled.

Dental care continues to be important. Ensure regular visits to the dentist. This is the easiest thing to do and the end results will mean less pain.

At this stage the Goat's nervous stomach may also be giving problems. This is likely to be inconvenient and irritating rather than serious. Flatulence may continue to bother, so try to ensure that he consumes food at a reasonable rate. The gobbler is sure to suffer. You can also be certain that any mysterious stomach ailments that appear to baffle the entire medical profession are the results of worry and tension. The sooner you discover just what it is that is worrying the child the better, and the ailment will soon vanish once its cause is out in the open.

The Goat is generally a healthy specimen, although most of his problems will be self-inflicted for one reason or another. Therefore, it is up to the parent to find out the cause of these problems, the child's worries and tensions.

Friends

The young Capricorn may be extremely anti-social on occasions, apparently in no need of companionship. This type really does enjoy his own company. He is also a rather suspicious individual and it takes time for someone to win his trust and approval. Therefore, don't expect a continual stream of chums – one or two are basically all he needs to keep him content. And if he is happy, surely that is all that matters? Don't worry about the love of solitude too much; he will emerge from it when he is good and ready.

Interests and Games

Interests and games of the Capricornian tend to be traditional rather than modern. *Tales of Yore* at bedtime will enthral, where *Science Fiction Adventure* will bore. Later the volumes of Charles Dickens will prove to be a much-loved possession. The Goat is fascinated – even obsessed – by the past and this will be reflected in televiewing, play-acting and choice of reading material. Should you combine such a preoccupation with a love of bargain-hunting then you have a child who will be in his element at jumble sales, markets or junk-yards. A browse round an ancient, dusty bookshop will enthral, as will metal-detecting at the site of a past battle. The latter will keep the Goat absorbed for hours, especially if this activity can be shared with the family.

A party-goer the Goat is not. Sticky buns and wobbly jellies do not set his pulse aracing. And jolly party-games are viewed with scorn. Therefore, never insist that he attends parties unless, of course, they are elegant dinner-parties. You have to remember that you are dealing with an adult in disguise – a fact to be always borne in mind. Forget about all the usual childhood treats such as the circus. The circus? Juvenile and cruel. Clowns? Decidedly unfunny. Sporting events? Too taxing. Pantomime, theatre, cinema? Now you're talking his language. Outings such as these allow him to sit in the dark and give full vent to his imagination. He's right up there on the stage or screen with the characters, especially if they should be portraying royalty or rolling back the centuries before his eyes.

Treat your youngster as you would an adult and this will help you to achieve some insight into his complicated mind.

Accepting a New Baby

The Goat has great difficulty in coping with a new brother or sister, and the greatest danger exists in his apparent outward acceptance. He does not display open hostility as would his Scorpian counterpart, nor weep and sulk like the Cancerian. Rather he hides doubt, hurt and uncertainty behind an indifferent, even frigid, facade and bleeds inwardly. Should a situation like this exist for longer than six months the Goat will become emotionally constipated. He is now so well practised in self-control that he neither knows when or how to let go – a tendency that could stay with him for life, and might later damage his relationships. Emotionally speaking your Goat is not as mature as he is in other directions, and he needs help.

Should you be congratulating yourself upon the ease with which you introduced your new infant into the family without so much as a pout or tear from your Capricorn, then stop. It is question time.

Is that real acceptance, or resignation? Is school work suffering? Does he now have nightmares? Has he regressed in his development? Should any answers be in the affirmative then your Goat is inwardly dying for help. Take some time out now before it is too late. Lose the younger child to a sitter or an obliging relative for at least two full days. Permit your Goat to stay at home. If he asks why, be honest. Give him a big hug and say that you want him to yourself for a while. However, don't take him on a special trip, for while he will love it it will make him feel even more acutely just how much more fun he could have had if that small object had not been brought into the family. Rather, treat him to favoured meals and play favourite games. When you sense that he is totally relaxed, make some attempt at real communication: school, friends, anything to start him talking. Once he begins to open up, ask how he feels about the baby. This will not be easy, for the natural instinct will be to hide true feelings. Gently refuse to allow this to happen. Quite suddenly and to your amazement he will become as passionate as the Scorpion and as vulnerable as the Piscean. Allow him to cry out frustration, anger and love. Once this has been done it will then be up to both parents to get him to freely express feelings in the future. Lots of love and displays of caring are the only ways in which this can be achieved.

Given time, this practical child will be able to put his fears in perspective. But don't let him bottle up precious emotions. Should he believe that you cannot understand him, he will bury them deep inside. Win his confidence and you will not be sorry.

Discipline

The Goat is one of the easiest children to discipline. He is naturally so well behaved, so sensible, that firm, well-meaning words will always fall on receptive ears, where hot bottoms will merely create resentment. Should he abuse your fair-minded treatment, remarks such as, 'Well, if you aren't as responsible as I thought, I shall have to treat you like a child!' will be guaranteed to make him sit up and take notice. The withdrawal of one privilege will make such an impression that parents are unlikely to find a second withdrawal necessary. He is sensible, shrewd and mature and therefore easy to rear. Proceed with confidence, give him responsibilities and he will not let you down. If he does, find out just what it is that is bothering him, for a disobedient, rebellious Capricorn has an axe to grind and he will use your heart for this purpose.

Sex

It is important that the advice given at the end of the book be followed. To avoid offering sexual education until your Goat is approximately ten only to follow this with an unexpected assault of the facts will only acutely embarrass him.

He feels he hasn't survived that first decade without learning something. Do you really think he hasn't noticed the difference between the sexes? If you haven't taught him anything, by now he will have a very confused idea of what is what and is probably well on his way to inhibition. Give him the emotional and physical facts clearly over the years, and later you will be proud of your well-adjusted teenager. Ignore this advice and you do so at his peril.

Homework and Study

When it comes to learning and studying, the Goat is surprisingly late in development, but he gets there a step at a time with dogged determination. He feels inferior to friends, so don't parade their virtues in front of him; he will only become depressed and may give up. Practical help is the most useful thing you can give. He will not have a tantrum if hopelessly lost, but observe the leaden, depressed face, that far-away look, and make a point of discovering just how far behind he is. Hire a tutor if you can afford to. If not, get into those books and help him. Show him that he can catch up, with time and effort. Eventually he will. Show him faith in his ability to catch up and, with your assistance, he will never let you down.

The Goat is ambitious and has a thirst for accomplishment. Put it within his reach and watch him go.

Finding a Direction

Your Goat will be slow to decide just which way he wishes to go in life, but if you want to help, eliminate that which he definitely does not want. As far as exams are concerned he will get there, probably a little later than most others. Encourage that financial ability – you may well have a businessman in the house. Allow him to accompany you when you are bargain-hunting; his talents may lie in wheeling and dealing. Nurture that love of the past by visits to the library and museum. He may become an historian or an antique-dealer. Any of these ploys will stimulate, for a Goat left to his own devices can become depressive and apathetic. If this applies, it is time for some action before he becomes the domestic Goat who tries to climb the mountain but is forever falling back down hill. Assist him in working towards his objectives slowly, a step at a time. Be patient and persistent. Your Goat will eventually climb to the top of his mountain. He will be at his best between the ages of thirty and forty, so it is never too late for him. Do not instil panic at the age of fourteen, for he has time on his side. Let him make use of it.

THE CAPRICORN TEENAGER

Twelve to eighteen years of age

Adolescence can be a difficult phase both emotionally and physically, especially where sex education is confused or ill informed. This period can have a psychological effect right through to adult-hood. Puberty need not be too dramatic if the changes that occur happen in an atmosphere that can encourage the right emotional development, not only the sexual knowledge. A teenager's preoccupation with sex and the problems that can develop from either fear, or expecting too much from it, can cause headaches for parents and children alike. These problems can arise from an upbringing where sex was emphasized by its very absence (inhibited parents), or where it was excitedly over-stressed (by parents who wished to appear open and 'with it'). The natural approach discussed in the chapter at the end of the book is particularly helpful when coping with such an unapproachable character. How unapproachable depends entirely upon yourself and your success or failure at an earlier juncture, especially in establishing emotional and mental communication. If you are being treated to the big freeze, you have failed. It is doubtful now whether you will ever be able to penetrate the glacier at this late stage.

The Capricorn teenager is a worrier. He wonders whether he is good looking enough, clever enough. Will he ever grow any taller, lose that extra weight? The list is endless and each worry is a cry for reassurance of a practical nature. If he is too fat, then suggest a sensible diet. Not attractive enough? Then show how to make the best of what is already there. The more interest you show the closer will be your relationship. Indifference or intolerance will result in a Capricorn who is competing for the manic depressive of the year award! Furthermore, one with a good chance of winning!

This type may also prove to be something of a social climber. You won't change him, so don't try. Ideally, assist. Dancing, tennis, even elocution lessons will delight your Goat. You may not approve but this may well be what he needs. And he will get it – with or without your consent. This particular teenager is complex and sometimes impossible but not beyond average intelligent parents.

Dating

When it comes to the opposite sex the Goat is a late developer. Your Goat will attempt to attract the attention of a much-exalted god or goddess and as with all else the Goat proceeds a step at a time. No unwise teenage marriage for this character. Despite the fact that the first date will probably be the first love, your Capricorn will be in no hurry to tie himself down. This type is ambitious and has much to do before he gives up his independence. Nevertheless, prepare for regular heartbreak. This individual is not a born Don Juan and each new relationship has a special meaning for him. No point in telling him to be less serious. Be ready with tea and sympathy. You may give advice, but only when it is requested.

It takes time for all of us to learn about our emotions, our wants and our needs and this is very true of Capricorns.

Alcohol

With alcohol, again much depends upon the depth of your relationship. The Goat likes a drink – sometimes to excess. Problems may arise whenever he goes through a particularly depressive phase in life, for when the Goat cannot cope there is a real danger of alcohol being used as an escape. It is therefore worthwhile for parents to concern themselves when their Goat is low, nervous and worried. Try to become the bottle, just as you were when he was a baby. In this way you will minimize the drinking. Don't expect him to stop completely though. Capricorn is not a teetotal sign. Besides, with any luck, the tendency to late development may postpone his initiation and therefore save you from any early worries.

Drugs

The taking of drugs is *not* a Capricorn tendency. Later he may take the occasional sleeping-pill when under stress, but he would much prefer a drink, providing there is one around. As a teenager he may be vaguely curious when confronted with marijuana, but the Goat is not an experimenter, and the typical member of this sign will not give parents a moment's worry in this direction.

Besides, even if he should decide to take the occasional drug he possesses an iron will and he could drop any tendency to its becoming a habit whenever he feels so inclined. There must, on the law of averages, be one or two Capricorn addicts, but the odds are so great against it that generally parents can relax.

SUGGESTED CAREERS

The Capricorn needs security and a regular pay-cheque. This should be kept in mind when choosing a career. Any attempt to 'get rich quick' would be unlikely to appeal and it should be discouraged if it does. The Goat should always try to make steady progress, for in the long term the sky is the limit. By hook or by crook he usually reaches the top of his profession.

He likes fame and being in the public eye. His career can be so important to him that all else is excluded. Therefore, encourage him in any direction he chooses.

The following are strong possibilities:

Civil servant	Teacher	Builder
Mathematician	Engineer	Architect
Politician	Farmer	Surveyor
Osteopath	Mineralogist	Dentist
Scientist	Musician	Administrator

The Capricorn may even take his rock-climbing seriously and become a mountaineer.

AQUARIUS

THE THIRD AIR SIGN

Symbol The water bearer

Colour Electric blue

Metal Uranium

Planet Uranus

Motivation To seek the truth

Independent; detached; unusual; opionated; inspired; scientific

GENERAL CHARACTERISTICS

Dr Jekyll: positive

The Aquarian has a way of looking at life's problems from the outside rather than from the centre. Instead of trusting others he watches them, earnestly, patiently and carefully, scrutinizing their words and actions and if possible even their thoughts. Surprisingly he is also conscious of his own shortcomings but is not happy when others attempt to dissect him in his motives. Yes . . . the Aquarian is a far-reaching seeker of the truth. His attitude to the world is kindly and humane and he will go to any amount of trouble to increase the comfort and well being of those around him, finding great satisfaction in devising simple pleasures for others. Charities and societies whose concern is with the poor often find Aquarians to be willing contributors.

However, both Jekyll and Hyde spend a good deal of their time putting their feet in their mouths. The Aquarian simply cannot help himself. He is constantly getting into hot water through asking tactless and direct questions about the feelings and actions of others. He seems to lack intuition and cannot rest content until he has reached the heart of any mystery. He is often very disappointed to find that the hidden treasure didn't amount to much anyway, and quite apt to add insult to injury by naively expressing his opinion to that effect.

Aquarians are also full of eccentric ideas. They may suddenly decide to take up skate-boarding, meditation or joining the peace corps! Their dreams are different from other peoples' and, no matter how close others may attempt to get to them, those born under this sign always remain vaguely and elusively out of reach.

Mr Hyde: negative

The wonderfully broad-minded Aquarian is distorted here, for his vision has grown too wide, thus creating inefficiency. Practical considerations are totally lost in confusion and, although this character will know there are many things that could be done, deciding where and when to start is something he is incapable of doing. Opportunities are lost through wavering and time is wasted over trifles. Difficulties are blundered into through lack of tact and consideration. The power of concentration is almost non-existent. On top of all this, the worst type of Aquarian can frequently be accused of cowardice. Mr Hyde tends to dislike unpleasantness and will do all in his power to avoid it. Romantic young girls looking for a knight on a white charger will need to look elsewhere, for at the first puff of smoke from the dragon's nostrils the Aquarian Mr Hyde will be conspicuous by his absence.

Is Your Child a Typical Aquarian?

Answer the questions below honestly, scoring three for every 'Yes', two for every 'Sometimes' and one for every 'No', totalling your score as you go. Turn to page 216 for the answers.

1 Does your child mix easily with children of his/her own age?
2 Is he totally trusting?
3 Have you noticed a streak of cowardice in your child?
4 Does your child regularly attempt to give his toys away?
5 Is the child determined?
6 Do you find the child detached?
7 Would you say your child is eccentric?
8 Is your child oblivious to the time?
9 Is your child free from jealousy?
10 Is your child always truthful?
11 Is your child optimistic?
12 Is your child's voice gentle?
13 Does poor circulation bother the child?
14 Does the child tell Daddy if you tell fibs, Mummy?
15 Is the child inquisitive?
16 Does the child have difficulty distinguishing between tidiness and untidiness.
17 Is your child constantly experimenting?
18 Does the child have a weird sense of humour?
19 Does the child have the bluest eyes you have ever seen?
20 Is the child disinterested in cuddly toys?

THE AQUARIAN BABY

Up to four years of age

Naturally, every parent believes his child to be special, unique or somehow different in comparison to other children. In this case they are probably a hundred per cent correct. There is absolutely no strict code of behaviour for those born under this sign. Both boys and girls can be calm and docile on the outside but a sudden sharp wind can turn and they will be totally confused and irritable. As soon as this character is out of his cot you will find him absorbed in experiments of one sort or another. Buy him a shiny red car for Christmas and he will turn it upside down and use it as a boat! Give the Aquarian girl her very own cooker and before you know where you are she is using it as a bookcase! There is no point in expecting children of this sign to conform, and parents who expect them to do so are in for a considerable amount of heartache – not to mention frustration. The mind combines uncanny perception and sharp, probing logic. Stir it all together and there will be occasions when you can later expect to be acutely embarrassed by your child!

When Mummy's friend appears after a three-week stay in hospital this little individual will enquire, in a loud, clear voice – 'Why are Aunty's boobs bigger now, Mummy? They weren't like that before she went away!!' Should your next-door neighbour pop in to borrow the shears to trim his hedge don't be surprised when that voice makes itself heard again – 'Who was that yellow-haired lady in your car the other night? Why were you cuddling? It wasn't your wife, I know her!!': Yes . . . the Aquarian will pursue the truth in the face of all opposition. The fact is he doesn't recognize opposition even when he runs head on into it. Bear in mind that a parent caught lying will lose the respect which had been given unquestioningly up to this point.

Popularity is enjoyed by this type, but the main cause for concern may be his detached and seemingly unaffectionate nature. But this child loves in his own way. Friendship and the sharing of interests are substituted where a kiss and a cuddle is needed by another more sensitive child. It may be possible to teach this child warmth by example, providing this is not overdone.

Health

Aquarius rules the blood, so sluggish circulation is fairly common among members of this sign, and if your infant is the possessor of constantly cold hands and feet you would be wise to pay a visit to the doctor. Also, check the elastic on baby-clothes, especially on mittens and bootees. If it is too tight replace it immediately. Your young Aquarian's blood needs to flow without restriction. A well-balanced diet will also help to keep this type healthy, for it is this baby who will be the first one to suffer from anaemia, especially if the diet is lacking in some way. However, at this stage in life your Aquarian should be getting most of the vitamins needed from the breast or the bottle, and the remainder can be extracted from fruit juice or regular doses of rose-hip syrup. As the Aquarian grows, do try to plan the diet carefully and always include foods that are rich in iron.

Usually the Aquarian is a healthy specimen, and common children's ailments are avoided altogether or thrown off effortlessly. (See the chapter at the end of the book for symptoms of child ailments.)

Food

The Aquarian child is worth his weight in gold nappy-pins when meal-times arrive. He is not fastidious and is therefore easy to please. Neither is he excessive, so that unlike his Taurean or Cancerian counterpart he is rarely likely to suffer health hazards brought on by over-weight. Nevertheless, there is one basic rule that must be observed. Few of us eat absolutely anything – we all have our idiosyncrasies and your child is, after all, only human. Possibly he will be revolted by the sight of, say, eggs. If so, do not attempt to coerce him by telling him that he will not grow into a big, strong lad without them. Remember, this is the truth seeker, and it is not going to take your Aquarian long to work out the stupidity of such a statement. Once this occurs the child will quickly decide that he has been lumbered with an idiot for a parent. Should the refusal of meat, eggs or milk cause you concern then check with your doctor. He will no doubt inform you that your child, if necessary, could grow big and healthy on plenty of water, bread, cheese and the occasional apple. He is also likely to say that most babies of the western world are over-fed anyway.

Allow your Aquarian baby to have some individuality, refrain from over-loading his plate and he will not give you a moment's concern at meal-times.

Crying

This infant's wails do not shatter your best crystal or your eardrums at twenty paces – not without a very good reason, anyway. The Aquarian is neither possessive nor in constant need of displays of affection. He believes the best of others, so he feels that of course you love him and are doing your very best. You would have to be pretty heartless and incompetent before he would change his mind. Apart from the usual reasons for distress – a wet nappy, hunger, and so on – Aquarians can also add hyper-sensitivity to temperature to this list. Naturally all young babies can be upset by excessive cold and heat, but room temperatures are particularly important to the young Aquarian. During the first year this baby needs a warm room both night and day, preferably 65 to 70 degrees fahrenheit (18-20°C). You may be a fresh air freak but it can be dangerous to this young baby.

The Aquarian may not be demanding but do try to coddle him in the aforementioned directions.

Teething

There's no point in expecting your unpredictable Aquarian child to cut his teeth obligingly by the baby books! He may cut the bottom teeth first, the back before the front, or he may not have a tooth in his head until he is fourteen months old. But what does it matter as long as they finally arrive? Besides, your Aquarian has not read the baby books, so how is he to know just when he should be cutting his first molar? However, when the moment finally arrives the expected symptoms are a rise in temperature plus a rash. He may also be distressed, but the typical member of this sign may look as if he is threatening to give you a hard time, but his threats rarely materialize. Such an infant warns you about the forthcoming events and then blithely waits for you to rally round and help. However, if teething proves to be unusually painful and you are unable to relieve it in any way then he will decide that you are completely incompetent and yell in an effort to inform the rest of the world of your ineffectiveness! So don't suffer in silence for too long: call in the nurse.

Bath-time

It really doesn't matter at what time you bath the Aquarian baby. This is a flexible individual, one who enjoys minor changes in routine. Do bear in mind that the temperature of the water is all important to this baby. Never allow your Aquarian toddler to sit in the water until it is almost cold. Conversely, over-heating should, of course, be avoided. Basically this infant has an empathy with water and his feelings towards it will not change unless you give him reasons to have second thoughts. Observe all safety precautions and this will not occur. The sharing of a bath will be greatly enjoyed, but should this be your only child plop him in with mum or dad. This will not only be enjoyable for him, but it will also help to cement relationships. The Aquarian is not in the least house-proud, so water games should not be allowed to go to extremes. If they do you will regret it later.

Interests and Games

All preconceived ideas about young children's games and interests can be thrown out of the window when considering the Aquarian child. Nursery rhymes and fairy stories may send his Piscean, Taurean and Cancerian counterparts into ecstasies, but not the Aquarian. Tradition leaves him cold. This doesn't mean he doesn't need fantasy, but it has to be of the right variety. Fairies do not excite unless they are the type who inhabit some far-away planet, walk on their heads and live exclusively on nuts and bolts, for example. Dressing up will be a bore unless it is a space-suit with full kit, but cowboys, knights in shining armour, or nurses do absolutely nothing for him.

Games with a sense of logic can be utilized and will stimulate, whether they be various kinds of puzzles or the placing of shapes inside one another or into some container. Maths will appeal later, so at this stage your Aquarian can be amused with any kind of counting or number games.

Bear in mind this child's truth-probing instinct, for because of it any game or story which helps him to distinguish between truth and fantasy is recommended. Be prepared to be constantly surprised by your Aquarian's interests and try to share in as many of them as possible.

Walking and Talking

As has been mentioned, the Aquarian is a seeker of the truth, but one who can hardly conduct a third degree when only verbally in possession of several variations on baby noises. Obviously a full vocabulary is therefore desirable; the sooner the better as far as he is concerned. Once your little Waterbearer has mastered the obligatory 'Mamma/Daddy' he gathers confidence and grasps the rudimentary rules of the language in record time. Once this happens you should take a crash course in science for, thus armed, you may just be able to answer those penetrating questions with which you will later be bombarded.

A word of advice; when stuck for the correct answer don't make up a reply, no matter how creative or witty. Your Aquarian will store such information and use it as ammunition later. Naturally, with all this mental activity gcing on, physical development may suffer. Observe your Aquarian; the experimentor should be clearly identifiable. It may be that he is happy to answer his own questions by utilizing some kind of physical action, such as touching, even if it does result in destruction. In this case it is quite possible that he may walk first though this would be unusual.

Toilet-training

The easiest way to train the Aquarian is by example. Once he is old enough to understand that the lavatory or the potty is the way to tackle his wet nappy problem, and that the rest of the family have solved the same problem in an identical fashion, he will be happy to conform. Make the most of this, for it is probably the only time he will. But do not imagine for a moment that perching him on the potty at the age of six months will do the trick. Any result will only be accidental. He cannot control either his bowel or bladder until at least eighteen months, and you will be letting yourself in for a further year of falsely raised hopes and disappointments if you are too premature. Therefore, wait. The Aquarian will take this stage of development in his own stride. You cannot push or coax him.

Starting School

Parents can use the weeks preceding that all-important first day at school to their advantage. Occasionally adopt a blank expression when subjected to a battery of questions, but don't overdo it. Occasionally utter, 'Oh . . . I don't know, but we'll ask your teacher as soon as you start school.' Also, curb any drama, or your Aquarian will smell a rat. The object of this exercise is to arouse the curiosity even before school begins. This accomplished, he will itch to actually experience this new, exciting part of life. His need to acquire knowledge, together with the fact that the Aquarian does not cling, should mean that your child will be able to take school as a natural progression. Aquarians love to meet and mix freely with other people, so the chances of his standing alone for longer than five seconds are remote. Naturally, if his mother is going to cry and clasp her infant to her bosom the emotion is sure to affect the child, filling him with confusion and conflict. So keep calm, let your baby go — he's not going to change overnight. Your Aquarian needs other in order to grow and function normally.

THE AQUARIAN CHILD
Four to twelve years of age

Health

Blood disorders continue to be the area that demands plenty of attention. Inspect and clean injuries thoroughly and, if they do not heal within a reasonable period, go to the doctor. Don't run risks of blood-poisoning. Also, keep an eye on diet, making certain that it is well balanced. If anyone is going to develop anaemia it is going to be the young Aquarian.

Poor circulation could develop at this age, too. Continually cold hands and feet, perhaps tinged with blue, are symptoms not to be disregarded.

As Aquarius also rules the calves, protection should be provided during sports. Football in particular can play havoc with this part of the Aquarian's anatomy.

An alert parent will ensure a healthy, happy Aquarian.

Friends

Your Aquarian may conform to the various stages in his development, but this is the only concession he will make to convention. He sees no reason at all why Christmas cannot be celebrated on 25 June or why he cannot have his birthday-party in December, despite the fact that he was born in February! Not surprisingly, other children are attracted in droves to such an eccentric character. The Aquarian's tendency to experiment continually with life is also appealing to young children. They want to share in his ideas and listen to those crazy plans. They may not understand them and very often children of his own age will be in awe of him. Because of this they are quite happy to concede leadership to him.

Furthermore, the Aquarian is a good friend and should someone be in difficulty he will be there in a flash to assist. However, help is always given in a rather detached manner. This makes other children grateful but intrigued. They soon learn that anything is liable to happen around an Aquarian. As a result this child is never alone, and never lonely.

Interests and Games

What interests an Aquarian? Anything. There is nothing which, at some time or another, will not come under his scrutiny in his bid to uncover the truth. A good deal of time is spent doing favours for friends – he will rescue a pal from a soaking in a pond, bring him home to dry off, place the wet clothing in the cooker for this reason and discover later that the garments have burned to a crisp! The Aquarian is quite likely to arrive home with his best overcoat wrapped around a shivering, sick bundle which turns out to be a flea-infested stray dog. On such occasions parents will not know whether to laugh or be angry, but they had better make up their minds – and quickly. These situations occur with alarming regularity.

The Aquarian has idealistic dreams and perhaps the thought of being a missionary dedicated to a cause will appeal. Conversely, a scientist suffering deprivation in order to find a cure for cancer might be of interest. All Aquarians dream. They may grow up, but the first dream will always be with them somewhere. Oddly enough this character can sometimes realize those dreams simply by concentrating upon them with a heart full of hope.

Reading-matter for both sexes will centre around science fiction, or science fact. The Aquarian boy will spend hours making solutions with his chemistry set – the girl may be located in deep thought somewhere in the house; Mum may be highly delighted if she finds her in the kitchen, and could be forgiven for thinking that her daughter is considering a female occupation such as cooking. But don't be fooled, Mum, for, quite suddenly out of the blue, your hopes will be dashed to the ground. Young Aquarian daughter announces that she thinks she has invented a way of mixing an egg before the shell is broken! What can you do?

Encourage your child's involvement in invention. You never know, for your Aquarian could well develop a device that could make him or her rich and famous. Not that such an individual would notice the money – he'd be on to the next invention.

All group activities appeal to the Aquarian, providing there is a common goal. Later your child could be a tireless charity worker; give the Aquarian a cause and he'll dedicate himself to it.

Accepting a New Baby

A new baby? What new baby? The chances are that your Aquarian hasn't even noticed one. This is perhaps an exaggeration, but don't expect the Aquarian to give the new baby much thought. Your first born may cast a paternal or maternal eye over the new arrival in order to check that you are looking after it, but once satisfied that you are in control of the situation you will be on your own. This type won't offer assistance unless an emergency arises. Should this occur your Aquarian will be efficiency personified. Because of this it could be an idea to contrive the occasional panic, if only to remind your Aquarian of the baby's existence. Later, when the new infant begins to walk and talk, your Aquarian will take an interest, for here is a friend in the making. Once this stage has been reached, you will lose both of them, for the younger child will follow big brother or sister everywhere.

Aquarians make ideal big brothers or sisters, providing you can wait for them to assume the protective role when they are good and ready.

Discipline

Certain problems are specially applicable to the Aquarian. Picture this: an Aquarian child goes to the shops for some milk. Half an hour – one hour – two hours elapse. Panic! The child's mother rings the police, the hospitals and her husband. Suddenly the door opens and there is the erring child smiling sheepishly. Apologies – he hadn't realized the passing of time and had finished up the other side of town!

Worrying? Yes, but what can you do apart from buying an enormous dog, one that can be trained to bring home your daydreaming Aquarian occasionally.

The Aquarian doesn't mean to hurt or worry you, and he isn't really being naughty, so it is difficult for you to scold. However, you should be quite certain that you can trust this child in traffic and that he knows how dangerous it can be to converse with just anyone. Your Aquarian must be taught to organize his thoughts into some sort of order, or the potential genius will be lost in eccentricity. Encourage physical action, or hours will be wasted daydreaming. Also, there are many occasions when he will take the path of least resistance. Explain then how he is kidding himself, let him take decisions and act upon them.

Unspoken tension will disturb the Aquarian for he can read your stifled utterances. Displeasure then must be aired, discussed and forgotten. You must remember that you are dealing with a truth seeker. So give it to him. This way your Aquarian will always retain respect for you and you will be more than three-quarters of the way towards bringing up a responsible adult.

Sex

The Aquarian is rarely, at any stage, obsessed with sex, either physically or mentally. However, it will distress him quite considerably if he believes himself, or his knowledge, to be deficient in some way. Here again the truth – the whole truth and nothing but – is essential. Once in possession of the facts he will concentrate interest elsewhere. Any preoccupation with sex is a sure sign of uncertainty. Follow the advice given in the section at the end of the book and you will raise a well-adjusted adult. So it is a case of forgetting inhibition, or tales of the stork. The latter will only convulse the Aquarian anyway, and the thought that you have treated him to nonsense will result in hurt feelings and insult his adequate intelligence.

Homework and Study

Teachers may complain that your Aquarian's gift of self-expression is somewhat lacking, for he cannot explain how he arrives at some amazing answers to difficult maths problems, for instance, before the teacher had even finished chalking it up on the board. The answer is one that a mere mortal, such as the teacher, cannot possibly understand. The Aquarian mind was sparked off by some unseen wave which took him through the problem so quickly that he is unable to explain in a step by step process. Some call it inspiration, and this is the only practical way of describing it. Your Aquarian probably has a poor memory and concentration, and he cannot study when there is too much distraction. Homework periods should be set at a special time each day. He could be allocated a remote niche in the house, and while that brain is whirring he will appreciate the absence of his parents, working best in an atmosphere of peace, quiet and harmony. With these ingredients he will be happy to work; without them the only thing he can do effectively is day-dream.

Finding a Direction

To keep that inspired mind in top gear it is necessary to steer the Aquarian away from physical laziness or he will, as already stated, waste his life dreaming. You should therefore encourage some kind of sport. This applies regardless of the sex of your child. Dancing lessons could be the answer, especially if your Aquarian shows a complete lack of stimulation.

Mentally your Aquarian needs a hero or heroine, probably a dedicated person who helps humanity. Buy or borrow books on the same personality. And if you have the time you should read them yourself, for in this way you can converse with your child about the particular idol. The next requirement for all Aquarians is a cause. It may be a charity, such as raising money for the local church hall, although it is more likely to be raising funds for the Third World. Later he will take practical steps to help the world, either by taking part in its politics or becoming a scientist or inventor, for instance. There may be times when parents will feel that perhaps this individual should pay more attention to those in his own backyard, but the Aquarian cannot find his interest in this way. His concern is for the whole world.

Visits to exhibitions dealing with space travel and science in general will also appeal. But don't expect him to go into ecstasy when confronted with a bed that Henry VIII slept in, or any other antique for that matter. History and antiques belong in the past and this is a child of the future.

Bear this in mind and you will not only be able to understand him but offer the valuable support that is needed.

THE AQUARIAN TEENAGER
Twelve to eighteen years of age

The typical Aquarian teenager's usual choice of wardrobe makes parents suspect that he or she has just escaped from the influence of Dr. Frankenstein. He or she picks up on any current weird trend and adapts it, usually making it appear even more weird. One week this character will resemble a demented old English sheepdog who has recently fallen into the sheep dip, the next he looks particularly elegant. However, this is probably the only phase in life when your Aquarian's appearance will give you some indication as to what is going on inside that eccentric head. What are you to do when confronted with such visions? The answer, in a word, is nothing. Interfere, mock or chastise and you will prolong this phase; indifference will cut it short.

It's perfectly true that your teenager could wander into an important dinner party displaying newly dyed green hair to shock what he might describe as your bourgeois friends, but remarks such as 'I didn't know the circus had hit town' or an embarrassed rush towards him in the hope that you can reach him before your friends catch a glimpse of his eccentricity is not the way. Try instead – 'You know, darling, I can't help feeling that bright green really does not go with that cerise shirt or dress, but it's different. Just give me a couple of weeks to get used to it'. In this way you will have made it perfectly clear that you are not in the least bit shocked, merely wish to help him or her make the most of the newly acquired brilliant locks.

However, if incidents such as these do not lead you into cancelling various social functions then perhaps your Aquarian teenager's natural talent for faux pas will. Picture: Boss and wife happily seated at your house in front of a delicious plate of Profiteroles when in strolls your Aquarian teen. He states – 'Middle aged people really should be more careful with their diet, then they would be slimmer, younger and wouldn't constantly need to keep dieting or be embarrassed when sitting on a beach like a bloated lobster' – whether the boss or his wife are dieting is beside the point! The fact is your Aquarian teen has made it quite clear that they need to. If you cannot handle this situation what will you do when your teen proudly informs the party that – 'Isn't it incredible . . . Mum only looks 35, but y'know she's pushing 42!' Naturally, you will smile and blush, but in the end you are quite likely to decide that the only time for dinner parties is when your Aquarian is many miles from home.

Faux-pas and bizarre wardrobe aside, what else can you expect? Your Aquarian will be prone to ideas and inspirations that are beyond the scope of other more normal people. You will need to take him seriously however, for among that hopelessly impractical stream of suggestions is likely to lurk a grain of genius. How can you set those ideas down into some logical and understandable order? Be a friend. Gently point out that although the plans are good they lack sensible presentation. Teach him this, ignore his often bizarre appearance and, unlike many parents, you will not lose your offspring at this sensitive time in life.

Dating

Dating to this character is not to be confused with romancing. What it means is simply being friendly. So you'll have to control your reactions when your son brings home a nightclub stripper or your daughter asks the local undertaker to tea. Display horror, nag or criticise and your Aquarian will fly to the defence of his friend and may, for the first time, consider romance.

People fascinate the Aquarian. He helps, befriends and learns from them. Attempt to do the same and you'll earn his undying gratitude and respect. Romantically and sexually this type is a very slow starter. You mean there is some difference between the stripper and himself? 'Oh that,' he will say, dismissing the thought before it has had a chance to take root. Eventually your teenager will no doubt become attached to a member of the opposite sex, but initially they will simply be friends. Friendship always take priority over romance, and parents may find this a little hard to grasp. But it is a fact. You cannot change an Aquarian and, if you try, all you will acquire is a rebel. Let your waterbearer grow and develop in his or her own way.

This type is a sucker for causes, particularly lost ones. You cannot prevent him from waving a placard under your nose so you may as well discover what it is that is overheating his adrenalin. The Aquarian wants his parents to be friends, just as he would anyone else.

Alcohol

Aquarians may embarrass parents with a tendency to state the unvarnished truth, they may surprise with their clothes, but they will not attempt to walk all over your dining-room table while drunk! The Aquarians' appetities are, possibly, the only moderate things about them. The Aquarian may drink to be sociable but he is not a budding alcoholic, so lectures on the demon drink are quite out of place. Set a good example yourself and your Aquarian will not give you a moment's concern in this quarter.

Drugs

The Aquarian may possess a slight preference for drugs to drink, but again it is unlikely to go to extremes. An Aquarian drug-addict is a fairly rare occurrence. He may try them to be sociable, and he may even attempt to discover some source of truth through them, but he is an intelligent individual. He realizes that the elusive truth is as far away as ever and will rapidly lose interest.

Keep your eyes open and your nose at the ready. If you suspect that your child is experimenting, don't lecture or panic. Ask for his impressions. The Aquarian will wish to discuss them with someone and it may as well be you. At least you will be fully aware of the situation. It is easy, of course, to give advice, but a calm and interested attitude will see your Aquarian through a couple of months of experiment which will soon pass and will not be repeated unless you force him into rebellion.

Suggested Careers

Independence, originality and scope for inventiveness must be used by the Aquarian if he or she is to be happy in work. Dull routine will bore. This type can do a dull job, but will be wasted in it. Given his or her head they are capable of great invention and will bring a fresh approach undertaken.

Occupations that may appeal are:

Scientist	Astrologer	Radiographer
Writer	Astronomer	Inventor
Sociologist	Archaeologist	Air Force or
Charity worker	Industrial worker (ie, TV)	United Nations

PISCES

THE THIRD WATER SIGN

Symbol The Fish

Colour Sea green

Metal Tin

Planet Neptune

Motivation To interpret

Versatile; emotionally sensitive; idealistic; easily influenced; strong artistic and religious feelings; lacks concentration and a grasp of practical affairs

GENERAL CHARACTERISTICS

Dr Jekyll: positive

Pisceans are difficult to analyse, being very complex human beings. They are indifferent to limitations and restrictions provided that their inner selves are free to dream, feel and grow according to their own natures. They do not compete in the rat-race and dislike competition and rivalry. They are attracted to the sea, to writing and to anything that will permit them to create when free from pressure. It is quite common for these types to enter the entertainment industry, where they can use their gifts of interpretation. Experiencing great satisfaction when slipping into another identity, they also are at their best when interpreting this in front of an audience. Those born under this sign are receptive, emotional and contemplative and, despite the fact that others may construe their gentleness as weakness, Pisceans possess a strong inner being together with a heart filled with inexhaustible love for all living things.

They have no prejudices and they refuse to judge other people until they have mentally changed places with them. Even when this operation has been completed they will understand and not pass critical judgement. The true Piscean is short on cold, blunt accusations but long on warm tolerance.

Mr Hyde: negative

These individuals are totally unable to make decisions or exercise any kind of discrimination in their life. Friends rush around like demented wildcats, desperately attempting to rescue them from the frying-pan, only to discover that they have leaped, feet first, into the fire. The root of the problem lies in their receptive powers which are generally far too susceptible. They can listen to one person and act on his advice, then change direction after receiving more advice from another. Naturally enough it is easy to understand why these Fishes all too often tend to drift through life in a sea of trouble. Such Fishes are also prone to strange antipathies and attractions which they make no effort to control. Their desires for their own secret world are stimulated by over-indulgence in alcohol. This, together with a certain degree of bad luck, seems to prove that either a Piscean swims high and is good, or swims low and is bad.

Financially speaking these characters can only be described as inept. Totally unable to budget, forever up to their necks in debt and sparing little or no thought to discharging their creditors. The charming and sensitive side to the Piscean is distorted and used for his own end; this type usually makes a successful con-man.

Is Your Child a Typical Piscean?

Answer the questions honestly. Score three for every 'Yes', two for every 'Sometimes' and one for every 'No'. Turn to page 216 for the answers.

1 Is the child secretive?
2 Does the child seem to be constantly thirsty?
3 Does the child suffer from short, but deep, depression?
4 Is the child cowardly when faced with unpleasantness?
5 Does the child's fantasy world get out of hand?
6 Is your child torn in two directions whenever a decision is necessary?
7 Is your child a hypochondriac?
8 Is the child fond of animals?
9 Does your child enjoy his or her own company?
10 Is your child hypersensitive?
11 Is your child a nervous chatterer?
12 Is your child frightened of water?
13 Is the child jealous?
14 Is the child sensitive to the feel of soft fabrics?
15 Does the child cry easily?
16 Do you believe there is something mentally elusive about the child?
17 Does the child have strange likes and dislikes?
18 Does the child suffer from nightmares?
19 Does your child cling?
20 Does your child frequently tell lies?

THE PISCEAN BABY
Up to four years of age

As soon as you set eyes on your Piscean baby, there is no way you will ever believe that he or she is real. No, your child quite clearly came from some mythical place. The magic may almost have disappeared, but not quite, for it glistens in that silken hair. It is possible that you have been foolish enough to think that, once you have tended and cared for your little one for a certain amount of time, you may be able to get that dreamy look out of his or her eyes and mould him into any shape you like. After all, he seems so sensitive, gentle and fragile. But stop – right there! The young Piscean can get what he wants from life just as effectively as a proud Leo, the determined Capricorn or the little Taurean. The only difference is that tactics vary. This individual achieves his ends by charming his parents and drowning them in oceans of angelic smiles and affectionate gestures. Parents have been known to murmur 'Why do small children have to grow up into nasty adults' – and that wish may be granted! This is the original Peter Pan, and the passing of years hardly seems to leave an impression.

This type is always dreamily magical and possesses a quality of make-believe. No matter what you say, such a little character believes that life is all mystery, fantasy and adventure. Parents will need to harden their hearts occasionally to persuade a Piscean that this just isn't so, but never overdo it for if you do the child will retreat into his fantasy world, close the door and lock you out forever.

Health

The Piscean baby makes it easy for parents to believe that he must have been found under a toadstool. These types are typically frail and almost ethereal in appearance. It is this that makes parents handle such an infant with the utmost care. Fortunately, the Fish is rarely as fragile as he appears. However, this sign does rule the feet and bad influences on the natal chart may result in slight deformities to this part of the anatomy. A twisted foot, a toe which looks for all the world as if it grew as an afterthought are all possibilities. Tummies may be disturbed and food poisoning and allergies may develop later. Because of this it could be useful for parents to be well acquainted with the symptoms of food poisoning. They are sudden vomiting, diarrhoea and stomach pains. Inform your doctor immediately any of these symptoms appear; he will prescribe the necessary treatment. Don't experiment with remedies yourself.

The Piscean's emotions match his physical appearance and, when a Piscean is deeply upset, they can react adversely on health. This type needs gentle love and a harmonious environment to remain hale and hearty. Despite this, refrain from treating your infant as if he were made of crystal. This is an intuitive type, one who will sense any apprehension which would worry him. Besides, he is tougher than he looks so do not be fooled.

Food

The important thing to bear in mind with food is that you are dealing with a fish, so plenty of water is needed to avoid dehydration. Liquids are readily accepted but solids can be difficult to introduce in the diet. Your Piscean may therefore be a little late in this direction. The Piscean appetite ranges from average to impossible, but never excessive. As this type's preferences are closely tied in with mood, meal-times can be sheer agony. Poor mother will serve a meal that was last week considered ideal and consumed with relish, but which is now greeted with a flat refusal. To make matters worse the Piscean is easily upset. Mother, not surprisingly, can become rather exasperated while the baby dissolves in tears. To avoid a Piscean breakdown right then, force feeding, threatening behaviour or anger are strictly out. To minimize mum's exasperation the best thing to do is to present the meal and to take it away if it is refused and unacceptable. Eventually your Fish will learn that if he doesn't eat when he can he will have to go hungry. This type is not an idiot and he will not starve to death. However, it will help if you can remember that Piscean babies live life upside down. They may sleep all day and stay awake all night, or may only eat when they are hungry and sleep when they are tired. Unfortunately this may not fit in with your routine, but training him into it is quite a task and you may as well adjust your routine to his, for while he may not throw a tantrum, he will somehow or other get his own way in any case.

Another useful fact for frustrated parents: the Piscean has a keen sense of the ridiculous and is a born clown. If you are similarly inclined the feeding situation could be eased considerably. The more you are able to act the fool at meal-times the more the Piscean will relax and the greater his appetite will become. Tell him, for instance, that the peas will be upset if he doesn't eat them, that if he listens he can hear the cabbage asking him to be consumed and you may make some progress. Any talents you possess as a ventriloquist will come in handy. The Piscean loves to be fooled and he also appreciates a funny mother.

The mood at meal-times should thus range from indifference to slapstick comedy; try the heavy hand and a mental block will develop. The situation then becomes impossible and, not only that, will probably continue for the next ten years.

Crying

When expressing or communicating distress the Piscean gets all the prizes. This type can sob for thirty seconds and make it seem that he has been neglected for at least three hours. In a split second the expressive eyes fill and overflow with big, wet tears. The face breaks out into a blotchy rash and, just to complete the picture of misery, your Fish will dribble with the efficiency of the Niagara Falls. Parents needs hearts of stone to ignore this character for he can consume you with a vast amount of guilt. He will cry torrents for all kinds of reasons, a wet nappy, hunger, thirst, sickness and so on. Mostly this type will sob his heart out for extra affection, and be warned that the little Fish can never have too much of it.

When you have eliminated all the obvious causes for upset and ladled out lots of love and the little Fish is still wailing, then consider one obvious fact. That Piscean child just isn't sleepy – yet. Tiny babies do not know night from day; they only know they get hungry about every four hours. Why not try singing your Piscean to sleep? Rocking the cradle? Conversely you can leave the radio on quietly and wheel him backwards and forwards for a little while.

Whatever you do *don't* take a tiny baby into bed with you. It is easy to fall asleep and either smother the child or push it out of bed on to the floor. Don't expect the Piscean to fit in with convention – that is the last thing he has on his mind.

Teething

Pisceans are average in this stage of development, although you can be quite sure that they will make the most of the situation. This is another excuse to extract some extra affection and the little Fish will not let such a chance slip by! The first symptom of teething is sure to be oceans of saliva, and the constant wearing of a bib is going to be necessary, quite possibly for you both! Everthing is going to be soaked, clothes, cot and you. A runny nose may also be added to the flood. Read the section at the end of the book for further advice, give lots of love and it will not be necessary for your infant to scream for attention. Do this and you will both emerge a good deal wetter but closer.

Bath-time

If there is one thing in life the Piscean adores it is water. Hot or cold, the Piscean doesn't mind, just give him lots of it! This individual needs a daily bath, not because of that constant dribbling, wetting and crying but because the Fish anticipates that daily dunking. Soap, however, isn't part of the deal, so be wise and purchase sting-free bubble-baths and shampoos. This done, your infant will continue to enjoy bath-time. Now a warning: *never* leave the Piscean unattended, for as soon as he is strong enough he will make a bee-line for the taps. Even if he manages to avoid being burned by the hot tap, your child is not yet at the age to understand that it is possible to overfill a bath.

Interests and Games

Any games that an inventive parent can develop which utilizes water can be guaranteed to bring a smile to the Piscean. Toy tea-sets filled with water, a plastic bowl with soapy water to wash socks or dolls' clothes . . . this may be messy but what bliss your Piscean will have. This individual has the most vivid imagination plus a sense of the dramatic, so he leans heavily on fantasy. Such a child may well create his own language or give life to inanimate objects like a simple spoon, a scrap of rag or a teddy bear. He creates voices and personalities for them all. Fairy stories are also a source of wonderment and a dose of fantasy should be administered at bed-time. The Piscean must, however, be taught the difference between truth and fiction, although this is not possible at such a young age. The Fish's sense of theatricals often leads to a love of dressing up, and applies to both sexes. Reading-material filled with magic adventures will encourage an interest in reading that otherwise may not be there. Concentration is not good in the Piscean so don't labour the point too much.

Keep a tight rein on television viewing, as it takes little to upset the Piscean. A short but sad piece of music can instigate a flood of tears. And the sight of violence or some much-feared monster will lead to troubled nightmares or prey on the imaginative brain. Watch him carefully and at the first sign of distress switch off. The right kind of play will help your Piscean grow into the sensitive, creative person he is meant to be; the wrong kind will encourage neurosis.

Walking and Talking

Pisceans possess a strong inner life and are therefore more mental than physical characters. Talking may be well developed long before the Fish starts to crawl and walk. Naturally the presence of other children will affect this individual, perhaps more than most. The Fish has a heart filled to bursting with love, and he will totter adoringly around after an older brother or sister. Without such incentive your baby Piscean will be quite happy to sit observing the activity around him.

Such an infant's preference for his own language may mean that he will prefer to learn speech with unbelievable complications. Take a simple, uncomplicated word like car. Firstly, it may be 'babbum' then 'bam' and a little later 'gar', finally becoming 'car'. Parents will wonder if such a state of affairs will ever lead to coherent speech. Strangely enough, as soon as he discovers a more satisfactory way of flexing that imagination, he becomes quite eloquent.

Toilet-training

The important thing to remember with toilet-training is that your Piscean wants to please you. The Fish is never *deliberately* naughty and is naturally well behaved, so accidents are just that – accidents, and as such they do not warrant punishment or anger. In fact, either will distress this sensitive character to the extreme, resulting in floods of tears for a considerable time. When eventually you start training, ideally around eighteen months, make it a game in any way that you can devise. In this way the Piscean will actually look forward to the experience, especially if he is rewarded by an extra dose of silliness. Failure should be ignored. The fact that you are silent is sufficient to make the point to this intuitive infant.

Generally speaking, free from pressure the Piscean learns quickly. Therefore you will do yourself a favour if you take toilet-training easily and with a sense of humour. Better still – a sense of the ridiculous.

Starting School

Leaving mother will be a traumatic experience for Pisceans and half a day at school is infinitely preferable to a whole day at least for a few months. Emotionally, the Piscean is as sensitive as the Cancerian, so the procedure set out in this section in the Cancerian chapter is recommended reading.

THE PISCEAN CHILD
Four to twelve years of age

Health

Where illness is concerned the Piscean seems to deliberately go out of his way to be unconventional. Put your little Fish in a room crammed with children infested with chicken pox and he will emerge spotless. Prepare a chicken paprika for your infant only to discover later that he has broken out into an angry red rash. Scarlet fever? Shingles? No. He is allergic to paprika. The parents of the Piscean should hesitate before diagnosing a rash: leave it to the professionals. Let them inspect your Fish on all occasions. It is all too easy to confuse one rash with another and a professional eye is needed for identification.

As previously mentioned, Pisces rules the feet, and infections and ailments to these parts are fairly common. You can expect a stream of irritating diseases such as chilblains, athletes foot, corns. . . . Choose wisely when purchasing shoes and this will help to minimize this tendency. Healthwise, expect the unexpected and don't expect the more usual illnesses. By doing this you will become acquainted with the right way to approach the Pisces and his illnesses.

Friends

The Piscean child does not, like the Leo, make a dramatic entrance into a room full of children and take over. Neither does he win friends and influence people with a razor-sharp wit. That particular talent is reserved for the Geminian. The Piscean is shy and nervous when confronted with strangers. Nevertheless, other children are attracted to this type. They sense the natural Piscean gentleness and kindness. Friends are therefore made slowly, and invariably for life. When the Fish gives love or friendship it is complete. He will stick loyally through fire, flood and pestilence. However, this character is instinctively selective, and loud, cruel or bullying children will fill him with horror. He is drawn to those as sensitive as himself or to those who can make him laugh. Extra caution is advised when accepting party invitations, for he will be reluctant, even nervous, about attending unless one or two of his special chums are also to be present. Furthermore, there will be some children in your neighbourhood who are bound to intimidate him and the infant will not thank you should you insist on pushing him into their company. Permit this child to sift through any invitations. Never apply pressure, nor demand. He will probably be a social butterfly. Simply welcome that small selective band of friends into your home and leave the rest to him.

Interests and Games

The Piscean needs to be free to grow and develop and express himself in his own way, and the arts often assist him in this particular respect. Pisceans usually love to paint, dance, write poetry or play an instrument and it is important for both their mental and emotional development. Discover which appeals and encourage it, perhaps arranging specialized tuition. Nijinsky was Piscean and so is Nureyev. Fathers should not scorn or discourage a Piscean boy who wishes to take dancing-lessons. The Fish is not sporty and no amount of bullying will change this. However, if your particular Piscean's chart is a good one then he will adore water and all kinds of water-sports. But if that Pisces is afflicted and there is an acute fear of water, love and encouragement *may* at least teach him to swim, if only a little – a wise move for obvious safety reasons. However, don't push the point – nor him into the water. Fantasy and a sense of the ridiculous will continue to absorb the Piscean at this age. Walt Disney must have had the Piscean in mind, for his films are avidly consumed by this child.

The Piscean also needs a pet. It may only be a goldfish, but it will be the best-kept and most-loved fish for miles around. The more love-objects in his life the better.

If your Piscean child still refuses to give up his comforter, be it an earless rabbit or a piece of smelly rag, don't worry. He'll give it up one day – possibly when he is twenty-one! But don't remove it without permission.

Keep those bed-time stories flowing – that hour at the end of the day is important to both him and your relationship, for it enables you to establish contact daily. This must be good, for the Piscean child is naturally secretive, so these moments are invaluable for the unburdening of problems. Later, when those teenage years arrive, you'll be glad you kept communication lines well and truly open.

Accepting a New Baby

Because the Piscean is so sensitive and ready to enter into a fantasy world at the slightest provocation, his acceptance of a new baby needs careful handling. Initially the new infant is greeted with a heart full of love and arms ever open to give affection. Because of this parents may be fooled into premature self-congratulation. They regard themselves as understanding and loving parents giving extra love and attention to the first-born child. Then why does your Piscean child become so impossible a year or so later? The answer is that parents may be unconscious ever of placing a time-limit on the careful nurturing of their Piscean, probably because he seems content. After all, raising two infants can be time-consuming. Parents should ask themselves whether their Piscean is still enjoying the attention he had had when he was a single child, and also during the six months following the birth of the second child. If the answer is in the negative then that is the reason for those delayed tantrums, sulks, nightmares or withdrawal. But fortunately, no matter how objectionable the Piscean may appear to be, that sensitive and loving heart is never far away and with patience the situation might be rectified.

First make a point of taking your Piscean out on regular little trips without the new baby. Once a month is sufficient, but do make an occasion of them. Secondly, once the baby is settled for the night accompany your Piscean to his room and spend half an hour with him, reading, playing or talking. Lastly, allow this little character to help with the new child. The symptoms of unrest and conflict are easily recognized in the Piscean. Secrecy, regression or withdrawal should not be ignored. Lots of love, together with the advice given here, will soon put a smile back on your Piscean's face.

Discipline

Whether to wallop, beat or smack is the question. The answer is *no*. The Piscean is terrified of violence and in most cases a raised voice is sufficient to send him taking refuge behind the nearest piece of furniture. But he doesn't listen when I attempt to talk sensibly to him, his mother cries. True. But think again. When exactly did you attempt to establish communication? At mealtimes? In the middle of a cartoon on television? Remember that it is difficult to make contact with this type and to attempt to when any kind of distraction is around is totally impossible. Save words of wisdom and advice for the appropriate time, namely, just before bed-time. You are alone, the television is silent and all friends have departed. Try it and you'll notice the difference. Remember the Fish is never knowingly naughty or hurtful, and if he appears to be so then your child is attention-seeking. Answer the call and remedy the situation.

Sex

If you are going to stick your head in the sand and refuse to discuss sex until your Piscean is about ten then he will not only be completely shattered but will resent this intrusion of reality into his world of fantasy. Somehow Walt Disney and sex are just not compatible, and the facts may even be rejected.

Certain truths must never be confused with fantasy and sex is one of them. Follow the advice given in the section at the end of the book and you will raise a sexually well-adjusted Piscean. Allow him to twist the facts by leaving his education incomplete and hoping that school friends will finish it off for you and his sexual fantasies will literally take root and may later lead to unhappiness and perversion, i.e. he may not be able to function without the use of pornography. The responsibility is the parents'. Do the child a favour and give him *all* the facts of life.

Homework and Study

Concentration is one of your Piscean's biggest problems, this plus the fact that he can never decide where to start. In order to assist with the first problem do provide a quiet niche somewhere. Here peace and lack of distraction can be located. Also, discover exactly what has to be done to help him through it, finding a clear format. Furthermore, make yourself readily available for advice and brain-probing.

Allot a time of day for study and eventually this individual will reluctantly accept that between six and seven pm is homework time and that he may just as well get on with it.

Finding a Direction

Before a Piscean can even begin to sift through his interests and find the correct road in life, he needs one thing: the ability to make a decision and stick to it. At this age the Fish cannot decide even whether to don a coat or an anorak, shoes or boots. This character will always waver, but how much sometimes depends on his parents. The Piscean needs to be brought up to be accustomed to decision-making and the earlier parents start the better. Restrict the choice of decisions, initially, to two. Once this has been mastered step them up to three, and so on until the child can make up his mind almost immediately. It may be a long process but it is an important lesson for the Fish to learn.

By the time your Piscean approaches the teen years you should have some idea of his more hopeless areas in life. If you are still unsure of his actual talents, don't worry. Should you decide that your Fish will never learn mathematics then discard any interests or careers that are likely to rest on him gaining a grasp of this subject. Refrain from insisting that just because his father is a financial wizard, he must be; it doesn't follow. Having accepted his weak points, try to discover whether he is artistically or scientifically inclined. Your Fish may not be a Picasso or André Previn, but he needs an art form in order to find peace. Therefore, encourage any inclination in these directions. This will later reward him if not with a career then at least with a hobby. Besides, he may just turn out to be a famous painter or conductor. Many Pisceans also become vets, so if he displays a detached but strong affection for animals allow him as many pets as is feasible and buy books on their care.

If you still draw a blank after trying almost everything, then you have one of those unambitious Pisceans. There are some and, in this instance, you have no alternative but to stifle those ambitious plans for your child and try to understand that this one is not interested in knocking himself out in an effort to get to the top. Give a lesson in economics and attempt to make him understand that work usually means money, and he may just as well do something he enjoys. Pushing a Piscean where he doesn't want to go is like fishing with a hole in your net: he keeps swimming out.

The Fish has no natural ability with money. Educate him from an early age and budget pocket-money. Once he reaches the age of fourteen, extra money will have to be worked for. This way he will learn that money means work and instead of drifting he may later realize that he has to pay his own way.

THE PISCEAN TEENAGER

Twelve to eighteen years of age

The Piscean's gullability and sensitivity can mean a traumatic adolescence, and Pisces girls especially need a certain amount of protection, although this does not mean smothering them.

When the Fish is depressed he will be really low and you will need to lend an ear and a shoulder on many occasions. It is also important that you attempt to find the reasons for this melancholia. The root cause may be laughable to a sophisticated adult, but laugh at your peril. Once ridiculed the Fish withdraws and you will have lost your teenager's trust for good.

Encourage daughters to make the most of their femininity. Female Pisceans are certain to be budding beauties with natural grace, but you can be quite certain that they don't think so. 'Look at these awful freckles . . . pounds of fat . . .' they wail.

What about the male Piscean? Observe. He will turn a beautiful shade of pink or develop a stammer in the company of strangers. He too despairs, though in this instance it is likely to be a lack of beard, etc. Problems like these weigh heavily on the not-so-broad Piscean shoulders and they are just as important as the parents' mortgage payments, wrinkles or lack of promotion. Give confidence whenever and wherever you can. Complete sex education without over-stressing it and you will be doing your best.

Dating

I do not believe that dating at twelve and sex at thirteen is either healthy or desirable for young teenagers and this is especially true of the Fish variety, females in particular. Water signs possess such complex emotions that they cannot possibly hope to understand them at such a young age. A boy of fourteen is basically hoping to learn and to appear more mature; a girl desires romance, and sex in the back of a car with some callow youth hardly qualifies and will break her heart. However, it is necessary to add a rider here. For once she has matured, perhaps around eighteen, then there must be no distinctions between the sexes, in the meantime she needs a chance to discover those varying emotions. Only time can aid her in this direction.

The Piscean teenager of both sexes is romantic in the extreme, although somewhat timid and shy. They arouse paternal and maternal instincts in the opposite sex and this in itself may delay premature promiscuity. Parents should avoid destroying romantic notions while at the same time emphasizing that it is quite possible to be attracted to one person by a sense of humour, another by physical attributes and yet another by intellect.

Help your teenager to understand his emotions, teach contraception and explain the possibilities of veneral disease. However, should your Piscean launch into a sexual affair before the age of sixteen, then don't preach, it is too late. Instead, be a friend and purchase bulk supplies of tissues, you are going to need them when the affair goes wrong.

If your Piscean is still disinterested in the opposite sex at the age of sixteen, do refrain from applying pressure, as this would only encourage him to feel that he should be raving around as the various media suggest and that there is something wrong with him because he isn't. Your Fish will swim out into the open when he is good and ready and not before.

Alcohol

Naturally the Piscean is attracted to liquids, so if you were hoping to have reared a teetotaller, then you will need to go back to the beginning and start again! Nevertheless, heavy drinking before eighteen isn't typical unless your Piscean wishes to court disaster in later years. Should drinking at a young age occur, discover just what particular sorrow or problem he is trying to solve. The Fish tends to ease pressure or escape from it by drinking alcohol. Obviously, a happy teenager is not a regular drunk and shandy, watered wines and cider are quite acceptable around the house at sixteen and ideally this should be the limit. Once your Piscean leaves home he is out of your control, but while under your roof certain rules should be observed. Besides, your Fish loves you and he doesn't wish to upset you unless he feels you are the type who is always upset about something.

Parents of teenagers should reserve recriminations and tears for serious problems only, not for minutiae. This way your Piscean will understand that he has really hurt you and that you are not angry or being neurotic for no reason.

Drugs

The advice given above also seems to cover drugs quite adequately. The Fish is not naturally drawn to drugs, although he may be when under extreme pressure. It is a possibility to be contemplated that friends may have led your gullible teenager to experiment, and one or two attempts with soft drugs will not do any lasting damage. However, should the situation get out of hand it is time he found a new and different circle of friends. Suggest that he join a club, maybe a musical or artistic one. This will enable him to meet new friends and with any luck he may then drop the undesirables of his own free will.

However, keep matters in proportion. The occasional smoke at a party will not lead to addiction, although naturally enough regular 'highs' need looking into. While he is in your home you have a perfect right to object to his home-grown marijuana plants! This is against the law in any case, and a police raid isn't everyone's idea of excitement!

Despite these warnings the Piscean is unlikely to become addicted, so try not to worry excessively about something that may never happen.

SUGGESTED CAREERS

The Piscean should not, in principle, contemplate a career in which noise or discipline play too great a part. However, he will accept the discipline of life in the nursing profession. Should the Fish become a professional dancer, he will find himself able to become part of a company and work well within that discipline because he has the capacity to mould himself to his work. Generally speaking the arts form the core of the Piscean personality and he is rarely drawn to the sciences. Suitable Piscean professions are as follows:

Actor	Fishmonger	Hypnotist
Dancer	The shoe trade	Illusionist
Writer	The navy	Photographer
Poet	Nursing and the medical profession	The Church

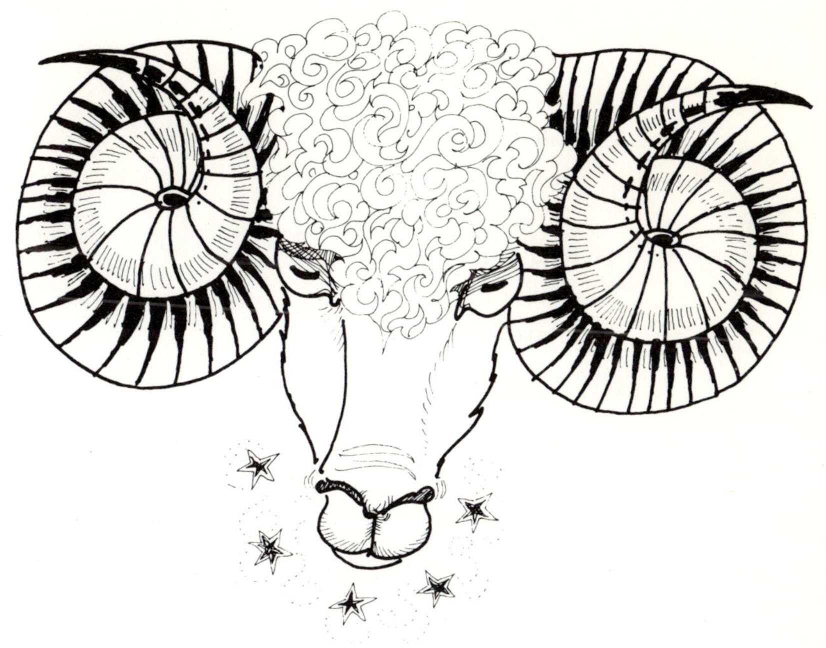

ARIES

THE FIRST FIRE SIGN

Symbol The Ram

Colour Red

Metal Iron

Planet Mars

Motivation To fight and pioneer

Assertive; sexually vital; energetic in personal and professional life

GENERAL CHARACTERISTICS

Dr Jekyll: positive

Arietians positively burst with energy. In fact no one could be more enthusiastic or pioneering. Their desire for action is strong, and they need a job where they have a challenge, although they are more comfortable as leaders than followers. They are forever in sympathy with new thoughts, ideas and ways of life. They are go-getters whose enthusiasm is so great that they can inspire others to go along with them. They expect to achieve plenty in life and push ahead in an independent fashion. As a result, this type not surprisingly frets considerably when forced to take a subordinate position.

Arietians are full of enterprise, energy and ambition. Provided these characteristics are projected wisely, it can only be a matter of time before they climb to the tops of their own particular ladders. Rams are always hopeful, no matter where life takes them and, luckily for them, they have a happy knack of forgetting failure. Will-power is strong, but ideals can be extreme and a critical attitude needs to be adopted towards them. Those born under this sign are all or nothing people, disliking compromise whether it exists in professional or personal problems.

On the personal side of life love and friendship play an important part, and the same impetuosity and ardour goes into it. They are frank in showing affection – in fact they find it difficult to restrain themselves once deeply aroused or committed. Love is a sort of Tarzan and Jane affair, with lots of fun and games and a constant struggle for domination. However, when happily mated they can remain loyal and faithful, though this can take a considerable length of time. Many relationships are tried and tested before the Aries finds the right partner.

Mr Hyde: negative

When Arietians are frustrated in their professional lives and ambitions remain unrealized, their hopes and enthusiasms are replaced by fickleness and restlessness. They are forever engaged in some new project or idea which is rarely, if ever, taken through to any kind of conclusion. They often bring failure on themselves by rushing headlong into situations that require tact and thought. Past mistakes are rarely dwelt upon and the same situation therefore arises again and again. Enterprises are abandoned as soon as the going gets tough.

To a Ram this is the easiest way of solving problems. It doesn't matter how much loved-ones point out that one cannot progress in life unless some road to success is followed; these reckless and impulsive characters are simply not listening.

In love they rush in and out of relationships as often as other characters change their socks, and when involved with the wrong mate they become unbearably selfish. Their plans, ideas and thoughts are the only ones that count. They can be exasperatingly intolerant, thoughtless, selfish and demanding. These characteristics emerge whenever Arietians are thwarted in any direction. There is no time for sentimentality – they have no patience for such trivia and ignore birthdays and anniversaries unless, of course, that anniversary or birthday happens to be their own! In this case they sit, optimistically, hoping for the most.

In relationships, whether as lover or friend, there is no point in expecting to change the Ram. Neither should one hesitate if it comes to discarding him. His memory is short and by the time he has woken up after the event, the departed lover is completely forgotten.

Is Your Child a Typical Aries?

Answer the questions honestly. Score three for every 'Yes', two for every 'Sometimes' and one for every 'No'. Turn to page 217 for the answers.

1 Does your child have a pink complexion?
2 Is your child frustrated easily?
3 Is your little ram bossy?
4 Is your child accident prone?
5 Is your child affectionate?
6 Does the child dislike water or bathing?
7 Does the child dislike taking orders?
8 Is your child impulsive?
9 Is your child impatient?
10 Is your child arrogant?
11 Is your Arietian short tempered?
12 Does he adore physical exercise?
13 Is he generous?
14 Is the little ram adventurous?
15 Is he a fighter?
16 Does he try hard not to cry?
17 Do you detect a sense of urgency about the child?
18 Is your Arietian a positive character?
19 Is he given to exaggeration?
20 Is he full of good ideas?

THE ARIES BABY
Up to four years of age

While proud father is wetting the baby's head and mother is unsuccessfully trying to disguise her post-natal blues with a smile and the dark circles under her eyes with heavy make-up the reason for her strained behavior will probably be screaming itself more scarlet with every passing second. Even more probable is the fact that junior will be in the room next door hopefully out of earshot. The baby Arietian rarely stops demanding attention. How could you just walk away from him? Who's the boss around here anyway? There is, without doubt, only one answer to that: your seven-pound baby, that's who!

There are going to be many occasions over the next month when mother in particular is going to wonder why on earth she ever bothered to have a baby. And she will probably vow to herself that it is going to be the first and the last. That is, of course, until the baby Ram gives her that first gummy grin. Then she is hopelessly lost. The best she can do is to go on a course of vitamins and get help when she feels most desperate. Ideally, to cope with the Arietian infant one needs patience, mechanical ability and strength. As this probably doesn't apply to most people, read on.

Health

Aries rules the head. The head is, of course, vulnerable in any baby, but in the Aries child particular attention and precautions need to be taken. Furthermore, the child is usually accident prone and this doesn't help matters much, particularly where heat and sharp objects are concerned. You will need to be on your guard against injuries to that small head and face. Whatever you do keep sharp objects out of reach and watch out for burns and scalds. There is no point in screaming, 'Don't touch!' Anything forbidden naturally becomes more exciting. The best thing is to try to anticipate trouble. A safety guard on the cooker is a worthwhile investment with this infant because the steam from saucepans is going to be a source of fascination to him. Where there are open fires, whether they be gas, electricity or coal, always fix a fire-guard and never drape clothes over it. If you use a paraffin heater always make certain that it cannot tip over, that it is properly guarded and placed well away from draughts.

This type is also particularly sensitive to colds and as we are dealing with a Fire subject don't forget that it may take some weeks before breathing and temperature are back to normal. This baby needs a constant room temperature of between 18°C (65°F) and 21°C (70°F). And don't think he needs airing, like a dog, in all weathers; he doesn't. He should be kept indoors when it is very cold or foggy or very hot and humid. The Arietian baby dislikes and reacts against intense heat too. That sensitive head of his is likely to get sunstroke far quicker than any of the other zodiac signs.

Ears can be another source of problems. Again, take preventive action. Many babies have soft wax in their ears, and this can be gently wiped away with a piece of cotton wool as it appears. *Never* poke in babies' ears with anything stiff or sharp as this always causes some damage. If there is a runny or smelly discharge or one that looks blood-stained, don't hesitate and take the baby to a doctor immediately.

Poisonings are another Arietian health hazard. When your little Ram begins to toddle it is important that all poisonous substances, cleaning fluids, bleach, and so on be locked away well out of reach.

One last word – you may well find that the Arietian baby in particular runs a temperature at the slightest provocation. In some cases this can be caused by excitement but do not wait if further symptoms develop. Fevers, too, are a health hazard to baby Aries.

Food

If you have any doubts about your Arietian's impatience, short temper or the assertion that he is the boss in your house, your doubts will disappear at meal-times. As soon as your Ram is big enough to sit in his high chair he will scream and throw the nearest object, possibly at you, if you desert him for too long or his dinner isn't placed in front of him immediately! When it comes to content, the Aries will leave you in no doubt about his preferred foods. His likes and dislikes are very apparent. Remember that there isn't a diplomatic bone in his entire anatomy. Try coaxing this child into something he doesn't want and he will spit it out, pick up the offending meal and place it on his head, or yours!

There are several important things to remember. As with all babies, one should be very particular about cleanliness and sterilization. It won't take much to infect this little character. Always follow the instructions on tins or packets to the letter. It will also save you a great deal of aggravation if you can arrange to have meals and bottles ready five minutes before the young Ram starts to scream. A child that has been screaming itself hoarse for five to ten minutes is quite likely to either lose its appetite or fill itself up with wind. Furthermore, this little Arietian dictator will not take too kindly to sloppy foods which tend to make a mess. Surprisingly enough, the Ram dislikes messy clothes and appearance.

As far as routine is concerned the Arietian is the boss and he won't let you forget it. There is no point in trying to foist your own routine on to this child as he will have other ideas about that. You may as well give in to him and save yourself a whole load of aggravation.

Crying

Babies cry for many reasons, at first mainly from hunger. You soon realize your little Arietian has different cries which mean different things. Boredom, for instance, often produces cries of frustration. Then there are the little tuning-up cries which mean that the baby has woken up and it is close to feed time. With this you won't get too much warming up, not with the Arietian baby – he goes into full throttle in a matter of seconds. Then again there are the rhythmic bouts of crying associated with colic, or the wails of diappointment when baby Ram is laid to rest and he doesn't want to be. In spite of what most books say on this subject, when you become a mother for the first time don't feel inadequate should you not be able to distinguish one cry from another: you'll soon learn.

Each baby expresses itself differently and, whereas one zodiac sign will be furious when left unattended, another will be quite happy on his own for a reasonable length of time. The Aries baby shouts the loudest when he's wet or teething. Again you must bear in mind that you are dealing with a fire sign, and he doesn't like this wet stuff! Some people will advise you to let the child cry for a while. The problem in this case is that the Aries baby has such a bad temper and it doesn't take him long to get into a very distressed state.

However, there is one compensation connected with an Aries baby. It always *knows* why it is crying, and it is always for a good reason. Because of this, don't be afraid to give an extra cuddle here and there thinking that you may spoil the child. This type rarely cries out of loneliness. For a while he will enjoy his own company, but should a favoured toy or comforter be out of reach then it is the end of the world and unless you are deaf there is no way you will be able to escape from that piercing, shrieking fury.

Temperature is, of course, another reason for a baby's discomfort. In this instance we are dealing with a child who will be too cold more than he will be too hot. If you are instinctive, with any luck you will be able to anticipate his wants, and the screams from the direction of the nursery will be minimal.

Teething

The Aries child can suffer quite considerably from teething problems, mainly because Aries rules the head and the teeth are located in this region. When he's teething, your little Ram will be even more short tempered than usual, feverish, and may even bang his head against the wall or cot. This strange activity usually indicates a headache, and junior aspirin, in the recommended dosage, will work wonders.

There are, of course, various aids one can buy to help the Aries baby through this difficult period. An invaluable preparation is a teething gel. This numbs the gums, therefore taking away some of the irritation. A teething-ring is naturally a must at this time. Buy a red one for your Ram as this colour is sure to fascinate him.

Lastly, as any adult knows, the teeth can affect not only the head and mouth but also the eyes and ears. In this particular case the latter seem to suffer the most. If you see your Aries child pulling at its ears, and you know there is nothing wrong in this direction, it is quite likely that this is a symptom of teething. However, whenever you are in doubt *always* consult your doctor. For the progress of the child's teeth see the section at the end of this book. But don't be put out if your particular Aries progresses at a different rate, as babies progress at their own sweet pace and there is nothing parents can do about it.

Bath-time

The average Scorpio or Cancer may delight in the feel of fluid lapping all over his body, but to the Aries child this is an unpleasant experience. Remember that Aries is a fire sign. The way around the bathing problem is to give your Aries baby frequent but short baths. Eventually he will get used to the idea that his mother deems it necessary to dunk him in this wet stuff at least once a day. When the child is older, of course, you can make it more fun. If there is a mirror round the bath, the baby can sit for hours making silly faces at himself. If the child has a sense of humour, utilize it.

A word of warning: do not expect baby to like having his face and ears washed. And washing the hair of this child can be a nightmare. However, there are a couple of aids. One is a face shield, which will help keep the water off the face of the child, and the other is a special baby shampoo, specially made so that it doesn't irritate the eyes. There is also a wonder product that doesn't require rinsing. These products are invaluable when dealing with this type of baby.

Never expect the Aries baby to enjoy being submerged in water; this feeling will stay with him too, as you will find when attempting to teach him to swim.

Interests and Games

The Aries child is quite raucous and anything that makes a loud noise will appeal to him. However, while it may be fun for him, it won't be for you! Any game where patience is encouraged and developed is a good idea, but do take heart if he initially tosses this type of game aside. Simply put it away and resurrect it a week or so later. Red will be his favourite colour and will immediately attract, a point to be borne in mind. On no account introduce young Ram to books made of paper. Rag-books are a better idea. There is also an in-born fascination for engines and mechanics, so clockwork toys are a good purchase.

Lastly, this little chap may enjoy rough games. Don't overdo these, though, or you will finish up with a really rough, tough character. Passable in boys, but hardly welcome in girls!

Walking and Talking

Naturally, parents always worry about their own baby's development. You may be disappointed if John from down the road walks a little earlier than your baby, but you shouldn't worry about this. Each baby develops his own way of doing things, be it walking or crawling, and has his own time-table. Some children crawl until they are eighteen months old and others walk at nine months.

As far as the Aries baby is concerned he will get from point A to point B quicker than most others, but remember that once he starts it will be you who will need to go into training to keep up with him! Bear in mind the Arietian proneness to accidents, for you will need to be on your guard against bumps and other injuries to that vulnerable head and face.

The process of learning to walk, or even stand, is extremely frustrating to this type. The Aries is an impatient animal. When some desired object is out of reach, this child will scream so loudly as to startle the neighbours. Also, try to remember that fat babies get on to their wobbly legs a lot later than their slimmer brother or sister.

Speech is also a source of worry to some parents. Generally speaking the Aries child learns to talk fairly early, but this does of course depend on other influences. Usually the first word the little Ram learns is not 'Mummy' or 'Daddy' but 'No'! There will be many brief altercations between you, but the Arietian child usually forgives and forgets and the sweet smile or the winning grin will start you wondering whether or not the earlier tantrum ever occurred.

As always and as with everything connected with progress, there is basically no fixed rule. Attempts to apply pressure will only make you and the child nervous wrecks. However, the typically Arietian child usually develops quickly, for he cannot wait to become a part of that big wide world. Even if this should prove not to be the case, don't fly into a panic. Just wait; the child will get there eventually.

Toilet-training

Most children are not physically able to control their bowels or bladder until between one and a half and two and a half years of age and much heartache is caused by trying to make toddlers dry before they are ready. You won't save yourself much work in any case, for instead of wet nappies you will have to cope with soaking pants and puddles on the floor. A good time to introduce the potty is at about eighteen months, but don't expect instant success and never get worked up about it. A child cannot do as you desire when he is frightened and upset or too young to understand just what it is you expect from him. With this type you will only frustrate the impatient child if you expect him to sit on the offending, cold plastic object for hours at a time. Because of his impetuous nature he will want to get this operation over and done with as quickly as possible, so if the child understands he will use the potty immediately, if not you are wasting your time.

The first indication that your Aries baby is attempting to

control himself is when he remains dry overnight. There is no game on earth that will induce the little Ram to sit anywhere for very long, but what may produce results are a big fuss and a lot of affection when he kindly obliges. As with all children, if the child is unsuccessful with the potty his failure should be ignored. Should the child think that he has disappointed you he will have accidents, and these are the rule rather than the exception.

Starting School

Starting school is, of course, the first step towards independence and adulthood, and a step that most parents dread. The child's doting mother simply has to face the fact that the little Ram is growing up. In fact, in many instances, and with this type in particular, it is likely to prove a more traumatic experience for the mother than for the child.

The most important thing to remember is that the parents must not make a fuss. Of course one has to be prepared, and the best way to do this is to talk about the fun the child can have with the other children. Remember that the Aries child is rather independent, and when the big day finally arrives parents must try hard to be casual and hide any fears they may have. Children are often more intelligent than parents give them credit for. They can sense tension and apprehension, and this in turn will make them feel uncomfortable. It will not occur to the little Ram that he should miss either parent just for a few hours. That is, of course, unless the thought is put into his head by well-meaning mother stating, 'Don't worry, darling, Mummy is coming back later. Don't cry!' As far as this little character is concerned he is not worried at all. He can glimpse, through the school door, an exciting new world, full of new faces and things to explore. Parents can be assured that they aren't in the child's thoughts at all, unless the tears welling up in his mother's eyes make him think that the paradise ahead is not going to be as much fun as he initially thought.

It may also be a good idea to inform the child that he will have his favourite meal upon returning home. Anticipating this, the child will know that at some point he is going home to his familiar surroundings.

Lastly, although circumstances may dictate otherwise, it is not a good idea to change schools too often. Security is important to children and the more changes there are the more threatened they will feel.

THE ARIETIAN CHILD

Four to twelve years of age

Health

Your Arietian child doesn't get any less accident prone as he grows older. If you are wise you will instil in your child a healthy respect for sharp objects and fire. You will have to resign yourself to the never-ending stream of minor cuts, bruises and scratches, especially where the face and the head are concerned. The vulnerability to infection is also carried over into childhood and cleanliness needs to be taught at an early age. Washing grubby hands before meal-times is always an important act to stress, especially with the little Ram, for should the child's temperature shoot up within a matter of seconds you can be fairly certain that some laws of hygiene have been broken.

A tendency to headaches also continues, especially should the child be under any form of stress or when dental problems begin. Ear-ache is another common occurrence, and never underestimate infection here. Should this important part of the anatomy continue to be aggravated a visit to your docotor is invariably the wisest course.

Nightmares are a problem in the Ram child and they can often be traced back to some kind of friction at school. It is important that you communicate and discover what is worrying the child. The Aries infant does have a tendency to keep worries and problems to himself. Gentle persuasion will help to unlock any mental doors the child may attempt to keep shut.

A list of childhood ailments appears in the section at the end of the book.

Friends

Young Rams display many war-like traits! Although on occasions these can lead to physical violence the Aries child will generally prefer to fight verbally. Conflict stimulates the Arietian and arguments among friends will be the rule rather than the exception. A bloodied nose and a bruised lip can usually be traced back to a best friend and not to an enemy.

Such a child is independent, original and sports-loving. He will usually be found taking part in all school activities, the usual result of which is popularity. Loneliness in the Aries child is a rare thing indeed.

Small Rams take the lead with playmates. They're the ones who start the new games, the brilliant ideas. Only one rule exists – they must have their own way! Not unexpectedly this tendency leads to a constantly changing series of 'best' friends. The little Ram falls in and out of friendships the same way that he will fall in and out of love at a later date. If you are a wise parent you will attempt to make the child realize that he is being unreasonable and that his own way cannot always come first, no matter how much he might want it to. Failure to do this will lead the child to grow into an unreasonable adult. Also, if there is a gang of children in your neighbourhood, you can bet that your little Aries will be the leader, and the instigator of most of their activities. Should this crowd get into any sort of trouble and your young Ram turns big eyes of innocence at you, don't believe it! Whatever the trouble happened to be, he was in it right up to his neck.

Clever parents realize the importance of entertaining children's friends. If the child gets accustomed to bringing home loud and noisy friends now, it will be natural to do likewise when older. If you are fiercely houseproud and don't like the thought of being invaded, set aside a couple of rooms (if possible) for the use of your Aries child and his followers, buy some ear-plugs and prepare for the mess once the party has departed. Better this than a child who sneaks off to Heaven knows where later on.

Interests and Games

The Aries child is a great innovator who takes the lead in games and projects but who moves on to new fields when things get boring or complicated. Hearts are worn on sleeves and you will be left in no doubt when the child is disgruntled or fed up. This is not a natural student and, if you are wise, you'll get the child into books at a very early age. Don't expect him to become engrossed in anything too academic, just get the child used to the idea of looking, touching and seeing books around the house, and referring to them for information as well as fun. Failure to gain the child's interest in this area could lead to tremendous problems later on and spelling and reading could well suffer as a result.

An Arietian doesn't naturally take to sitting still for any length of time. Sports, especially running and gymnastics, appeal to both sexes. If you are a devious parent you will reward any good efforts by buying books on a much-loved sport. In this way you will kill two birds with one stone.

Drama also appeals to the egotistical Ram and this should be encouraged. The Arietian imagination isn't strong, but such an activity will aid its stimulation. When telling stories, at bedtime or otherwise, try to use as your subjects those people who have conquered the world, almost! Any pioneer or army general will do for the boy Ram; girl Rams should be treated to innovative women like Florence Nightingale.

The Arietian child needs a flesh and blood hero or heroine to look up to. Nevertheless, they can be easily persuaded that there really are fairies at the bottom of the garden! However, reality is much more important to the Aries child than fantasy.

You are also likely to discover that your child is attracted to speed. Skating, scooters, skateboarding and so on will all appeal, but remember that accident-prone head and buy protective clothing. Both sexes also love climbing and here common sense should be taught. Steer them away from tall buildings and very high trees! Dressing up does not usually appeal unless uniforms are involved. An Aries girl would adore a nurse's outfit or the like, and there is an infinite selection for boy Rams.

A word of warning – don't encourage a liking for weapons of any description. In some Arietians, and it could be in yours, there lurks a streak of violence and the last thing you want to do is to encourage its emergence.

Lastly, because of the Arietian's love of comradeship and uniforms the scouts or the girl guides will have a particular attraction. These organizations are also recommended because they help to keep young Ram children out of mischief.

Accepting a New Baby

Don't expect shrieks of excitement or joy when the prospect of a new addition to the family is imminent. In fact, your Aries child will initially be downright indifferent. But don't be fooled: such coolness is uncharacteristic and soon fades away to be replaced by fiery possessiveness of one or both parents. Again, communication is the keyword, as always. You must encourage your child to talk about any fears he may have. He won't do this naturally and he will need a little coaxing. You can explain the better side of his having a little friend to play with, but your Ram will not be convinced. Rather, it is your attitude to him and love for him which will prove that his fears are groundless.

It is important to set aside at least forty-five minutes when either parent, preferably the mother, devotes full attention to the Aries infant. This must be for the child alone and no one else. In fact the new baby's home should not even be mentioned unless the Ram brings it up. Also, during holiday periods there should be at least one day when he can be with his mother or father on his own. On these occasions he or she should be treated as an adult. You can, of course, apply the old ploy of placing both children in the bath together, under supervision. With some Arietian children this may work (on those with other zodiac influences anyway) but for a die-hard Arietian, boy or girl, the thought of a small infant creating waves in the tub is quite a terrifying experience. If you must plonk your little Ram in the bath with someone, then it should ideally be with one of the parents.

Another golden rule to observe with a new baby is to make sure that he is put to bed a good deal earlier than the elder Aries child. Neither should you ever punish your little Ram in front of the baby. He will be unaware of the fact that the baby couldn't care less what is happening, but the Aries child has an ego. Scoldings should therefore be kept strictly between the parent and child. It won't do any harm, however, to scold the new baby or at least pretend to; that will make the little Ram feel good!

There are a myriad ways of boosting the Aries child's ego and the more you do it, during the first months of the new baby's life the better. Naturally a change of tactics is going to be needed later when the baby grows into an understanding child. In the meantime, encourage your Ram to teach the baby to talk, smile and wave. All this will appeal to the ego. There won't be a lot of patience, however, and discipline should not be resorted to when young Ram walks away in disgust at the baby's failure to add two and two together! Conversely, if the Ram is reluctant to help in any way, never force the issue. The best thing in this instance is for the parent to look helpless as the Arietian child can never resist rushing to the rescue.

Side-effects may follow the birth and introduction into the family of the new baby. One of these is the Arietian's school report, which may suffer for a while, although you should avoid drawing attention to it unless it goes on for longer than three or four terms. Then you could try a casual reference such as, 'Oh dear, if you aren't careful baby will learn to spell before you!' No way will your Arietian child allow that to happen!

Another side-effect could be a temporary relapse into bed-wetting or nightmares. Where the latter is concerned a safe night-light should be placed in the child's bedroom. With the former, change the bed without fuss or retribution and give lots of love before leaving the child alone. Ideally stay with the little Ram until sleep returns. It may be asking a lot if you have to get up early, but the more you give during this period the quicker he or she will get over the disappointment of being presented with a rival.

Fortunately, the typical Arietian child will take life in his stride and with any luck the above may not apply. But remember to ignore any regression. Give plenty of love and the infant Ram will soon accept the new member of the family. You may even be surprised when he becomes extremely protective. For instance, tell your Ram that a neighbour said the baby was rather ugly and notice the response. It is perfectly acceptable for the Aries child to say unpleasant things about the new brother or sister, but when strangers attempt it that is a different and unacceptable matter.

Discipline

This can be quite difficult with Arietians. It is quite likely that catching your child with a hand in the peanut butter you make the mistake of stamping your foot in fury. This will not only surprise him, but also outrage your Ram into stamping one of his own feet! As this type gets bigger and stronger you will notice that he can be at his most unreasonable when denied anything. Fortunately the anger doesn't last too long and after a violent outburst this child will beam at you and you will wonder whether you are dealing with a Jekyll and Hyde character. Any havoc he may wreak on the world later may not only be financially expensive, but will also take its toll in his mental anguish. The Arietian child who is not trained to obey, up to the point that doesn't break his spirit of course, will be taught some hurtful lessons in maturity.

Believe it or not, that Aries heart is pretty soft. The Arietian hides deep fears of being disliked and unloved despite the bravado, and any rejection of dreams or the dampening of enthusiasm will send him running home in tears. He or she needs to be loved when any of these things happen or its hearts will be broken. For all its brash and domineering ways the Arietian can be sensitive and bruised at the slightest bump.

Discipline needs to be firm and gentle, but love should always be on tap. Little Rams will have a few disappointments in life, but they will get up, dust themselves off and push forward once again, determined to teach the unimaginative world a thing or two. Obviously, they will gather a few scars as they go through life but you can certainly count on your child to put up a good fight.

Above all else you need to cultivate patience, consideration for others, concentration on objectives and financial common sense. Arietians are the last of the big spenders if you allow them to be. Although it is unwise to keep a child short of money, you should not lavish money on children either. If you do, the Aries will never learn the value of it and life could be very tough indeed later.

Be gentle in your teaching until the age of ten. After this, if your child wishes to purchase a Christmas or birthday present he should be made to save up for it well in advance. Observe this simple rule of discipline and the rest of the world will be appreciative to you later on.

Sex

Although the general rules that apply to any child are covered at the end of the book there are one or two things particularly applicable to the Arietian child.

This sign is particularly sensitive to the feel and smell of textures. Don't throw up your hands in horror and assume that this will lead to some weird sexual deviation. It is perfectly normal, for most children and many adults are sensualists and they show this trait in various ways. If his mother gets embarrassed when he strokes her satin-clad thigh, the Ram will assume that this is wrong and could develop a positive hang-up in this direction.

Aries children can also be rather cruel, and in some cases even sadistic. Naturally all cruelty should be discouraged gently but firmly, although never violently as violence begets violence and with this particular type the repercussions could be quite enormous. If you are the type of person who finds it difficult to discuss sex without becoming embarrassed, then try a more humorous approach. It matters not how you relate facts to the child provided you do so clearly, honestly and factually. And don't leave it too late. There is no point in leaving the Ram in ignorance until the age of ten or eleven and all questions must be honestly answered as they arise.

Homework and Study

Arietian boys and girls usually easily fall into the habit of forgetting homework. Life is so exciting to the young Ram that he can think of a million things he would rather be doing. And there is no point in your saying that other children are good and do all their homework every day — this ploy is a waste of time. Instead, you should dig at that sensitive ego. Try shaming the child into action; issue a challenge; simply tell him or her that it really doesn't matter too much, you could even suggest that he or she is just a little slow or not quite as clever as some of the other students.

By making the Arietian feel inferior in this way, action will follow. Watch your Arietian child put his nose to the grindstone in an effort to show you how ridiculous it is that anyone could do better than him.

Finding a Direction

Some children are self-motivated while others need gentle guidance without pressure. For the most part an Aries child takes the initiative and is definite about hobbies, interests and an eventual career. But what of the drifter? It is possible that your particular Aries starts many things and finishes none.

Every child should have a hobby, and the Arietian will be interested in either a sport or a society of some kind like drama, science or a charity. Between them, one of the parents should decide who is best qualified to encourage or support the chosen interest. Possibly the father if we are dealing with sports; he could then find out about the subject and arrange outings to various events. The mother could allow the drama group to meet at home occasionally. The parent could suggest that the child helps to prepare refreshment. A cake could even be baked if the Aries is anxious to impress, which this sign usually is. This way an interest in cooking can be developed, not to mention the helpful asset of playing host or hostess. But try suggesting that an Aries child should learn to cook and she/he would probably laugh.

Assuming then that a hobby has been established, what about a possible career? It may be a little early but these are important years. You would be most unwise to push the child in any direction, so take things slowly. But take a child who needs to improve his history, for instance. Bullying and threatening get nowhere, so an appeal to the warrior or pioneer within the child is the best approach. Obtain a book from the library and learn the facts and tactics regarding one famous battle, then at the right time you can explain colourfully and with as much excitement and enthusiasm as possible what is happening. Watch that Arietian face and you will see how much interest you have managed to stimulate. Don't push your point home, but wait until another opportunity arises and let him or her have it again, varying your story a little but sticking to the facts. You can follow this with trips to museums and later with books so you can study along with the child. Before your Arietian child knows what has happened his curiosity will have been aroused. A natural progression from this is to discover what was involved in such battles, like names, places and winners. Such a method can be used for any topic. Take a subject, enlarge upon it and enlighten the child. If your child is obsessed with pop music, do your homework. For instance a certain pop record may have been based on a piece by Chopin, a pop singer could be a fan of Tchaikovsky.

Facts like these may interest the child. It is quite possible to stimulate and educate from the humblest of beginnings.

Some unwise parents ignore their children's intellects altogether and threateningly suggest that they should shut up and watch the television. At a later date these parents wonder why their child's head is completely empty. So the more effort you put in at pre-puberty the easier time you are going to have later.

THE ARIETIAN TEENAGER
Twelve to eighteen years of age

If you have taken time with your child's intellect then adolescence need not be a daunting prospect. The luckiest parent will be the one who can vividly recall what it was like to be stranded in the no-man's-land of being neither adult nor child. Remember how you were just too everything? Too tall? Too short? Too fat? Too thin? Fair when you wanted to be dark and vice-versa? Remember that smooth chin that was shaved religiously every morning? And that silly voice that broke mid-sentence? And those spots? For both sexes spots are the absolute end of the world. If you can remember all of this then half the battle is won. No matter how tempted you may be to laugh or patronize such problems of adolescence – don't! All dramas must be taken seriously and advice given on demand. Be thankful that you are even being consulted. Suffer these teenage years with understanding and you will have a friend for life.

In what way is your Arietian youngster a special case? The pubescent Arietian is always in a hurry, so a good deal of impatience and frustration will be experienced. This will reveal itself in arrogance and general egotistical behaviour. But don't drag your bleeting Ram to a psychiatrist unless he becomes extremely violent. If this occurs you have failed in communication somewhere along the line.

The Arietian teenager needs a sounding-board, but this type is never helpless and, because of his or her fierce pride, will only come to you if he or she feels confidence in you. Fortunately the Arietian teenager is not too difficult, and problems will be shared provided you are willing to listen.

Your female Ram is a tom-boy – untidy, bossy and unhelpful. Rise above it all, for as soon as the opposite sex appears on the scene she will change overnight into a well-organized, clean and tidy young woman.

Her male counterpart is very similar. He proclaims total disinterest in females, although blushing furiously when in their company. He is noisy, untidy and always hungry. But from the moment he starts to be interested in girls you can bet that he is well on the road to reform and within a few months you won't recognize him. Providing the sexual side to life has been handled wisely and naturally no great problems will be encountered.

All in all the Arietian teenager is not too difficult. Take problems a step at a time, never look too far ahead and, above all else, be totally honest. In this way you will not only retain the love of your offspring but also their respect.

Dating

Some parents go into a frenzy when their children start to think about the opposite sex. They think the child is either premature and in danger of becoming a sex maniac at twelve or still too unconcerned at the age of fifteen. This is only another stage in a child's development and, like walking and talking, let your child take this step when he feels ready for it.

Arietian youngsters are fairly uncomplicated in this respect. They are constantly in love and one finds it difficult to keep up with the current object of affection, they change so often. However, if your Arietian is used to bringing friends home then he or she will see no reason to change this arrangement just because the friend happens to be of the opposite sex. When a friend is brought home, trust is the first prerequisite. If you suspect that your Arietian is sexually experimenting there is nothing you should do about it. It might just as well be in your own home as in the back of a car on a patch of waste ground. Conversely, don't actually push them into the bedroom with sly innuendo. If you can provide a room furnished with some chairs, a record-player and possibly a television let them have reasonable privacy. Providing you have taught common sense you will have nothing to worry about. Nobody is going to make the little Ram do anything he or she doesn't want to do.

Double standards should also be discarded. You cannot possibly tell your son to go out and have fun while chaining your daughter to her bed. However, certain rules must exist and here are a sample:

1 As a parent you should be consulted before friends are invited home. The Aries teen won't think about this unless you draw his or her attention to it.

2 You have every right, for their protection, and your peace of mind, to know where the children are going.

3 A reasonable time for returning home should be established and kept to. A sixteen-year-old Arietian is far too immature and impulsive to be allowed out all night, unless undertaken in special circumstances.

4 Make absolutely certain that in your conversations about sex the matters of contraception and venereal disease are freely discussed and properly understood.

If your child is female you certainly don't want her living in fear of getting pregnant. And besides she must understand that it would be irresponsible to bring another being into the world unless it were really wanted. The same goes for the male, he must understand that if an unwanted child is born through his irresponsibility then he will be made to share in its upkeep. Responsibility is a word the Arietian male loathes and should be enough of a deterrent to ensure his mature and common sense approach to the opposite sex.

Alcohol

According to many doctors teenage drinking is becoming a bigger problem than drug-taking but you cannot prevent your child from having the occasional drink unless of course you intend to follow him or her around all the time. Not an ideal state of affairs. Ideally then alcohol should be introduced by the parents within the home, especially in this particular case, for forbidden fruit is always attractive to the Arietian. A glass of wine at the dinner table or perhaps a nightcap is a good idea; make it a good strong one. An assault on those yet untried taste buds will prove to be such a shock that you are likely to postpone any alcoholic experimentation for another six months to a year. This particular teenager is usually full of bravado, wait for such a mood to descend then allow him or her to drink at home with you freely, and let him mix his drinks and go against all the known practical rules such as drinking on an empty stomach. It is often the case with this type that they have to learn the hard way and the unpleasant vomiting and hangover which can accompany an evening of drinking is something they will not forget for some time to come. This dispensed with then it is time to sit down and sensibly discuss all the 'dos' and 'don'ts' of alcoholic consumption. Lastly there is no reason if you enjoy a drink why you should feel that you can only drink soft drinks in front of your teenager. On the other hand you would be most unwise to treat him or her to the vision of your good self more than a little worse for wear. A good example is most important where this type is concerned.

Drugs

Fortunately Aries is a sign rarely attracted to drug-taking, but don't ignore the fact that the child may attend parties where marijuana and pills are passed around. To the best of your own knowledge explain the different types of drugs, addiction and its awful consequences, and allow the child to watch any programmes about drug-addiction that appear on television. This should be enough to deter any potential interest.

It is wise not to come out too firmly against any one thing, or the rebellious Arietian may just decide to try things for the hell of it. The secret is to be very casual on anything you feel strongly about.

SUGGESTED CAREERS

It is quite possible that your Arietian teenager may go through an anti-materialistic stage, but he or she never loses his sense of competition. And you'll need to be clever. When study for examinations is put off arguments and outbursts will get you nowhere. But an – 'OK if you're going to leave it, it is your life, but I never thought I'd see the day when you were happy to let that creep John Smith get four A levels while you failed, but then you always had trouble keeping up with him, didn't you?' – remarks like this are enough to send your average Arietian into a frenzy of activity, cancelling all dates and engagements and going to earth in his room with his books in order to study. No one is going to do better than him and you'd better believe it.

A straightforward Arietian child will either find a good position in the professions noted below or will do well freelancing in them. The weaker kind of Ram tends to drift through life. But if you have managed to stimulate the mind while it was receptive you should have provided some sort of direction and all you then need to do is use it as a base. Broaden and stretch it; the thirst for information will then take over. Remember that this teenager has the energy of three people, help him to channel it and the child will be on the way to a happy adulthood.

Careers

Psychologist	Explorer	Trade Unionist
Psychiatrist	Engineer	Mechanic
Butcher	Engine driver	Dentist
Foundry worker	Fireman	Professional sportsman or sportswoman
Metal worker	Arms manufacturer	

A slow, plodding, safe job is exactly what the Arietian does not need. They will be best in competitive work in a noisy, busy atmosphere where they can be in charge. Arietians should not be trapped permanently behind desks, unable to use their splendid initiative. Their high energy-level and enterprise must have release if they are not to burst.

The pioneering spirit could lead the child into becoming an explorer – it will certainly feel like one as it finds its way around untried ground, trading in new areas or developing fresh lines of scientific research. Carving will satisfy the talent and interest shown in sharp instruments, rally-driving or racing the thirst for speed, danger and noise. Female Arietians will get a good deal of satisfaction from ice-skating and hockey.

TAURUS

THE FIRST EARTH SIGN

Symbol The Bull

Colour Blue and pink

Metal Copper

Planet Venus

Motivation To build and protect

Hardworking; practical; loyal in affections; loves luxury, music and art; opinionated and fixed in ways

GENERAL CHARACTERISTICS

Is Your Child a Typical Taurus?

THE TAURUS BABY

Health

Food

Crying

Teething

Bath-time

Interests and Games

Walking and Talking

Toilet-training

Starting School

THE TAURUS CHILD

Health

Friends

Interests and Games

Accepting a New Baby

Discipline

Sex

Homework and Study

Finding a Direction

THE TAURUS TEENAGER

Dating

Alcohol

Drugs

Suggested Careers

GENERAL CHARACTERISTICS

Dr Jekyll: positive

The Taurean has a keen sense of purpose and stability, a fixed mind unshaken by any opposition and a quiet persistence when confronted by obstacles. The Bull is also artistic, enjoying music, poetry and painting. Sensuality is well developed and the true Taurean is anaesthetized by colours, especially pastel shades. Green will also attract, for this is the colour of money. This type is practical. The Bull loathes to part with his hard-earned cash and you won't find many born under this sign standing in a queue for free soup. This type progresses slowly but surely, always starting on solid foundations, and the achievements in life are accomplished by sheer hard work, strength of character, determination and stubbornness. Even the nicest Bull has a strong obstinate streak. However, to this individual this isn't stubbornness but merely patience, and he doesn't feel he's hard headed but just sensible and firm.

The Taurean gives enduring loyalty and devotion and a faithful heart, and this adds up to emotional security combined with financial ability and a strong romantic streak.

Mr Hyde: negative

This character's biggest fault is sheer bloody-mindedness. Put this together with a violent temper and there are times when you will have a fairly unpleasant individual. However, to be fair, the Bull rarely starts a quarrel and for the most part he is too content or lazy to be easily irritated. But when pressurized or positively shoved then onlookers had better prepare for a violent outburst, during the course of which he will abuse anyone both physically and verbally until those around him wish the floor could swallow them up. Once this type has cooled there is no point in trying to introduce a humorous element into the situation or you will wish you had left him alone to sulk. Furthermore, this particular Mr Hyde is also a rather selfish and slow individual. It's true that the Bull is capable of hard work, but labour is interspersed with periods of rest and general lethargy.

There is little point in trying to introduce change, for this subject lives his life at a leisurely pace and will refuse to be rushed or pushed. He has a speedometer set at one speed – slow. Even then there is only one motivation and that is self.

Is Your Child a Typical Taurean?

Answer the questions honestly. Score three for every 'Yes', two for every 'Sometimes' and one for every 'No'. Turn to page 217 for the answers.

1 Does your Taurean over-indulge in food?

2 Can you persuade the child to do practically anything for a slice of cake?

3 Does your child know exactly what he wants?
4 Does the sight of grass and trees relax the child?
5 Does your child have a weight problem?
6 Is your child possessive?
7 Does your child sulk whenever it is denied anything?
8 Does the child like a fixed routine?
9 Is your child lazy?
10 Does your child watch while you cook?
11 Do throat problems plague your child?
12 Does he recuperate quickly from illness?
13 Is your child reserved?
14 Does the child have a violent temper?
15 Is the child quiet when faced with strangers?
16 Is it a lover of music?
17 Is your Taurean persistent?
18 Does the child prefer to watch physical activity rather than take part?
19 Does your child refuse to share his toys?
20 Would your child notice if you wore something different?

THE TAURUS BABY
Up to four years of age

You'll know what it is to have a Taurean child even before you leave the nursing-home or hospital, for to get him home you will need to change the routine he's grown to love. If there is anything a Taurean child hates it is change. Your baby will be as unco-operative as possible while being dressed for the first time.

Notice the purple face, the loud cries and the stiff limbs. Don't think that his father could do any better. This is a performance that will be repeated whenever the general routine is disturbed. There is no point in your worrying what the neighbours will think, they'll have to get used to it.

The parents of this baby will either lose pounds or develop muscles they didn't know they had. This aside, however, you will be glad to hear that the baby can be a delight, for the little Bull is cuddly and loving and adores being squeezed, hugged and petted. The tiny Taurean girl will flirt with her father in an effort to get an extra mouthful of dessert, and he will have a hard time resisting her charm. Regardless of sex the Bull is strong and healthy. Taurean children seem to be more confident than others, they are generally stable and seldom subject to depression. This type possesses a maturity all his own and never embarrasses parents with arrogance or rudeness. If you challenge his temper by teasing or by applying pressure, the child will turn belligerent, paw the ground and charge!

Health

Taurus rules the throat and most health problems lead from this part of the anatomy. This child never knows when he is sated and is usually fairly greedy. This is turn leads to over-weight and more than a fair share of colic. The extra pounds that he has to carry typically leads this type into late development, for all the fat round the tummy makes it extremely difficult for the child to learn to sit up, stand and walk.

The throat is also prone to inflammations and to accident. When the little Bull begins to toddle around and puts everything in his mouth you'll need to be on your guard against choking. Learn to anticipate this and you will save both yourself and the child a lot of trouble.

Food

Meal-times present few problems as children born under this sign will eat pretty well anything. Beef dishes are a particular favourite. Your Bull is sure to be precocious in this respect and mixed feeding usually starts earlier than normal. However, if for some reason your Bull decides that he doesn't want to eat, you could be in trouble. If you think you are going to push that meal past those unrelenting, tightly closed lips you are wrong. Fortunately these occasions are rare, but when the meal is rejected you can bet your life that it smells or looks wrong. The Taurean is a sensual character with a keen sense of smell and touch. He may not like the colour, the odour or the texture of the meal. When he does refuse, watch for the protruding bottom lip.

When dealing with the Taurean child, it cannot be overstressed that it is all too easy to continually refill that ever-open mouth! You may be delighted with the gain in weight, but it won't be much fun when the doctor suggests that the child go on a diet. The Taurean baby, though usually good, can be a monster when he feels his stomach is too empty. Never lose sight of the fact that nine times out of ten, fat babies grow into fat children who in turn grow into even fatter adults.

Crying

As previously stated, the Taurean baby is usually content as long as his stomach is well lined. But when overfed, colic is usually the result and you are the one who is going to suffer at night when this occurs. A high percentage of the Taurean baby's tears are connected with food and the lack or surplus of it. Too much, not enough, wrong diet; if the Bull is bad tempered you can bet that food is the cause of it and with this problem out of the way you are left with a docile child. He doesn't exert himself purely for the sake of it.

Another possible reason for distress could be sensuality, for this child loves the smell and feel of his parents. The child can be easily soothed by music, so try a lullaby even at four in the morning. Avoid hard rock, though, for this will offend those sensitive ears. This Bull needs harmony and serenity.

The novice mother need not get tense or nervous with this baby, for in a very short time she will recognize all those insistent cries. The Taurean baby is positive and uncomplicated and parents will soon identify what feelings the baby is trying to communicate by crying.

Teething

The true Taurean baby is average with teething problems so you should refer to the section at the end of the book. If any problem arises it is going to be lack of teeth by the time the baby is a year old. But each baby progresses at a different rate, and lack of teeth won't stop the Bull munching on the hardest biscuits or chocolates! When he does finally being to teethe the symptoms will be a runny nose plus throat problems and swollen glands. When sore gums interfere with meal-times you will be subjected to an infuriated baby.

During these distressing times the child's sensuality is not far away, so abandon that metal spoon and try utensils that are warm, soft and plastic.

Lastly, buy pink or blue teething-rings. These are Taurean colours and they help to calm the savage breast!

Bath-time

Naturally enough with an earth sign, the Taurean child will love getting dirty and you are going to have the grubbiest child on the block! Fortunately, this little person also adores bath-time, so refuse to be deterred by the screams when he's first put into the water! Once the warm water envelopes and slides into the crevices of the body, the screams are only surpassed when you attempt to remove the soaking creature!

Children born under this sign are rarely afraid of water unless experience teaches them to be so. Nevertheless, do not leave the child alone, for not only is this dangerous but the little Bull does need your company. Use this half an hour as a rest period. Take a coffee with you and relax while your child enjoys the bath. Better still, climb in with him.

Provided accidents are avoided and soap is kept out of the eyes, bath-time will really be a joy to your Taurean.

Interests and Games

The young Taurean is very patient and will stick with a game long after his Arietian counterpart has given up. Therefore, puzzles are particularly beneficial although you mustn't rush him. If all the pieces are in place with the exception of one or two, don't cajole or coax the child as this will make him throw the whole object at you; rather leave it for a couple of days and then get the puzzle out again.

As previously mentioned, food and its preparation is an all-consuming passion! The child will play for hours with pots and pans and empty yogurt tubs serve very well. Naturally enough a tea-set or a plastic oven is very nice, but this type can manage equally well with a few of your bits and pieces and a cardboard box. Besides, this helps to exercise the imagination, something that bright, pleasantly made toys rarely do, for they are ready made and the child generally gets bored if things are too easy. You could try sitting the Taurean in the high chair while you prepare dinner. The chances are that the child will sit for hours provided you explain what you are doing. You may feel rather silly at first, but after a while you'll begin to suspect that you are being understood and your frustration shared when the soufflé collapses, or your sauce curdles!

Lastly, the Bull is not as physically active as other children and they get bored with toys that can be jumped on, ridden or pedalled. All that is far too exhausting! This type prefers to exercise the imagination and intellect. Painting and drawing are therefore a keen absorption provided you can stand the mess. Singing and dancing are also enjoyed, so there is plenty to be done to keep this child happy.

Walking and Talking

The average Bull is usually rather slow physically and is sometimes downright lazy. Because of this you needn't worry if the child is still inactive at the age of eighteen months. The time he sits up is usually a good guide to his future development. If he is late in this respect you can be sure that he will shy away from walking for some time. Also bear in mind that weight will play a part. If your Taurean is naturally lazy and also fat, it will be some time before he or she is up and about.

Though physically lethargic, the Taurean will usually make up for it mentally. After all, the child has to do something while he is lying around, and usually that is learning to talk. You will probably swear that your little Bull uttered the word 'Mummy' when he was three months old and you may well be right. But whether late or early, what does it matter as long as your little Bull is happy and healthy – you have nothing to worry about.

Toilet-training

There isn't a sign in the zodiac or a baby in the world which will respond to pressure when it comes to toilet-training. A tensed-up individual of any age will find difficulties in relieving himself under pressure and in your baby's instance it will become confused and neurotic as well. Furthermore, you may even inhibit the natural development. A general rule is to ignore disasters and reward achievements.

With the Taurean child, life is a little easier than with the highly strung Gemini, for instance, or the impatient Aries. The

Taurean will quite happily spend time on the potty surrounded by his favourite toys and things until his rear end is bright red! If the baby is happy, why not? But don't imagine that any results you get are intentional unless the child is over eighteen months. But at least the accidental fruits will give you something to make a fuss about!

Also remember the child's sensuality. If you aren't getting anywhere with your two- to three-year-old on that shiny red but cold potty, get a warm pink or blue plastic one. The different colour may just do the trick. And if the child is an early developer in this direction, don't be surprised if natural progression, in other words sitting on the lavatory, is delayed. It is quite likely that the child will baulk at sitting over that big, cavernous hole which looks cold and seems to threaten to engulf the child.

School usually resolves this problem. When your Taurean sees other children squatting on the lavatory and surviving the ordeal, then it won't want to be placed on a baby's potty.

Starting School

The Taurean is a conservative and sometimes shy child who needs school to learn to adapt to other people. Flexibility does not come easily. Ideally, on the first day the mother should stay at school with the child until he makes some attempt at communicating with others. As soon as this occurs she can casually, but not stealthily, slip away, possibly explaining that she is leaving to buy this child's favourite meal for tea. No Taurean is going to argue where the stomach is concerned. This type isn't emotional in front of others, unless he observes a distressed mother and if the parent behaves correctly then the child will naturally accept without too much reassurance that the parent will be back later. This should be a secure child, and it will take a lot to make an insecure Bull!

If you have brought up the child properly he will feel well loved, in which case he knows that his parents wouldn't leave him for too long. Suggest to the teacher that the child be given paints or crayons and it is unlikely that he will even notice your absence. Far from being distressed your young Bull will later hold up his painting in multi-coloured hands! Make a fuss and say you'd like another and he will be impatient to get back to school the following day.

THE TAUREAN CHILD
Four to twelve years of age

Health

Childhood for the young Bull can be a succession of throat problems like tonsilitis or swollen glands and there is an obvious off-shoot from this that should perhaps be discussed.

The Taurean child begins most children's illnesses with the same symptoms as those experienced by all children, but you will need to guard against dismissing things as just 'another one of those throats'! Also, whenever school seems an unpleasant prospect your Taurean child may feign some kind of throat infection, so a thermometer will be your greatest ally while this child is growing up. Furthermore, there may also be some parents who recognize their offspring as the greedy, overweight individual mentioned in the previous section. If so, it is essential that you remember that he is not going to get any slimmer or healthier unless you do something about it. This is the ideal stage in life for action, for at present it is not too late and you are still in control of the child's appetite! You are likely to find that by simply substituting slimming bread for the real thing, and reducing the number of potatoes, that he or she will slim down. If not – seek professional dietary advice. Also, little Bulls tend to compensate through their appetite. Therefore see that he or she is not lacking in any way. Lastly, this is naturally a strong sign, and one with excellent powers of recovery, therefore all that is basically needed to keep such a child healthy is common sense.

Friends

If the parents of the Taurean child are social butterflies, they may be disappointed by their offspring, for this type is selective and does not attempt to hide his disgust for people who do not come up to scratch. This is also a reserved and conservative individual, one who is easily embarrassed and one who thinks twice before romping around the floor when any strangers are present. Parties can be a real trial and the wise parent won't insist that the child should go, or demand that he or she has fun. If you feel that you must coax your child out of his shell then it would be a good idea to take both your child and his closest friend to the party or gathering. This way, at least, there will be one close friend around. In fact, one close friend is all he may have or desire to have. However, don't imagine that this one treasured relationship will be free from problems. The Taurean child is possessive, and the relationship will be continually up or down. The parent will have to be able to provide a big shoulder when the friendship is going through a negative phase.

The little Bull is a practical joker, a facet of the character that should not be allowed to get out of hand. It may be necessary for you to play one or two nasty little tricks on your child to make him conclude that humiliation is unpleasant. Lastly, ensure that your child feels perfectly free to extend invitations to his friends. This type will not fill the house with screaming monsters in any case, but if he feels that his close friend isn't welcome it is quite likely that he will cut himself off, possibly watching television and doing nothing else. If this does occur, he or she will not be easily budged.

Interests and Games

The important thing to remember about the Taurean's interests is that inside that solid, possibly lazy character is a budding artist. If your child doesn't leap into action at the sight of paint and brushes, crayons and paper, then try music. But do try to make it an active participation rather than simply mental preoccupation. The guitar should be your first choice of instrument, or the violin. The Bull also likes to watch things grow, so although the child may be a little too young for gardening, you could start him off on mustard and cress grown on blotting-paper, and take it from there.

History and the past in general is another Taurean interest. You could begin buying a few very simple history books and start to build up his education. Also, although it may be difficult to believe, this character is quite a romantic, a theme you should observe running through most of his games. A space-suit, for example, will do little to excite the adrenalin, but a suit of armour is a different matter. The same applies to your female Taurean. Forget the nurse's uniform and try a wig, which is sure to delight. Both sexes are budding cooks, and any toys that encourage this will please them. A child's cookery book may possibly lead to a messy kitchen but will also lead to hours of fun and education.

Accepting a New Baby

The Taurean is a practical animal who will understand all the caring that a little brother or sister needs. However, what will be resented is the time the never-ending changing, feeding and bathing seems to take and the only sensible answer to this is to extract some help from your Bull. However, you would be ill advised to scold him if he shows no inclination in this direction.

With any luck the Taurean should delight in helping to feed the baby and he will excel when it comes to singing lullabies. But don't overlook the Taurean's stubbornness – once those heels are dug in you'll be fighting a losing battle. If help is refused despite your smiles and requests, proceed without it. Later on invent an emergency, during which you can frantically plead for help – if the odd tear can be squeezed out then all the better. When the supposed drama is all over, place the Bull on your lap, give him a grateful hug and say that you don't know what may have happened without his assistance. Watch your child look proud. After this, if you are lucky, the Bull will take it upon himself to render assistance whenever called upon.

Don't forget to allow your child to join in with the fun too. Try making houses for both of them out of boxes or a tablecloth. Such a game is no fun for the child alone and the Taurean will soon come to realize that even a gurgling toddler is better than no one at all. However, when baby grabs one of those precious possessions retrieve it quickly. The Bull is possessive with his toys, just as it is with people, and baby must be taught to respect the older child's property from the word go.

These simple rules will lead to an easing of family tensions, but it won't ever be easy going. Use your heart with your head and you will not go wrong.

Discipline

Pressure will get you nowhere with the little Bull, and if you apply it you will only arouse his belligerence. The only way out is love. If a Taurean is forced all his life into doing things for which he is unsuited he will turn into a silent, moody, cruel adult. A young Bull cannot stay stubborn against physical demonstrations of affection. A big kiss and a cheerful smile coaxes out the obstinacy whereas yelling and harsh voices raised in command will just lead this type to shut his eyes and ears. Discipline will be resisted from an early age although resistance to affection is very short. The young Taurean's mind responds to common sense provided it sounds reasonable. This individual will do whatever is needed provided it is given a practical, uncomplicated, truthful explanation. 'You're not going out now because I say so' will get the parent nowhere, whereas 'You aren't going out because it is cold' or 'You haven't a pair of decent shoes' will be easily understood.

It is important that you do not lose contact with your child at this stage. If you do you will be faced with a very disgruntled and obstinate teenager and one who has an unpleasant tendency to sulk, with the irritating habit of always knowing best. To avoid this state of affairs, it is worth putting yourself out now.

Whenever you observe those eyes clouding over and the chin jutting out, control yourself. Don't lash out or demand explanations but find out exactly what it is that has upset him. This will give you a chance to exercise not only your own logic and reason, but the child's, although keep it simple. You are trying to make the child open up, not to subject him to a stream of your own thoughts.

On those rare occasions when your bull does lose his temper, try not to react violently yourself. This type does not lose its temper without very good reason. Don't adopt a humorous attitude to his anger. This individual will be thoroughly ashamed of any outburst, for he is normally self controlled.

Lastly, on to that age-old question of spanking. I believe that 99% of the time this should be avoided and should only be utilized once two warnings have been issued regarding a serious offence. If your warnings are ignored then you will need to carry these warnings through to their ultimate conclusion. The next time a first warning will be sufficient. On the whole the Taurean child is well behaved in any case, so problems should be minimal.

Sex

Bearing in mind the conservative and reticent character of the Bull your biggest problem will be the apparent total lack of interest in the sexual side to life. Don't be fooled, though. This type is easily embarrassed and as a result you are going to be the last person to whom he could go for advice. Therefore, the section at the end of this book about the acceptance of sex and the body is particularly important. Any embarrassment you feel will be picked up by the Taurean child.

Because of the apparent lack of interest it may be necessary for the parent to regularly broach the subject. Circumstances will arise for this to happen quite naturally. A pregnant friend, a woman in the street, or better still a pregnant mother. There are also news items on television and other programmes. It is not impossible to imagine a situation arising approximately once a month which should prompt discussion. You won't corrupt. The child, whether you like it or not, isn't going to stay permanently innocent and unless you educate him someone else, probably a mis-informed school-mate, will.

The importance of instilling a sexually enlightened and informed mind within your Taurean cannot be over-stressed. Taurus is a sign somewhat prone to inhibition which can lead to sex problems later. Present your facts clearly and sensitively, avoiding innuendo and any kind of vulgarity even in jest.

As the little Bull has a vivid imagination and a sense of delicacy, a crude introduction to the physical side of life is enough to put him off for good. By utilizing the above advice you should be able to eventually produce a sexually well-developed and well-balanced adult.

Homework and Study

Teachers generally have an easy time with Taureans, for these boys and girls are industrious, learn their lessons methodically and have excellent concentration. They are not the type of children to be late or throw ink pellets when the teacher isn't looking. They do have a wicked sense of humour and will convulse if the teacher crushes her fingers in the door. However, with education, parents of a Taurean child are lucky provided he is positive and not negative. The typical Bull instinctively knows when to take life seriously and he is quite happy with responsibility. This does not necessarily mean that he is a genius, and there will be times when the opposite may seem true, for the Bull is a slow developer. He works laboriously to keep abreast of speedier friends. The least you can do is to celebrate his effort and to reward his success. The actual process of persuading the Bull to get on with homework is not difficult. He likes routine, so set aside a homework period. After a while it will be done automatically.

So much for the positive Taurean. The negative Bull is petulant, lazy and incredibly stubborn. The very suggestion of home study is enough to send him pawing the ground in preparation for a full battle. Use the child's appetite as a weapon. Most children come home from school feeling hungry. Offer a small snack, something to take the edge off the appetite and say that you haven't had time to prepare dinner but will have it ready by the time homework has been finished. Add that there is no need to be too quick as you need sufficient time to cook it properly. This rider is an insurance policy against any slapdash work that may have been contemplated. But even a negative Taurean likes routine, so it is still vital to set aside a study hour. Routine breeds security. This little Bull can be difficult but only impossible when you allow him to be.

Finding a Direction

Although a direction can mean, in many instances, finding any job to keep the wolf from the door, those forced into such an existence can never really find fulfilment and they will suffer many frustrations. Frequently such a way of life is compensated for in private life, perhaps in the form of a creative hobby, although some people cannot express themselves in this way not because they are stupid but because they are too exhausted after a day at school or work. It may be that others cannot think of anything that particularly excites them. The Taurean's excellent common sense means that he will understand the practical reasons for mental stimulation in later work, but if the parent isn't careful the practical consideration will over-ride all else at a later date. The entire life will then be devoted to the pursuit of money. Ideally the Taurean child needs to acquire self-knowledge, for only this will allow the subject to live life to the fullest. Stimulation is the key-word and the parent should strive to achieve it in the child as early as possible. All adults should be able to express themselves not only at work but also at play or within a hobby.

Broadly speaking any contact with music, the arts, gardening or history will enthral. If the child has lost interest in learning a musical instrument you may be able to reactivate it by opening your child's eyes to the romantic side of some famous composer. You will need to read about the subject yourself, and much will depend upon the age of your child. The under nines, for example, cannot be expected to wade through volumes devoted to Chopin. But his life-story, presented by mother or father in the form of an interesting and romantic story, should appeal. Later, the purchase of a record devoted to your subject's creativity will add another dimension to your story.

Naturally enough this ploy does not have to be confined to the classics and the same approach can be adapted to jazz or pop music and probably should be, for your child needs to broaden his mind. As time passes your stories can be replaced by books. Your end product should be a child who is fully acquainted with the romance of Tchaikovsky, has heard and can recognize his music and has been sufficiently stimulated to thirst for more knowledge.

You will not only stimulate interest, but you will also encourage your child to learn to read and to spell. This method can be applied to anything, painters, writers, and so on. Feel your way before deciding which route to take; music lessons, visits to art galleries, perhaps a concert, all may give some indication and maybe radio or television can provide a clue. Another Taurean passion is gardening and gardening parents should allow the Taurean child to take an active part in the work, for growing anything provides relaxation to this child especially if the end product is something to eat! Also, simple cookery is a joy, so buy a child's cook-book. This is an excellent way to teach reading and even mathematics, for weights and measures are part and parcel of the preparation of food. The great thing about all these methods is that your Taurean child will not even realize that he or she is being educated.

THE TAUREAN TEENAGER
Twelve to eighteen years of age

Adolescence is a word to send a shiver down the spin of the most confident parents. They can relax, though, if they are still communicating by the time the child is thirteen, when any problems should not be too world-shattering. Also, of course, much will depend on their ability to recall the rigours of their own growing-pains, and an active imagination helps. Can you, for example, remember what it felt like to be as graceless as Tyrannosaurus Rex? Yes? Well . . . there is hope for your Taurean child. By now the Taurean child will be a bundle of complexes and not helped by a probable weight problem. The Taurean girl desperately wants to be as elegant as a fashion model but whenever she enters a room occupied by strangers her feet seem to grow and grow until she cannot move without tripping over them!

The Taurean boy, on the other hand, wants to saunter in like James Bond, but as every room turns into an obstacle course all he can do is hope that he can make his way around it without incident, something he rarely does. It wouldn't be so bad if Taurean teenagers were able to shrug off clumsiness with a glib, clever remark, but this type is rarely that mentally agile. All Taureans can manage when embarrassed is a mumbled apology, usually aimed in the direction of their chests, as they trip over the carpet on the way out!

Furthermore, this type is often teased unmercifully about size, which can result in some chaotic dietary habits. For example, one day this individual starves only to later raid the larder at four in the morning. Have you noticed that large appetite? And what about that laziness? 'You are young and in the prime of life. You should be filled with vitality!' you protest, only to be scowled at menacingly, which should temporarily still your tongue. And untidiness and the lack of help in the home should leave you speechless.

Adolescence seems to sap the Taurean's already sparse share of energy. Their bodies, glands and hormones are involved in all kinds of crazy activities and all this hidden activity will leave your Taurean feeling like a neglected and much-used dish-cloth. As when he was younger, try to keep that head busy, and overlook any physical imperfections. In a relaxed atmosphere they will pass away quickly, and unless you are really unlucky the Taurean isn't naturally untidy, so don't run after him like a martyr or nag the child into rebellion. Leave his possessions as he has left them, no matter how untidy, and your teenager will soon move himself when it is impossible to locate anything.

Your Taurean adolescent must know that you are always there to help if he wants it. It is also important he realizes that friends are welcome, and that there is love a-plenty. Emphasize that he or she will grow up soon enough.

Your Taurean may not listen to anyone, however, as the Taurean can be an opinionated character, a regular knowall. But after a few mistakes the Taurean child will soon realize that there is a lot to learn. Give your Taurus teenager some credit however difficult it may be at times.

Dating

The Taurean adolescent is usually extremely shy and self-conscious, and any blustering to the contrary is just show. Because of such reticence this type is frequently the original sufferer from the one-sided love affair. The Bull worships from afar, and all the parents' understanding will be needed to get him through a string of amours. However, once this type has finally taken the step successfully, he or she will take to love and sex like a veteran. The Bull likes method and habit, so your teenager will uncomplainingly arrange his or her social life around homework and the rules and regulations about dating shouldn't be a problem itself.

This character may secretly hope that he will be allowed out all night, but we are dealing with a realist and one that is not going to expect to be so lucky. Also, if your teenager has been accustomed to bringing home friends then this Taurean isn't about to change such habits.

Your child long ago went off with friends to play cowboys and Indians. Now the interest has changed to the opposite sex, and provided you have discussed it, and made emotional contact, then you have nothing to fear from your Taurean's going out with a girlfriend or boyfriend. The Bull is practical, sensible and responsible.

Lastly, don't make distinctions between sons and daughters. When sons live up to their sign don't deny daughters the same privilege. Taurean girls are strong-minded and the last people who should be incited into rebellion. Fortunately, this is normally a sign which likes to exercise moderation.

Alcohol

As with everything else a Taurean should be made to feel that there is nothing furtive or clever about becoming intoxicated. If he or she is allowed occasionally to drink at home, with meals for example, then life will not present any problems and one heavy drinking session at home is likely to put him or her off alcohol for quite a while. You'll also be well advised to emphasize the incoherent and incapable state to which the child at the time sank. How easy it would have been to cause an accident while under the influence and in possession of a car. And what about her? She could have been very easily seduced. It has got to happen sometime, but surely not under such circumstances. Introduce sensible rules for alcohol. It may be general to all signs but the Bull is more practical than most and so is likely to take more notice.

1 Don't drink on an empty stomach.
2 Explain how alcohol effects go far deeper when under stress.
3 The financial penalties for drinking. No Bull likes to throw money away.
4 The illegality of drinking and driving.
5 Explain that it is important to learn when his or her limit has been reached.

The wise parent will try to recall their own introduction to alcohol. It never fails to help when one is able to put oneself in someone else's shoes. If you suspect that your child is secretly drinking, then simply enquire why. After all, there is drink at home isn't there? Lastly, whatever you do don't dramatize the evils of alcohol or you are liable to make it far too attractive.

Drugs

Drugs are a rare problem for the Bull. Over-indulgence in drink, food and sex is likely, for the Bull likes the physical mechanics of all three, but he finds nothing sensual in popping a pill or smoking a joint. However, it is possible that your child may well try drugs once or even twice before abandoning them and when you suspect this has happened, talk about the experience. Taureans are strong-willed and the odd soft drug will not lead them on to the hard stuff. Handle the experiment as you would the first date. Drugs will be something that the Bull will dismiss quickly, especially should you draw attention to the financial outlay.

The whole drug-scene is against the Taurean grain, but keep your eyes open and act quickly by bringing it out into the open immediately you suspect your child has experimented with drugs.

SUGGESTED CAREERS

The Taurean is a positive individual who is usually very certain which way he wishes to go in life. The practical side of this sign may take your child into the monied professions like accounting or banking. The love of security could take it into property. If you are lucky, an artisitic hobby may slowly grow and take over until your Bull will be a totally fulfilled person.

Here are some further suggestions on Taurean careers:

Farmer	Surveyor	Model
Horticulturist	Jeweller	Art dealer
Businessman	Singer	Commercial artist
Builder	Civil Servant	Craftworker
Architect	Auctioneer	
Sculptor	Financier	

There are of course exceptions, but generally this sensible character will be drawn to a job or profession with a pay-packet at the end of the week. The more negative Taurean types will dislike any kind of physical work, and such a child should be stimulated mentally as early as possible. A lot of effort will be needed on the parents' part, but when the result is a well-adjusted contented adult it will have been worthwhile.

GEMINI

THE FIRST AIR SIGN

Symbol The Twins

Colour Yellow

Metal Quicksilver

Planet Mercury

Motivation To invent and create

Restless and mentally active; runs on nervous energy; quick-witted; adaptable; focuses on self-expression and communication; fickle

GENERAL CHARACTERISTICS

- Is Your Child a Typical Gemini?

THE GEMINI BABY

- Health
- Food
- Crying
- Teething
- Bath-time
- Interests and Games
- Walking and Talking
- Toilet-training
- Starting School

THE GEMINI CHILD

- Health
- Friends
- Interests and Games
- Accepting a New Baby
- Discipline
- Sex
- Homework and Study
- Finding a Direction

THE GEMINI TEENAGER

- Dating
- Alcohol
- Drugs
- Suggested Careers

GENERAL CHARACTERISTICS

Dr Jekyll: positive

The planet Mercury gives those born under this sign a surplus of intellectual energy that seeks constant expression. Those born under this sign also long for new interests and, when impatient with routine, can produce some incredible results in an artistic field. This type is at its happiest when expressing an essential part of his character. The Geminian's true desire in life is to make it more interesting and beautiful for everyone. The Gemini attempts to stimulate and refresh the minds of others, and the intellect is a driving force. When new problems arise that aren't at first understood, the Gemini will struggle with them until understanding is reached.

The positive Gemini can be observed at all types of gatherings matching their wits with interesting people. The interests encompass public relations, publishing, television and radio and in fact anything to do with communication. They can be found whereever they can meet interesting and lively minds. There is a certain eagerness about the Gemini, an immediate and sympathetic friendliness coupled with quick but graceful movement.

Almost every Gemini can speak, or understand, more than one language. This type can usually find some way of making words work for them, whether it be selling ice-cubes to Eskimoes or impractical dreams to pessimists! And when the Gemini is questioned on a subject about which he is ill informed, he will change the subject so quickly and direct the conversation to another area so adroitly that the whole affair ends with the questioner being questioned instead of himself. The Gemini also hates to be misunderstood, it frustrates and depresses him. When this occurs he will fly from one relationship to another seeking relief from his confused emotions.

Those born under this sign spend a great deal of their lives seeking information about themselves, the world in general and other people. It is the sign of the eternal student, and it is one that usually manages to attain a high order of intellect.

Mr Hyde: negative

The dual personality of Gemini is at its strongest in this more negative type. One day you are in their company and the hours rush past as you are cheered by their clever conversation and dazzled by their charm. The next you will appear to be totally ignored, causing you to imagine the worst possible things. Is he in trouble or are you? Your fears could be well based, of course, but then again perhaps they are not! A week later you will bump into this character, only to realize that yet again the mood has changed and now you are the best of friends once more.

This type has the unconscious urge to disguise his true intent, to disguise motives with dual actions. In general, such Geminis seek to confuse and, in true Gemini inconsistency, will turn right around and be so direct that they will fairly take your breath away! This particular Hyde generally throws away the familiar precious things and people in life too quickly, being attracted to the untried new. Later on it is no wonder that this particular type lives to regret the instant disposal.

In spite of the other people around this Gemini will share the deepest emotions only with one constant companion – the other twin self! You will feel drained when coming into contact with this individual for male or female, they demand sympathy, attention, consideration and time, believing these to be their right. And they will talk excessively in order to feed their rather inflated egos. Other people should ideally put their feet down a little more firmly at the beginning of any relationship, although the chances are that Mr and Miss Hyde will not even notice.

Is Your Child a Typical Gemini?

Answer honestly the questions below using Yes – (3 points) No – (2 points) Sometimes – (1 point), then turn to page 218 for the answers.

1 Does the child need constant mental stimulation?

2 Does he become impatient with reading and writing because his thoughts are running on ahead?

3 Does the child suffer from rapid changes of mood?

4 Is the child talkative?

5 Does he use his hands when trying to make a point?

6 Does fantasy play a larger part in his life than you would perhaps like?

7 Does silence unnerve the child?

8 Is his concentration poor?

9 Does the child loathe being restricted?

10 Is the child extremely mischievous?

11 Is the child excessively inquisitive?

12 Does the child take a long time to fall asleep?

13 Does the child love a challenge?

14 Does it sometimes push you away when you try to be affectionate?

15 Is the child critical?

16 Is it difficult for the child to sit still?

17 Does the child have a speech impediment such as a lisp or slight stammer?

18 Does the child like to do at least two things at once?

19 Is your child quite happy when strangers enter the room?

20 Is the child ambidextrous?

THE GEMINI BABY
Up to four years of age

If you have just arrived home with a Gemini baby in tow, then if you start now you will just about have enough time to look to your laurels before the child learns to ask questions. Once this starts you will need to be a walking encyclopaedia. You have two years then in which to bone up on all the useless information that happens to come your way and believe me you are going to need it. Questions – such as 'Which is the third highest mountain in the world?' 'Where is the shortest river in the world?' – may be an everyday occurrence, therefore you'll need either to learn the answers or become adept at bluff. Either way you have been warned.

It is important to remember that Gemini is an air sign and air must move. Because of this don't fence in your baby as he will not want to stay in any one place for too long. Once your child has learnt to use his vocal chords you will be surprised at how much noise can come from such a small mouth. If your nerves shatter easily or you like a quiet life then you are going to need large amounts of tolerance on which to draw. The quick bird-like movements, or constant fidgetting as it is sometimes called, will seem impossible for you to handle on occasions. Try to understand that doing two things at the same time is quite natural for the Gemini, and this is a normal state of activity. However, it might be a good idea to at least make attempts to teach him to do things a little slower for his own good. But the basic nature can be changed without causing a great deal of frustration. The best thing you can do to learn to love this child for what he or she is, outgoing, bright, curious and decidedly precocious. You cannot turn a cheetah into a tortoise, or vice versa, and if you try your Gemini child will end up a neurotic, unhappy being. Also, you will need to remember that this child has an active inner life which leads to a world of make-believe. Truth is often disguised as fantasy and vice versa. Your child may even give the impression of exaggeration or telling lies, but the Gemini just cannot help making life a little bigger than it really is. He may even convince himself that things really do happen that way!

If you have inexhaustible patience and energy you will make plenty of room for your Gemini and love every frantic, hectic and chaotic minute of his childhood.

Health

Gemini rules the lungs, and the Gemini baby needs plenty of preventive action to avoid the more complicated cold diseases such as pneumonia. Hygiene, of course, is always a must with small babies and should a member of your family catch cold you should be especially careful with the Gemini baby, as even a casually placed soiled tissue or hands that have used the tissue to blow a nose could lead to trouble. Parents should never attempt to treat the cold themselves; advice should be sought from the doctor.

This sign also rules the hands, arms and shoulders. After one year and above, a number of accidents to these parts should be expected. Geminian children are also quite highly strung, and sudden violent noises could prove to be most upsetting to them. Furthermore, there will be times when you'll wonder whether or not your Gemini will ever drop off to sleep. That little head is so full of curiosity that the child is frightened to switch it off in case it misses something! Not surprisingly many insomniacs are born under this sign.

Lastly, convulsions are associated with Gemini. They are mostly due to a sudden raised temperature, but they should never be underrated. Lay your baby on its stomach, head to one side, and ring the doctor. Fits are of course very upsetting to the parent, but don't panic, keep calm and get professional advice immediately.

Food

You may have noticed that your Gemini baby takes a considerable length of time to drink his bottles. It is not too difficult to understand why. Those eyes and that head appear to have been built on pivots, as they are forever trying to see just what is going on everywhere. If this exasperates you, wait until he or she can run – your child is not going to waste a moment sitting down even to eat. The wisest thing to do is to produce two special toys that the baby can touch and watch while you shovel the food into his mouth! The toys may also help to delay the feed until the child is really hungry. What does it matter if lunch is an hour late? The key word is adaptability. Naturally enough on no account should snacks between meals be encouraged. It does not take much to fill the Gemini child, and you are going to make meal-times more difficult if the child does not *want* to eat.

With regard to the meal content, this is not a fussy child, though he is one that is bored easily, and the same breakfast twice consecutively is once too many, so vary meals as much as possible.

Finally, the Gemini is somewhat a messy eater, not because he is naughty but because he is insatiably curious. That child wants to know exactly how the custard *feels* as well as tastes. Is it as wet as it looks? Are there any lumps? And this individual will not be satisfied until the truth has been revealed. So get plenty of paper napkins and keep them handy!

Crying

The lack of mental stimulation or boredom may not to the parent be a good reason for wailing, but it is to a Gemini. And to satisfy this infant there will be times when you will begin to feel like a court jester! Hopefully, you have a sense of humour. A cot strewn with bells and mobiles will help the child, but they will need rearranging occasionally if they are to retain their appeal. Of course, the child may occasionally scream for food or because of a wet nappy, but once these have been attended to and the child is still crying then you can be sure that boredom is the cause.

A general rule for all babies is that there is always a reason for their distress. You need not feel inadequate if you are unable to recognize each cry. You will learn from experience and you'll soon be able to understand when your child shrieks from either illness, boredom or loneliness. Hopefully your baby will be patient with you while you are finding your feet, although it must be added that the Gemini is not the most patient of creatures. Usually he wants everything immediately. However, keep calm and remember that the child must learn to adapt to you too.

Teething

If you were born under one of those over-rated 'lucky' stars, then one day you will discover something white flashing inside your baby's mouth – one, two or even four teeth! For generally the Gemini baby cuts his teeth earlier than most and with little apparent discomfort. (See the section at the end of the book.) But if your lucky star crashed to the ground with a *thud*, then your child will develop a heavy cold and be completely wretched. It may be difficult under the circumstances, but do try to be extra loving. Keep your Gemini warm and take it in turns to comfort him. Remind yourself just how miserable a heavy cold can be, add to this the discomfort of toothache, and you will imagine what the tot is going through.

Sit your baby in a baby-chair as often as possible at these times as this will help to keep the nose unblocked. Give him plenty of fruit-juices. Yellow is the colour to go for when you buy the first teething-ring. This will hold the child's attention. Apart from this advice, you can only hope that the teeth come through as quickly as possible.

Bath-time

It is not a good idea to bath your Gemini baby every day, especially in winter when a good wash from head to toes will suffice. When the child is older he will look forward to the bath-time ritual provided you allow the infant to take a number of toys in with him. This is necessary to prevent boredom, but do try to keep it within the bounds of reason or your bathroom carpet, along with the floorboards, will slowly rot with the daily puddles of water continually eddying over them!

Lastly, a word on safety. As previously mentioned the Gemini baby loathes to sit still for any length of time, but clambering in and out of the tub can be hazardous and jumping should be firmly discouraged from the moment it begins. Those taps can be awfully hard on little heads and bottoms. It is *never* safe to leave your baby unattended as he is far too active and curious, but with common sense prevailing bath-time will be tremendous fun.

Interests and Games

Your child does not need the most expensive toys that money can buy to stimulate games and play. The Gemini is stimulated by life itself. What it does need, however, is to learn the art of concentration, plus satisfying his eternal curiosity. However, at this stage your child will be interested in everything, although anything that requires time and patience is strictly out. Your Gemini child's immaturity will infuriate him at times. For example this individual may discover that he cannot obtain the desired result from paints or pencils and will be extremely frustrated with his poor efforts. The same can be said for puzzles. Once this occurs, abandon them until a later stage.

All Gemini children prefer objects that can be put into motion, such as a ball, dog, or cart on a leash to be dragged around. The baby will also enjoy self-propelling objects such as clockwork toys, cars and planes. The family cat is a continual source of enjoyment too, for unlike the toys it reacts unpredictably and keeps on making funny noises while tantalizingly out of reach. Expensive toys and dolls are a waste of time then, and too limiting. Puppets are a distinct possibility as they can be moved at will. Later on, your Gemini child will become an avid reader but at this stage books are far too static. It will not, however, do any harm to take the first steps in reading with alphabet bricks. T-E-A spells tea, not to mention ATE or EAT! What fun! One thing is certain, the Gemini may get bored himself but boredom for the rest of the family will be a thing of the past.

Walking and Talking

The Gemini baby cannot wait to be mobile and it's quite common for the typical member of this sign to be erect before the first birthday. Once this occurs you will need running shoes in an effort to keep up. He may even suspect that he has a twin brother or sister tucked away somewhere for it will seem that one moment you left him happily playing with his toys in one room while you rushed to the kitchen to rescue a burnt dinner only to discover within seconds he has joined you and has your best china strewn all over the kitchen floor in a flash.

Furthermore, there is no point in deceiving yourself into thinking you can outwit this type with a playpen. A restriction simply will not work with this sign. Confine such a child in a small space and it will consider this tantamount to cruelty! The whole personality wishes to explore and learn, and restriction will lead to emotional depression which will not be outgrown easily. Besides it is useless, for it is only a matter of seconds before he or she figures out a way of escape. The Gemini child's mind is as agile as his body.

Because of our little friend's speed, a word of warning. For heaven's sake, lock away all drugs and household goods. Out of reach is simply not good enough, and won't be for long. The same vitality that goes into physical exercise is channelled into speech. And although precocious the Gemini child seems determined to reach this particular stage through the most difficult route possible. He or she loves words. The sound of them. With a back to front, inside out, rhyming or even possibly the invention of his own language. Don't interfere, after all you may have given birth to an eminent literary personality. Lastly, because this is the sign of communication, sometimes distortions take place, due to various conflicting influences in their personal birth charts, and the Mercury child could, therefore, lisp or stammer.

Toilet-training

The Gemini child is reluctant to waste a second of his precious time sitting on the potty. As a result, he will either perform immediately or scream and shout if you insist on his sitting there until he cooperates.

As with all signs, applying too much pressure in toilet-training could put back the child's natural progress by six months or more. Forget training the baby when he's very young – eighteen months is soon enough. Any success before that is purely coincidental as a baby cannot control himself before this age. Express exaggerated delight with any success you finally get and ignore accidents in any form. It may be that your first clue will be a dry change one morning. However, if this doesn't occur don't fret, your child will certainly not have any trouble in asking for the potty, so let him or her be the boss in this very important stage.

Starting School

The Gemini child starting school is similar to the Arietian, so it is suggested you read and digest this section in the chapter The Aries Baby. Remember that your Gemini is bursting to explore and learn and once he has had a day at school without mishap he will be straining to return the next day. Don't feel rejected, just be thankful for that independent spirit.

THE GEMINI CHILD
Four to twelve years of age

Health

Your Gemini child's inability to relax may be your biggest headache at this stage. And although minor accidents to hands, arms and shoulders will continue, and colds develop rather too easily, these will seem as nothing compared to the anxiety of possessing a child who will simply not let up, a child who eats less than the other members of the family but who has twice as much energy. You will probably be right to be anxious. Your Gemini child feeds off nervous energy until it runs out, at which time the child will retire with half-a-dozen minor illnesses, most of them quite obscure. As a result, a good nourishing diet and plenty of rest are musts. If your Geminian cannot sleep until late because of his inability to switch off his active brain, then allow the child to sleep later the following morning. What does it matter if the others are up and about at eight? This child stores sleep like a hamster stores food. He will survive on the bare minimum of rest during schooldays, but at the weekends he should be allowed to rise when he wants to.

It is not unusual to find a left-handed Gemini, or an ambidextrous one for that matter. The child may write with one hand and draw with another. Neither should you become neurotic if you notice nibbled fingernails although if you wish this habit to cease you should endeavour to keep the child busier, for this is yet another side of boredom.

The Gemini is erratic in his methods and progress, but he keeps abreast and often overtakes his more orthodox contemporaries.

Friends

One of the more rewarding sides to possessing a Gemini child is that he has no trouble in mixing with other people. True, Geminians are fickle and forever involved in petty squabbles so best friends are changed within an hour, but it may be a wise move to make attempts at instilling some kind of loyalty. It is not a quality that comes naturally to this type. There is a natural opportunism and a tendency to use other people for the Geminian's own ends.

Apart from this your problems will be finding the house full of other children who follow your mischievous Gemini almost anywhere and will positively fall out of cupboards and other hidey-holes! They will crawl out from beneath beds, slip out of bathrooms and slide from behind the curtains! And when there is trouble in the neighbourhood, don't believe that innocent Gemini face as your child is sure to be mixed up in it somewhere along the line, probably as the ringleader of the local gang.

Interests and Games

At some point you are going to notice that your Gemini child has little trouble with reading. No Gemini will object when called upon to recite, for they all delight in communicating with others and sharing their knowledge, whether verbally or on paper. As for other interests, if one attempted to list one Gemini child's pursuits and passions it would fill the remainder of this chapter and perhaps the rest of this book.

Because of this, an attempt should be made to advise which activities should be encouraged. You need not worry about a physical hobby for fear of insufficient exercise for this type's everyday rush through life keeps him fit. Besides, any sports the child may be interested in will change daily, although sprinting will appeal and the child could go far with it.

Mentally, however, you do have a problem, for both positive

and negative Geminians find concentration difficult. Fiction will do almost nothing to hold the attention, but a book filled with facts and information will fascinate the child. The Gemini sense of humour is well developed and the more ridiculous the facts read, the better. Your child is an avid reader, and once he has mastered the art of sitting still, reading should be encouraged.

Don't ever attempt to take your Gemini to the cinema or theatre until approximately nine or ten unless you are quite happy to spend your time chasing after the infant all around the auditorium!

A suggestion for a musical instrument is the piano, the Gemini's instrument and one that is enjoyed, although practise will be erratic. However, the child is intelligent and will eventually realize that if anything is to be mastered it should be taken seriously.

Don't ever persecute those born under this sign of the Twins as it is the sign of the original rebel and one who will participate in anything that has been forbidden. Neither should parents despair if the Gemini child follows one hobby one week and another the next. This individual has a demanding intellect, one continuously searching for a subject that will engross him wholeheartedly.

Naturally, much depends on your relationship with the child, and if he should be close to a particular parent the child will earnestly strive to emulate that parent. The child knows that emulation will enable him to exchange thoughts and theories with the idolized one.

The Gemini needs to stretch that grey matter, so give your Mercury child space to breathe and the time to discover himself. Remember that the erratic path being followed is fairly straightforward to the child, though it may be a mystery and a complication to the rest of the family.

Accepting a New Baby

As repeatedly mentioned, the Gemini child's brain flutters not unlike a butterfly. Just for once, this could be a blessing in disguise as a new baby will be yet another novelty. Even when this wears off, your Gemini will be too engrossed elsewhere to worry about the time you are spending with the new baby and jealousy is unlikely unless you push your Gemini totally into the background.

Some children are extremely helpful and leap up whenever they are asked to assist. Such a child is helpful, but with one stipulation – help will only be given when the Gemini child *wants* to give it. If you pressurize your Gemini into assisting with the new infant you will have a rebellion on your hands. If you are clever you will show this type how much fun babies can be. For instance, bath-time can be fun, if disastrous for the decor! Plastic tea-sets provide parties – pouring water over everybody present will delight the Gemini child! Then, of course, there are meal-times! Probably a messy procedure, but why not let your Gemini feed the baby under supervision. This is something that should keep both youngsters happy. Furthermore, your Gemini child will be delighted with any progress the baby may make, for the sooner he grows up the sooner your first born will have a playmate, a fact that should be stressed. With a Gemini you are blessed with the most adaptable of children and because of this problems should not be insurmountable.

Discipline

If you are convinced that you have given birth to a barefaced liar, you should remember that this child needs to stretch his imagination. But if you honestly believe that this has gone a little too far, why not persuade the offender to write his stories down on paper? Once this has been mastered the child will be able to see the difference between dream and fact and he should recognize that something has been lost in the translation. As always, much depends on age in this case. However, you do have an intelligent child, and it is to this intelligence that you must continually appeal. Treat him like a fool and this child could detrimentally turn that splendid grey matter against you. Should this happen you will later discover that you have a most devious and cunning child. Also, physical violence can greatly disturb this highly strung individual, so much so that repercussions are sure to be felt, probably in the form of a conviction that he is unloved, which in turn leads to insecurity. If you do not make contact at this stage then you could be in for a very difficult time later, especially in adolescence, for this is the sign of the thief as well as the liar.

The only way to discipline this child is to make an appeal to his logic. When explaining why this or that must be done it is necessary to give a clear explanation. After all, certain actions can hurt people, so explain what they are and why. This is not the most considerate of signs and when it comes to other people the child can unintentionally hurt. Otherwise the Geminian is no fool, so don't treat him like one and always tell the truth if you expect it in return. Other than this, the Gemini child obviously needs love and logic in equal doses and both will see you through any difficulties.

Sex

Again, a truthful and natural approach is the only way to treat this subject. (See the section at the end of the book.) However, there may be one or two special Gemini problems you may have to solve.

1 Masturbation is not native to this sign alone, obviously. All children are curious about their and other people's genitals and it naturally follows that at some point they are going to want to touch them. This, in turn, applies to the average Gemini child. But it may seem that at times the child is taking this activity a little too zealously, and if this is the case then your child is probably bored to tears and finds this particular part of the anatomy the only thing worth

playing with! Control your anger, or you will give the child complexes that will later need to be sorted out. Try to draw his attention away elsewhere on a game or a book or perhaps painting. Mental stimulation is needed.

2 At some point this particular child will become very attached to a member of his or her own sex. The Gemini can easily identify with either sex quite happily, and this part of his development is quite natural. Don't over-react or you'll instil feelings of guilt, not to mention a feeling of isolation. This is a perfectly normal phase, and this child will only become submerged in it if the parents handle the situation with prejudice and fears. Stifle fears, be natural and recall that inquisitive mind, answer all questions honestly and your child will grow up sexually well adjusted.

Homework and Study

When your Gemini child is at school he will probably be the class impersonator because this type has the happy knack of being able to imitate most voices. This may lead to one or two unusual remarks on the school report, but in some instances this is a harmless enough phase while in others it is a lifelong talent. It is also a good idea to start your Gemini on a language early, for he will probably learn it effortlessly. Don't be surprised if your Gemini child insists he can do his homework quite adequately while listening to the radio. Believe it or not, this is probably true, and if progress continues, then why not? You will also have to remember that this child will never be satisfied with one pursuit at a time and the quicker you resign yourself to this fact the easier your life will be. The chief dangers are a lack of patience and an unwillingness to persist until anything is thoroughly learned. All Geminians need to be discouraged from a tendency to skim over knowledge without completely understanding it. You will also be infuriated when you are asked a question and then find that you are being interrupted before you have had a chance to reply. Geminians find it extremely difficult to listen without interrupting and this is a lesson you could do well to teach.

Furthermore, Geminians constantly repeat themselves but get extremely impatient when others do the same. If you learn that your Gemini is day-dreaming you should set about finding the reason for this dreamy state. If the child is typical to his sign you will probably find that he is fantasizing during the same lessons each time. This either means resignation to the fact that he will never master geography, for instance, or possibly that there may be a lack of communication between himself and his teacher.

As a general rule, your Gemini child can excel in whichever interest or activity he wishes to and when he does not wish to there is little you can do about it.

Finding a Direction

Geminians will not have one direction but rather directions, for everything in this sign is in the plural. This is perfectly normal for such a character, although clearly some kind of perspective needs to be exercised, for energies need some channelling.

The matter of time should also be considered. The message to be communicated is that if the child has six or seven all-consuming passions, three or four might be better. A set of encyclopaedias is a wise buy and will help to retain your child's interest in the world at large and will also improve reading and spelling.

This character will also be engrossed by the news in the media, an attempt to keep abreast of world events. Not surprisingly, many writers are born under this sign, so take particular note of the child's school essays. Never mind the punctuation or the grammar – extra tuition will help – but how is the content? You may have a journalist or an author in the making, and the school magazine may hold a strong attraction. Encourage membership of the local library as soon as reading becomes effortless. If your Gemini child is slow in geography or mathematics for example, then introduce an element of fun into the proceedings, at least at home. Allow a week for learning most of the world's important capitals, then, at the dinner-table or wherever, test the child. The whole family can join in and this will make the lesson not only enjoyable but casual, therefore relieving any tension or mental blocks that may have been building up in connection with the subject. The same ploy can obviously be used for other subjects such as spelling or history dates. The larger the family, the more fun you will have, although it goes without saying that some of you may need to check your facts yourself.

It is difficult to apply strict rules to such an airy subject as a Geminian, but encouragement and active participation on your part will increase your child's chances of finding that elusive direction in life.

THE GEMINI TEENAGER

Twelve to eighteen years of age

The Gemini's notorious impatience plays an important and unfortunate role in adolescence. There isn't any insult or statement the parents can level about impossible behaviour that the child doesn't concede to be the unblemished truth. If your Gemini isn't in open rebellion this honesty will serve as a bridge between parent and child. The Gemini teenager is either positive or negative, up or down, good or bad, all frequently during the course of one day. Such an individual has little time for wishy-washy or middle-of-the-road ways of life and adolescence to this type is an infuriating position to be in.

The Gemini can accept being a child or an adult but what sticks in his throat is being in the odious no-man's-land between the two. The result of this self-disgust is that one day your teenager is fighting to the death over the last cream cake and reading comics while the next he is demanding his first drink, cigarette or insisting that he is old enough to stay out all night. Such a paradox is clearly not easy to handle and no parent, however saintly, can be expected to bear the constant inconsistency.

Firstly – it is necessary for you to put yourself into your teenager's unkempt size eight shoes. This, at least, will give you some insight to his agony.

Make up your mind that this is an adult you are dealing with and treat the person accordingly. Responsibility should be meted out and most of the decisions that effect him or her should be laid out for attention. It is essential that the Gemini be allowed to choose his or her own wardrobe, advice only being given when asked for, which it won't be. This type needs to know that you respect his judgement and that you naturally expect him home at a reasonable hour. If it is made clear that you have no intention of laying down the law unless he or she is going to behave like an irresponsible child, then this individual is not going to give you the chance of accusing him of infantile behaviour and will then naturally respond to the responsibility that has been granted him.

If you are the nagging type of parent you will naturally incline to nag when studies are neglected. However, it is better to simply state that this is his or her own life and that if he wants to stay static while his friends get on then he should go ahead and tear up those books. Your Gemini likes to be ahead and will not like being left behind, so it will only be a matter of time before reason is shown in this respect.

Finally, it is important to keep open the lines of communication at all times. Provided you can force yourself to overlook the somewhat untidy exterior and take your Gemini out to dinner or for a drink, a feeling of comradeship can be developed. With a little luck you may find your Gemini beginning to confide in you. An unmeasurable amount of understanding and a keen sense of justice will help you through this, the most difficult of ages.

Dating

The Gemini will keep you on your toes and feeling young. The teenage Gemini boy will practically live on the phone, go steady with a different girl each week, change his mind a hundred times about his future career but . . . do it all with great panache.

The Gemini girl will be popular and able to turn on showers of tears or sunny smiles at the flick of a mental switch! Also, you'd better prepare your home, for it is about to be taken over, taking on the appearance of a railway station with people rushing in and out of your home. Better keep your temper and sanity pills! A lonely unpopular Gemini is not a typical specimen.

As previously mentioned, your Gemini will use the phone a great deal. You'll be forever opening and closing the front door, and why is it, you'll wonder, that your child always seems to be friendly with the noisiest teenagers? But where is your stiff upper lip? Force a grin and do try to go along with all of this, even if it necessitates buying ear-plugs. Besides, if you ban such happy chaos from your house, these high spirits may well find release on the streets.

On a romantic level you will never be able to keep abreast of the stream of admirers, so refrain from tearing your hair when your child brings home some friend of whom you disapprove. Forbid him or her to see any particular person and the object of your disapproval will become a hundred per cent more attractive. Remember, this type is bored easily and so you can expect many friends of the opposite sex rather than single relationships.

Sexually speaking, this type enjoys the thrill of the chase rather than the act itself and can certainly never be made to participate in anything he or she doesn't wish to. That Gemini boy of yours will eventually lose his virginity in order to impress his male friends rather than out of passion. Your Gemini girl is a flirt, preferring to remain unobtainable. No precocious sex-pert this! And what she doesn't know about female wiles could be written on the head of a pin! However, a word of advice. It won't do any harm to warn your daughter against extreme teasing, especially when dating the more mature male. Don't worry, she is willing to learn, so there is no need to be embarrassed and you can feel free to discuss anything with her.

Your Gemini teenager's dating habits will wear you to a frazzle, but with wise handling this child will grow into a charming, sociable if flirtatious adult.

Alcohol

The Gemini's need to grow up quickly may be reflected in his attitude to alcohol. A wise parent will allow this child to occasionally drink wine at home, especially with dinner. Furthermore, a trip to the local bar with his parents will take away the forbidden excitement of alcohol. However, it won't do any harm to point out the illegality of drinking and driving, and never complain if your teenager son abandons the car and arrives home in a cab. Encourage this sensible move; it may be expensive but it shows common sense.

Fortunately Gemini is not an alcoholic sign, so you can relax. Moderation is generally developed quite early on in life and quite naturally.

Drugs

Regrettably drug abuse is more frequently located under this sign than any other. It often begins with the Gemini's inclination towards insomnia. In an effort to minimize this situation allow and encourage your Gemini teenager to read late into the night. It will help to turn off that ever-active and whirling head. Secondly, your highly strung Gemini may consider drugs to keep himself calm during some important occasion. These types do tend to get wound up under stress – before interviews, for example – and probably do in fact need something to calm them down. And as this is not an alcoholic sign, a couple of stiff drinks will do equally well when it comes to calming shattered nerves.

Temptation can also be located at parties if soft drugs are part of the scene. Keep cool and keep your eyes peeled. Restrain yourself from anger and bear in mind that this is a rebel and one who will always do what you don't want him to. Make a casual observation. Ask him if he's been smoking or taking pills. Question him with as much interest as you can. What were his reactions to the experience? Inform him or her that you too have experimented even if you haven't, and have reached the conclusion that a couple of drinks are far more pleasurable. On reflection your Gemini may consider that if his antiquated parents have been turned on by drugs then it might be time for him to turn off as much of the excitement will have gone out of the operation.

Programmes on drug abuse can be switched on, too, but don't make a point of insisting that your teenager sit and watch them. View them without comment or scrutiny.

If these simple rules are observed you should be able to avert any great drama or tragedy with drugs.

SUGGESTED CAREERS

The Gemini teenager is not the most practical person in the world. The Gemini boy may decide to become a rock star – matters not that he is tone deaf and cannot sing. He may even decide that painting is his vocation and will be undeterred by the fact that he is only able to master matchstick men! It is the romantic or glamorous image that appeals. However, allow him to make such leanings while encouraging one of the Gemini careers mentioned below. And don't worry too much – he is not stupid. When he is booed off the stage at the local bar or the art expert falls about in hysterics, the Gemini will look elsewhere for glamour. Your child could be a second Elvis Presley or Gauguin, in which case you will have to forget your own ideas regarding his future and offer encouragement. When a Gemini is gifted he doesn't mess around, it is one hundred per cent commitment.

Here are some suggested Gemini careers:

Journalist	Lecturer	Chauffeur
Broadcaster	Linguist	Navigator
Commentator	Postman	Sales representative
Telephone operator	Secretary	Shop assistant
Teacher	Travel agent	Craftsman

The Gemini should obviously try to avoid any job that means working in one place all the time, or in work that is tedious or monotonous. Geminians need variety and should always be adding to their interest.

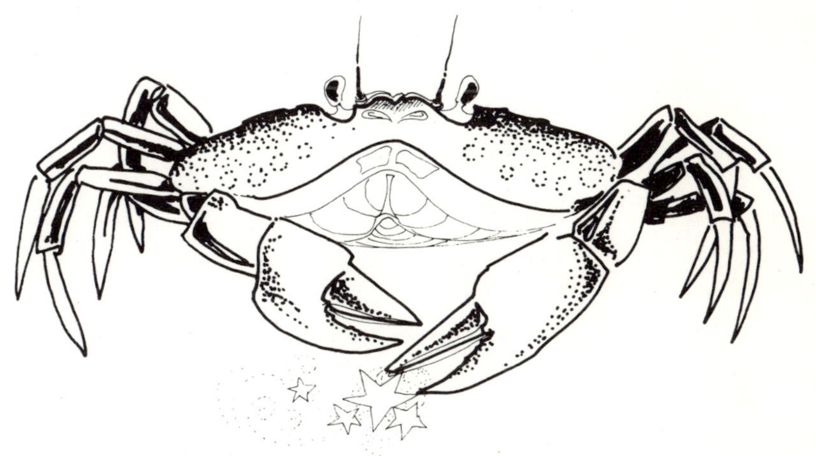

CANCER

THE FIRST WATER SIGN

Symbol The Crab

Colour Violet

Metal Silver

Planet The Moon

Motivation To prophesy and teach

Changeable; over-sensitive; imaginative; sensation-seeking

GENERAL CHARACTERISTICS

Is Your Child a Typical Cancer?

THE CANCERIAN BABY

Health

Food

Crying

Teething

Bath-time

Interests and Games

Walking and Talking

Toilet-training

Starting School

THE CANCERIAN CHILD

Health

Friends

Interests and Games

Accepting a New Baby

Discipline

Sex

Homework and Study

Finding a Direction

THE CANCERIAN TEENAGER

Dating

Alcohol

Drugs

Suggested Careers

GENERAL CHARACTERISTICS

Dr Jekyll: positive

Two of the most prominent Cancerian characteristics are tenacity and patience. Once a desired object, idea or person has come within this type's reach he will seize it and, like the Crab, would rather lose a limb than let it go. Rather like a pianist the Cancerian has every conceivable mood and emotion at his fingertips. Such a virtuoso can feel and make others experience joy, sorrow, compassion and horror. But the affections are deep and lasting. No distance or period of time can lessen family ties or dim a friendship. Because the Crab is naturally restless and changeable he is usually well travelled but, no matter how far or long he may wander, he will always return home, being a natural domesticate.

Financially this is a shrewd type and no matter how much money is acquired the Cancerian never feels really secure. Likewise, no matter how much love is acquired, he always wants more. Just to look at or feel his money makes him feel smug and secure, though other people will rarely be aware of the size of his bank-balance. The Cancerian believes himself to be just a poor soul struggling along to earn a crust! There are times when others feel that perhaps they can help this poor bankrupt and maybe acquire a loan from the bank for him, only to discover that 'bankrupt' means he is down to his last £1000. Don't be upset, this type simply cannot help himself. Insecurity runs strongly through the veins, hence the hoarding tendency. You will rarely run across a Crab who even throws an old postcard away, and Cancerians are hoarders too, probably keeping sufficient foodstuffs to keep a normal family for five weeks.

Such complexity makes this a difficult sign to understand, but if you love a Cancerian you'll just keep trying.

Mr Hyde: negative

This individual is completely ruled by emotions and selfishness and frantic worrying and apprehension can actually make him ill. While sympathy and cheerfulness often lead to a miraculous recovery, sleepless nights are often spent anticipating horrors that for the most part are never likely to strike. The active imagination can be morbid enough to turn a minor illness into a grave or chronic one.

Gloomy compassion may initially seem to be the answer, but don't you believe it! For once the limelight has been obtained this type will take twice as long to recover. Pessimism is never far away, always ready to spoil other people's flights of fancy or pleasure, and tears flow like deep rivers from his frantic heart. Sensitive feelings can be damaged by a harsh glance or a rough turn of phrase, and cruelty of any description brings on complete withdrawal. It won't be easy then to spot the Crab in this mood because, when hurt, he disappears into his shell of reproachful silence. It is extremely difficult for this type to enjoy professional or personal life as too much time is spent hiding within the protective shell. Once he regards himself injured by a broken love affair or by a professional rebuff do what you like but you'll never reach him. The phone will be ignored while he secretly revels in his misery.

Unless you are really ready to take on an adult who's like an emotional infant, or you possess a heart full of inexhaustible love, then it is probably best to leave this Crab well and truly alone.

Is Your Child a Typical Cancer?

Answer honestly the questions below, using 'Yes', 'No' or 'Sometimes' then turn to page 218 for the answer. Score 3 for Yes – 2 for Sometimes – 1 for No.

1 Does your child love water?

2 Does your child seem permanently thirsty?

3 Does he delight in brother or sister?

4 Does the child have a good memory?

5 Is the child greedy at meal times?

6 Does it suffer from nightmares?

7 Does the child enjoy the limelight?

8 Is it hurt easily?

9 Does the child refuse to throw away old toys?

10 Is the child possessive?

11 Does it cry easily?

12 Is the child over weight?

13 Does it reflect your moods?

14 Does the child dislike its own company?

15 Is the child shy?

16 Does the child have a sweet tooth?

17 Does the child dislike the company of children its own age?

18 Does the child prefer to stick to a routine?

19 Does the child become stubborn when you try to take something away from it?

20 Is the child extremely moody?

THE CANCER BABY
Up to four years of age

Unless you are walking around permanently blindfolded and ear-plugged you cannot help but have noticed just how expressively the new baby's crumpled face is. No matter how much the medics insist that he can see very little at present you are unlikely to believe this. Your little Crab is extremely impressionable and it has just entered a brand new fascinating world. All the new sensations that he is experiencing make a great impact on that indelible memory. From bed-time to bed-time the imaginative mind will be recalling what it has seen, heard and observed. The emotions are rich and full and your little pink bundle will react sometimes violently to everything that is going on around. It will take his parents some time to recognize all the baby's expressions and cries as they change with each emotion and mood, and right from birth the Cancerian is revelling in the sensations of life. Once you are used to the complexity of your Cancer infant the little Crab can be lots of fun. Your little angel's features can crumble easily into tears or spread wide with a beam of delight, and it is interesting to watch those very versatile expressions.

From infancy to adolescence those born under this sign are tremendously dependent on the actions of those around, especially in the family circle. They do not demand to be loved, they simply lie there hoping that someone will realize they desperately need to be cuddled and adored. Rejection or neglect will ruin this type. Later, your child will do or say anything in order to be loved. This includes giving away the contents of the toy cupboard to those whom he wishes to smile favourably upon him.

You will have your hands full, but the little Crab has so much to give and all you have to do is to get the most out of him.

Health

This child's often disastrously sweet tooth, in time, will lead to dental problems. If you cannot prevent the child from consuming large amounts of sweets and biscuits then at least make regular dental appointments. Not surprisingly the Cancerian is frequently an overweight child. This in turn can lead to fat tissue gathering on chest and complaints associated with this region such as asthma. The chesty child is the one who repeatedly suffers from colds that lead to continual catarrh and coughs. There will also be a tendency to wheeze. Although there may be nothing fundamentally wrong your doctor should be consulted. This type needs a good, well-balanced diet, which means nourishing rather than too filling foods. Try not to over-protect the chesty child. If you are worried, then the child will worry. Children may well grow out of their chesty condition and, in the meantime, need to lead as full a life as possible. No special precautions are necessary unless your doctor advises. It may also be a good idea to check whether your child is being greedy in an effort to compensate for something that is missing from life. In this case it is up to you to be honest with yourself and find out what it is.

Food

The Crab is frequently one of those perpetually hungry children and, as a baby, once this type is up to eight ounces of milk at a sitting it may well be time to start solids, despite the fact that four to six months is usually the age advised. Remember, age is just a guide and some larger and hungrier babies are ready for solids earlier than others. Bear in mind, however, that there could be other reasons for your baby's apparent hunger and fretfulness and it could be wise to first consult your doctor before acting. Also, you'll discover that your Cancerian, at all ages, will tend to prefer sweet, sticky things to the savoury. Try not to encourage this or you could run into the weight problems.

Generally speaking, the Cancer child is the easiest of all to please. The very sight of food being prepared is enough to send the adrenalin surging through any Cancerian's veins and this little character is a precocious feeder, one who will soon dispense with your services. It only takes a few months for baby to start to try to feed himself.

Always have food ready in advance. The little Crab gets extremely fretful when he is kept waiting. Fortunately for his parents food problems will probably be the last thing they will have to worry about.

Crying

The only possible way a small baby can attract your attention is by crying. To be ignored is extremely distressing for him. The small Crab needs to be constantly handled and reassured, and this in turn leads to security. This child has a vivid and over-active imagination and is regularly plagued at night by devils and hobgoblins! The only way they will disappear is by your presence and love and eventually, when the child has grown more and more secure, the monsters will begin to evaporate and leave him in peace. However, be warned that nightmares will occur whenever this type is under stress or physically below par.

There will, of course, be the usual reasons for tears – too hot, too cold, a wet nappy – but top of the list will be problems related to diet. Too much or not enough food, for example. This is a water sign and the little Crab also gets thirstier than most. Milk is simply not enough, so always have some fruit-juice or water available. Lastly, bear in mind that there is always a reason for the child's tears and do make a point of discovering what it is. This is your first lesson in communication, and it is probably the most important one when bringing up *any* child.

Teething

One of the first symptoms your Cancerian baby will display will be a constant gnawing of his or her knuckles. This is an attempt to ease his aching gums, and is not to be confused with hunger. It will probably be accompanied by yet another symptom, possibly constant dribbling. This other symptom will help to prevent the aforementioned confusion. There may also be, of course, a rise in temperature, a runny nose, or twenty-four hours' diarrhoea. Obviously should the latter continue for longer you should call in the doctor.

Fortunately the Cancerian usually cuts teeth at the expected time, although the eye teeth may appear before the front ones. (For further advice see the section at the end of this book.)

Bath-time

Cancerians like water and the Cancerian baby's favourite pastime after eating is bathing. It is as well to remember, though, that bathing after a meal may well upset a new Cancerian baby's delicate stomach. Furthermore, always completely run both hot and cold water before immersing the child. This applies to all children but to the Crab in particular, as the Cancerian simply adores this wet warm water and, as soon as possible, will be stretching out a little hand in an effort to touch that fascinating water. With common sense, this is one of the happiest parts of the child's day and it may be advisable for you to perhaps cover yourself from head to foot in protective clothing as this little character really enjoys a good splash.

Face- or hair-washing should present no problems, although it is kinder to purchase non-stinging shampoo. A bubble bath will also delight the child, but again buy non-stinging mixtures.

Your Crab will love the water, and if you try skipping the bath for a day the child will not be slow to communicate his absolute disgust!

Interests and Games

You cannot stimulate in your baby Crab an urge to read or write early enough, as when he is older he may have difficulty in learning to do so. Your Cancerian's imagination can be utilized for this purpose, so begin with fairy stories regardless of the child's sex, as he or she will love giants, gnomes and fairy queens. Then, as time passes, you should purchase some beautifully illustrated books centred around this theme. Later still you should locate volumes with less pictures and more words. Do save a 'happy-ever-after' story for bed-time as tales of witches devouring children, for instance, will not surprisingly play upon this sensitive child's imagination and you will be in for a very disturbed night.

Soft cuddly animals and toys are highly recommended. Your little Crab will cling to several, especially at bed-time. They will make the child more secure. Many parents worry should their three- or four-year-old begin to invent an imaginary friend. Should this occur, neither encourage or discourage the child, simply give him some extra love and introduce your child to children of his own age. Should this ploy fail then relax, for you will soon communicate your neurosis and, besides, this phase will soon pass.

Walking and Talking

The true, diehard Cancerian child is fairly slow with regard to these two milestones. Walking is often delayed by excess weight, but even a trim Cancerian is not as impatient for mobility as, say, the Gemini. The child quickly realizes that his parents will fetch and carry for him provided the object of desire is indicated to them. It doesn't matter if a neighbour's child is rushing around at fourteen months. Your baby will walk when he is ready to. If you try to plonk him on his wobbly legs he may oblige but don't be surprised if bandy legs develop. Besides, at a later date you will realize that a toddler needs constant supervision so enjoy the relative peace while it lasts.

Cancerians are frequently quite psychic and if their mothers are similarly inclined the need for speech may diminish. You may pride yourself on being able to anticipate your child's every need but you will then wonder why he hasn't said a word by the age of two. If your child is still speechless at eighteen months feign confusion when he points to an object and ask whether he wants, say, his teddy or ball. Eventually the child will finally realize it is necessary to make the effort to speak, for this evidently stupid parent simply cannot be relied upon to present the right article.

Toilet-training

Girls are often quicker to toilet-train than boys, but as always your Cancerian is very emotional and sensitive so a calm atmosphere is most important. Avoid starting toilet-training during any domestic upheaval such as moving house or when the child is going through an uncooperative or negative phase. Also, wait until the child is at least eighteen months as control is not normally possible before then. If you are pressurizing the little Crab into toilet-training, then a reaction to this may be constipation. If this occurs, stop at once and try again once a couple of months have passed.

During the summer the child can, of course, be stripped and allowed to run around the garden, perhaps with a potty nearby, but never ever make a fuss when there is an accident. Anxiety will interfere with the baby's natural development. As in everything your little Crab knows when he is ready, so let him or her be your guide. Give the child some credit! The Cancerian will soon discover that wet, dirty nappies are extremely unpleasant, not to mention uncomfortable, and he will rectify this matter just as soon as he can.

Starting School

Any parent should be advised against expecting the little Crab to stay all day at his first nursery school as this is simply too long. This type is very attached to his home base and he will be reluctant to leave it at all. But little ones have to eventually meet the outside world and, when this happens, during the first year at least, they should never be away from home for longer than half a day.

Ideally the Cancerian should be left casually and without ceremony on the first and second days for only an hour, on the third and fourth days for two hours. Providing all is sunshine and light the half day can commence after this, probably about ten to twelve days later. It will also help if the child's mother can remain with the child on the first day. This will help to ease the child into the new situation and introduce the new faces. After this, however, it is important that on the second day the child be alone.

Any emotion on the part of the parent should be disguised. The little Crab will sense it and cling, feeling the apprehension. Circumstances may make it difficult for the parent to devote ten days to this operation, but it is imperative, if you don't want months of tears, nights disturbed by nightmares and a regression in toilet-training and other directions. Even then, and in spite of all your care and love, there may still be some regression. If so, ignore it. And if after a few weeks the child shows a reluctance to go to school one day, be casual about it and give in. Providing the Cancerian believes that school is not obligatory he will not mind it too much, and the occasional day off will do a lot to promote security. But you must still take out an insurance policy and it is absolutely essential that any day spent at home with either parent be incredibly boring for the child; if a fun day is planned, the child will never wish to return to school.

Love and understanding are your best assets. Emotion, tears and secret forebodings are your worst enemies.

THE CANCER CHILD
Four to twelve years of age

Health

The comments already made on the health of the Cancerian baby continue to apply. If your baby was overweight he will most likely have turned into an overweight child, one continually plagued with chest problems of some description. This is the age when that sweet tooth will be at its sweetest and dental problems should be expected regularly. Keep those periodic dental appointments, ideally about every three months. Better still, assuming you are the one who pays for those sweets and biscuits and not the child himself, ration them to one day a week and if there is any complaint now is the chance to appeal to the Crab's shrewd mind. Save up the money usually spent on those goodies over a month and then show your Crab just how quickly it all mounts up. When you hand over the full amount, he will be unlikely to want to waste it all on bubblegum, sweets and lollipops.

If this sweet tooth of the Cancerian character is out of control then you would be wise to remember that it could be due to compensation. If you are continually finding sweet papers tucked in the most unlikely places, better ask yourself just what is missing from the child's life and attempt to put it right.

Your little Crab's whiter than white skin will need special attention from sunburn at this time. Bear this in mind each summer and take the necessary precautions.

Friends

Should your Cancerian be one of the overweight variety then he is in for a tough time where friends are concerned. Bullies invariably pick on the more vulnerable, and the Cancerian's sensitivity makes it an ideal victim for jokes. Eventually, the little Crab will develop a tough outer shell, but inside he will be lonely and very miserable. Remember that this type is not naturally gregarious and usually prefers to locate a kindred spirit and stick like glue with true Cancerian tenacity! Naturally when this precious bond is threatened in any way the bottom will fall out of your Cancerian's world and he will then need all the love you can muster to act as a buffer. However, in this situation the insensitive parent could begin to lose contact with his or her child, for when misunderstood the Crab will feel rejected and extremely depressed. This difficult side to the Cancerian's life will need careful handling. Never insist that he be sensible, pull himself together or apply pressure when party invitations are extended. Your Crab will know if a bully will be present, although he may not wish to tell you so. Bow to his wishes in this respect, for the Crab knows best.

What practical help can you give? The Cancerian loves to play host or hostess and this is the best way for him or her to keep unwanted guests at bay. Occasionally allow your little Crab to have small groups of favoured friends around, and suggest that he or she helps with the refreshments. This type loves to mess around in the kitchen and will be proud of that sticky, runny toffee or cakes. Your Cancerian may not have sufficient friends to make a small party possible, in which case allow that one and only precious friend to spend the night fairly frequently. It won't matter if the floor and a few cushions are the best you can do – in fact, the more chaotic the stay the more your Crab will enjoy it!

To sum up: be sympathetic at all times and try to view your child's problems through his or her eyes. In this way you will always be able to offer timely love and understanding.

Interests and Games

The Cancerian is a natural mother's helper, trailing behind her sweeping, cleaning and dusting. Baking time is seventh heaven. Give the little Crab a few scraps of pastry, a rolling-pin and peace will reign for hours! Any kind of toy that will encourage this domestic interest will be most pleasing – toy vacuum-cleaners, tea-sets, ironing boards. . . . Don't be put off if your Crab is a boy, it makes absolutely no difference.

The garden is another haven. Produce a packet of seeds and you will have an enthralled youngster.

The love of water in all Crabs means that toys for the bathroom are welcome. Painting may also appeal, but the Crab is rather clumsy and you may need to take precautions to avoid messy and hard-to-clean accidents. It is, however, worth making this effort to keep the Cancer child happy.

Accepting a New Baby

If you are wise you will pave the way for your Crab's acceptance of a new brother or sister by bringing other new babies to his attention. Nevertheless, the new brother's or sister's actual presence is going to be a big upheaval in this child's life. Fortunately the Cancerian child is maternal or paternal and, initially, will take to any helpless being. Later he may suddenly react, quite violently, with jealousy. Remember, your first born is not being naughty but feeling for some reason insecure. Should this occur temporary regression in his part may result: wet pants, returning to the bottle, and so on. This misguided child may think he has to behave badly to attract your attention or to discover whether your love is still strong. The ball will then be fairly and squarely in your court and you should set aside enough time to your elder child to show that your feelings for him haven't changed.

Never prevent your little Crab from kissing or cuddling the new baby. This type is full of love and the more people there are to shower it upon the better. Encourage the child to give active help with the new baby and put aside some part of every day for just him or her, a time when the new baby is safely out of the way. Extra attention now will pay off later when you watch both children walking hand in hand upstairs to play together.

Discipline

The Cancerian child is a strange one to discipline. There are times when he will appear to be pushing you to your absolute limit and even when this results in a smack on the bottom (never anywhere else!) he seems to be satisfied. What you need to understand when this occurs is the crab's logic; he feels that if he can make you sufficiently angry then quite obviously you still care and he is happy.

Parents always need to be open and honest with their children but in particular with the Cancerian. It does no harm whatsoever to confide your fears for his or her safety, especially when talking to strangers or crossing the road. After such a discussion, quite suddenly your emotional Crab will become filled with common sense and really sit up and take note of your advice. However, never nag, bully or remain angry for any length of time with this type. Never use your superiority with words to emphasize this child's inadequacies. The Crab will feel stupid and miserable enough when he understands that you are annoyed.

When the Crab is really naughty, openly show your anger and hurt. Be one big bundle of emotion and finish, later, with a big kiss and cuddle. Your Cancerian has no real intention of hurting you and when he realizes that this is what he has done, he will feel sufficiently punished.

An accidentally broken plate or cup does not constitute naughtiness, for Cancerians are naturally clumsy and these accidents generally occur when such a child is anxious to prove just how grown up he has become. Anxiety clouds his judgement. Screaming and nagging him will also lead to a string of mishaps. Better resign yourself to the breakages and buy cheap china. Generally, never lose sight of your Crab's sensitivity and you will not go far wrong.

Sex

While the section of sex at the end of the book holds good for the Cancerian, it is important to remember that this is a romantic and hypersensitive sign. Facts must therefore be related not only with sensitivity but also with understanding. Help your child to cope with his varying emotions. The most important lesson is perhaps the one in which you make him or her understand that sex is more gratifying, rewarding and satisfying where a deep love is shared. But, at the same time, it is important to make the point that lust does not necessarily have anything to do with love at all, that it is possible to want someone without loving them and even love them without physically wanting them.

If the facts of life are accepted as a natural human function then in time the Cancerian will gradually learn about the complexity of his or her own emotions, eventually being able to separate them whenever necessary.

Homework and Study

Teachers find the little Crab absorbed and fascinated by history. They seldom forget dates and events, and many of them excel at dramatics. However, this type may need an above average amount of help and support from the parent. Generally speaking, the Cancerian is rather like the Taurean and prefers to get homework finished and out of the way. Should you discover that he is procrastinating and finding excuses for not doing his homework then he is quite likely having difficulty in relating to his teacher or has fallen behind in some specific subject and now feels quite incapable of catching up. Extra tuition, of course, may do the trick, although it is more likely that your little Crab will learn more readily from yourself. Should there be some incompatibility between the teacher and your child then don't thunder into the school and grab the poor unfortunate teacher by the lapels and issue threats. Try a friendly phone call and a sensible discussion instead. In this way you will discover just what it is that is going wrong with the teacher/child communication.

The Cancerian child is frequently a late developer and the mental process seems to absorb facts slowly. If his father has more patience than his mother then he is the one to offer assistance – or vice versa, because a bad-tempered or irritated parent will only worsen the situation. Boost the child's confidence wherever possible. Even if he may not live up your expectations, try to hide your disappointment and reward any kind of effort.

Finding a Direction

An appeal to the romantic side of life can be of positive use when attempting to stimulate this type. In the previous section it was shown how fairy stories can help to stimulate, and when the child is maturing these stories can be of an historical nature. Any biography will do splendidly, whether the subject is an actor, composer or military person. Should your Cancerian be a boy, then you will find him transfixed with the tales of Lord Nelson and Lady Hamilton, for instance. A girl will enjoy reading about Henry the Eighth and his wives. A follow-up trip to an art gallery, museum or military exhibition will illustrate to your child just how life was during that era or century.

Remember when purchasing that biography or visiting the library to choose a relatively simple book. Reading is frequently difficult for the Crab and it needs to be stimulated and improved for a while before introducing weightier material to the child. A children's dictionary will prove invaluable provided you bring up your child to look up any strange words he or she hears.

Any subject you feel needs attention can be improved by the romantic approach. Should your Cancerian be weak in science, for example, it shouldn't be difficult for you to locate the story of a scientist who has suffered for his beliefs or ideals. In fact, the more acute the suffering the more it will appeal to the Cancerian. Naturally, after a while he or she will wish to understand just why the vaccine or invention was so important. Your child may even go so far as to wish to investigate just how the invention worked.

Never lose sight of the fact that your Crab is a born romantic and as bright as any other child but that those born under this sign need some special handling.

For recreation, while the Crab is rarely the energetic type, he could be interested in a water sport such as swimming or water-skiing. Water calms the Cancerian's turbulent emotion and even a walk by a pond or river will be thoroughly enjoyed.

To sum up, when your Crab appears listless or bored it is possible that he or she is not being stimulated in the right direction.

THE CANCER TEENAGER

Twelve to eighteen years of age

The Cancerian's sensitivity comes into play during his teenage years and can make this stage in life far more acute and dramatic than it actually is. Everything is dramatized, her introduction to menstruation, his to ejaculation. Hopefully you were wise enough to rear your Crab so that he or she feels perfectly able to discuss any disaster or new beginning with you at this stage. Both male and female teenagers should have been well prepared for the formerly mentioned experience. However, all phases of adolescence are equally important, and pimples receive the same status as more important problems. It is often a good idea to suggest a trip to the doctor, even though you may not feel it necessary. Bear in mind that your Crab loves a bit of a fuss, and a visit to the professional while not helping physically will do wonders mentally and emotionally. This is also the age when the clumsiness previously mentioned will loom large. Wise parents will remove obvious obstacles but they shouldn't draw too much attention to the young Crab's mishaps.

This sign doesn't excel at any kind of small talk, so be realistic. It's better that Cancer teenagers don't meet their parents' friends as they will have little to say to them. Furthermore, never discuss your Crab in front of your friends as if the child weren't there and do attempt to treat the child as the adult he or she will soon become.

Occasionally ask your Crab's advice on certain subjects. Obviously you cannot expect the child to understand that you are frantic with worry over unpaid bills, although it may be a good idea to acquaint it with exactly what they are, but you should keep things light. Ask for opinions on whether you should wear this suit or that, or should it be spaghetti or lasagne for dinner. Better still ask how you can prevent his younger brother from biting his nails. The Crab needs to be aware of responsibility and decision-making, and when you do occasionally turn to him or her for opinion or advice let the child know that what he or she thinks counts.

This is a shrewd individual, one who will puff up with pride when you bemoan the fact that you have overspent, or mislaid some money, and you ask him to help you in accounting for the day's movements or expenses. Bear in mind your own, possibly ghastly, adolescence to understand your teen. Let your Cancerian know that you were once a fallible human being of the same age, and you may be able to help and more importantly he may just let you.

Dating

The Crab will develop slowly in his or her relationships so if your sixteen-year-old son prefers to spend his time with his stamp collection or your daughter still remains enthused with the girl guides don't doubt their sexuality. You would probably soon complain and worry if she became a Lolita and he a pubescent Don Juan! When they do start dating, and rest assured they will, your problems will be minimal. The Cancerian reveres the home and is strongly attached to at least one parent. And when that parent says, 'Home by eleven!' the Cancer will uncomplainingly oblige.

The most sensitive area of dating lies in the fact that your Crab will take each relationship that little bit too seriously and will therefore be hurt quite regularly. All parents can do is to supply a shoulder to cry on and to offer as much comfort as possible. It may help if the mother tells some stories of her own teenage loves and if father can take his son aside and impart some friendly man to man advice. Don't ever ignore the agony you know your teenager is suffering, but coax it out into the open. Your Crab will then gather courage and rise to fight another day.

Alcohol

There is no doubt that alcohol could, in some instances, be a great problem. Cancer is a water sign and as such is attracted to all liquids. Even so, this does not constitute the need for a ban on alcohol and in fact that could be the worst thing to do, for unwittingly you will have made alcohol more attractive. The best thing is to encourage moderation by your own good example. Never allow your teenage Cancer to see you in a drunken state, neither should it be a witness to your habit, if possessed, of drowning your problems and sorrows in the bottom of a glass. Worse still, it should never discover that either parent is a secret drinker. Introduce your child to a glass of wine with a meal, or as a reason for celebration. There is no good reason why the child should not partake in a drink with friends to be sociable. You have to face the fact that you are not going to keep your Cancerian away from alcohol any more than you could from the larder or the bathtub. Therefore, let your Cancerian drink alcohol openly and moderately.

Drugs

Fortunately it is a rare Crab who is attracted to drugs. The positive members of this sign are almost completely immune from them. He or she may indulge in the odd drink and in sex. Only the more negative types, in searching for a thrill, will succumb. Should your child be the rare one to give into drugs, don't drive his search for escapism under ground by obvious disapproval. Your Cancer must feel he can count on you no matter what, so a serious talk at this point is called for, the object of which is to discover just why drugs were turned to in the first place. If it is possible to remove the reason then you should be able to prevent this unhappy matter from getting out of control. It may be that your Cancerian feels the pressure of study. If so, and despite your ambitions for him, it may be that your teenager is not fitted for an academic career so don't pressurize him into one at the risk of his health. The child in question may already be working, of course, in which case there is too much responsibility on him or the job may be too difficult. Whatever the reason, bring it out and confront it, talk about it and try to eradicate it.

SUGGESTED CAREERS

Your Crab is bound to have romantic ideas about a career at some point, so encourage it. Your teenager may want to be an archaeologist, but if he is later put off by the study then clearly he wasn't suited in the first place. Various Cancer careers are given below and should your Crab show interest in any of them you should encourage him for he may have found his way.

Caterer	Nurse	Sailor
Hotelier	Boatbuilder	Antique dealer
Fisherman	Kindergarten teacher	Museum curator
Businessman	Domestic science specialist	Historian

Cancerians may also do well as estate agents or market gardeners. Any career involving the sea is also positive.

LEO

THE SECOND FIRE SIGN

Symbol The Lion

Colour Orange

Metal Gold

Planet The sun

Motivation Power

Proud; bold; dramatic; full of warmth; dominating

GENERAL CHARACTERISTICS

Dr Jekyll: positive

There is absolutely no way you can overlook the Leo. The regal bearing and good appearance usually guarantee this. But the very presence commands attention. The Leo makes a wonderful friend, having fierce pride and taking naturally to the good things of life. Usually they are incredibly popular. Those born under this sign shine when being the host or hostess, delighting in giving their best to friend and stranger alike. Nothing is too good or too much trouble for those that are loved. However, the need to go first class all the way means that these types spend freely and financial common sense does not come naturally. In love the Lion possesses a strong nature which makes him passionate though for the most part sincere. Because emotional force springs from the heart the Lion can be sensitive, though frequently resorting to arrogance to hide it. The generosity and warmth given to this sign radiates most of the time, and the Lion adores flattery and admiration. Both are needed desperately.

It is important to remember that this sign represents the king of all animals, and because this is so the Leonine tends to dominate wherever possible. Usually where they fail, they withdraw.

Mr Hyde: negative

The love of flattery, in this particular instance, is perverted into an unquenchable need for personal glory. This type continually strives for positions in life which, if acquired, would be totally wasted for want of application. Airs of self-importance and delusions of grandeur are common. The Leonine tries to lord it over whoever he considers to be his inferior. In relationships this type does not only wish to be loved, but also to dominate. The secret fear is that he or she may fail in some way and feel ridiculous and this feeling is a constant source of inner conflict.

Many of those who fall into this category seek to associate with inferiors – far better to be a big fish in a small pond, they feel. Anything rather than be simply run-of-the-mill. Financially speaking, the desire to show off gets ridiculously out of hand. This is a character who will cheerfully roar in the pub at the top of his voice, 'The drinks are on me!' – probably using money that had been put away for the electricity bill! This type believes that the whole wide world revolves around him and would be most put off if he failed to hear about some happening in his sphere of life or circle of friends. This particular Lion believes that the rest of us are merely here for his convenience, in fact his subjects, to be commanded accordingly.

Is Your Child a Typical Leo?

Answer the questions honestly. Score three for every 'Yes', two for every 'Sometimes' and one for every 'No'. Turn to page 219 for the answers.

1. Does the child beam when flattered?
2. Do you find yourself thinking twice before saying no to the child?
3. Is your child over affectionate?
4. Does your child react quickly to the cold?
5. Does your child easily forgive your outbursts of irritation or anger?
6. Is the child generous with toys?
7. Does your Leo try to dominate others?
8. Does the child have a good sense of rhythm?
9. Does your child react violently to criticism?
10. Does your Leo have a lazy streak?
11. Does the child always expect its own way?
12. Is your child put out when the routine is changed?
13. Does your child sulk when ignored?
14. Does your child dislike the feel of water?
15. Is your child reluctant to cry in front of you?
16. Is your child attracted to your jewellery?
17. Does your child notice anything new you do to your appearance?
18. Is your child quite happy when you aren't there?
19. Is your child strongly attracted to the feel of soft objects?
20. Is it impossible to feed your Cub when it does not wish to be fed?

THE LEO BABY
Up to four years of age

The typical cub is charming, funny and playful, with one proviso – as long as he gets his own way. When he does not, the ensuing roar will be overheard by your deafest of neighbours. From the moment you bring your Leo baby home he will dominate the entire household. Orders are issued from the cot every minute of the day. What you must realize is that you don't possess any common or garden baby, but a little angel who regards himself with importance. If he wants his nappy changed, he wants it done *now*, not when you have finished your coffee. The scowling face of father leaning over the cot intimidates him? Not a jot! *This* particular subordinate is going to have to be taught to come to heel! Ignore him if you must but he will get his own way in the end, that you can depend upon.

The Leo child has a certain natural dignity. This is the only sign of the Zodiac able to sit in the high chair, covered head to foot in tomato soup with soiled nappy and still retain the aura of a monarch. And notice the happy knack this child has of being able to attract the attention of strangers? Watch the way he beams when they make a fuss of him. However, the Leo child may be a rather daunting prospect, but not an impossible one. But get out your vitamins to keep you on your toes and your best cap and apron – you're in service now and you will be unable to forget it.

Health

Leo is the sign that rules the back and later on accidents to this part of the anatomy should be expected. Also, the heart is governed by Leo, though at this stage it is simply a heart full to bursting-point with love. Circulation can also be a problem. Be conscious of room temperatures and make sure that the elastic around trousers and bootees is not too constricting. Some misguided parents dress their six-pound cub in one outfit and, later, attempt to squeeze their sixteen-pound Lion into the same outfit.

Furthermore, the Leo has a pale, sensitive skin and while he or she will love the sun it will burn easily. Therefore, sun-hats and canopies are a must. If the skin ever does get too burned, take him to the doctor as quickly as possible.

Some Leonines are born with a bit of a squint. In small babies the eyes can look as if they were put in separately. This usually rights itself, if you still notice it when the child is six months old, even though it only happens occasionally, tell the doctor. This is important because if neglected the squint may lead to the sight being affected.

Food

The cat is a fastidious eater, not being slow to let you know when the bottle is of an incorrect temperature, or if this or that particular brand of cereal does not happen to suit the palate. This picking and choosing is continued right through life. This type knows exactly what it wants, and when it finds something it likes the demand is for a lot of it. Don't insist that the Leo child eat anything because it happens to be good for him. Bear in mind that, generally speaking, parents over-feed their children to quite a shocking degree. So don't worry should the Lion skip an occasional meal; besides, a missed lunch in a healthy child means an eagerly devoured dinner. Also, any talents you may possess as a chef will not go unrewarded or unnoticed, for the more attractive the food the more stimulated will be your Lion. You cannot bully a Leo and, if you do, expect it to become arrogant and angry. So, when greeted with a blank refusal, capitulate. The Lion will eat when it is ready.

Bear in mind that the Lion likes to eat small but frequent meals. Mountains of pasta or potatoes will completely put him off. However, this type is not as fussy as some, so thank your lucky stars he isn't a Virgo, for example.

Crying

The Leo cub will, of course, cry for the usual reasons – a wet nappy, hunger, thirst . . . But mostly he will assault your ear-drums for attention. This is a royal sign and if the child decides that he is being neglected you are going to be made aware of the fact in no uncertain terms. He is also a child who will quickly outgrow the need for an afternoon nap, so don't insist upon one. Mostly, however, this child is content just as long as you are there and talking to him.

It will become necessary for you to cart him around as you clean the house, cook the dinner, and so on. Don't hesitate to explain just what you are doing. Initially, of course, the child will not understand, but at least you will be conveying the fact that you think it important enough to communicate with him. Eventually the child will try to participate in answering you. If he is distressed at night your Lion may simply be feeling neglected, especially if there's no other reason for his distress. A lullaby, a cuddle, will reassure. He will not quieten down if he is ignored, for this type will simply get more and more angry and insecure. But the Leo cub is a lovable little soul. Look at that dazzling smile of recognition! It isn't that difficult to indulge him!

Teething

The Lion rarely does anything in halves. This child will either cut teeth according to the book and unknown to you or he will scream at every molar. A raised temperature and a piercing scream will be your first indication. Should things get totally out of hand then don't hesitate to visit the doctor. He will be most concerned if you are worn to a frazzle and will give practical advice. For further information you should refer to the chapter at the end of the book.

Bath-time

The Leo's attitude to this particular ritual is not unlike his brother Aries. The reason for this is simple: both signs are fire, and when you mix fire and water you generally get steam. In this instance the steam is quite likely to be coming out of your Lion's ears. Your child may tolerate bath-time if you are lucky, but don't expect him to enjoy it. Even while still relatively tiny, it is imperative that the Leo be held firmly, but lovingly, while submerged – obvious for reasons of safety but mostly for reassurance. Never run the water while he is in the bath, for the sound of running water will unnerve this little character.

If you are still suffering from problems with bath-time when the Leo is older you may be able to encourage and interest him by adding to the water a few drops of cochineal. One day you could make the water pink, next red and, with a different colouring, blue, and so on. Make sure, however, that any colourings you use are perfectly safe. Don't overdo it, unless you wish your Cub to emerge with a brand new complexion! With any luck this ploy will intrigue your little Cub to the extent that he will be too busy considering the change that has occurred and will not think about the feel of this wet liquid.

You would also be wise to take advantage of all the non-sting products on the market – shampoos, soaps, etc. Don't give him a practical reason for disliking his bath or he will refuse to go in without a fight that wouldn't put a professional boxer to shame!

If, despite all your ploys, the Lion still loathes bath-time, then cut out the daily agony and make it every other day. Remember not to splash the Leo: he is not there to have fun, he wants to be in and out of the water and dry again as quickly as possible.

Interests and Games

The most important thing to bear in mind with games is that the Leo is not a loner. He dislikes his own company and ideally needs a small group of people of the same age. Even now, the need to exercise authority is strong. At bedtime this type will enjoy stories about kings and the like. King Arthur and his knights is a good example. You can forget fairy stories, or Snow White; he just isn't interested.

Just as soon as the Lion can toddle it will want to dress up. The theatrical streak blossoms at an extremely early age.

Regarding the ideal kind of toy – the Leo loves music, so musical trains, balls, clocks, and so on, will satisfy and fascinate. This child may learn to sing before he can speak!

The sensational streak will also be quite apparent and the Cub will be attracted to wild outfits such as those that allow him to believe he is Batman or Batgirl. Forget cowboys and Indians; this character demands something far more dramatic. If you can find or make a golden crown he will really come into his own. You will be able to observe him strutting up and down attempting to issue orders to the bewildered family cat or dog!

It is a good idea for all Lions to have their own pets, even if only a solitary goldfish, for the Lion needs to learn early on consideration for others. Caring for an animal, under supervision of course, is a good place to start.

Walking and Talking

The Leo does everything with style and panache, of that you can be sure, but an innate laziness is likely to make him a late walker. However, once the Lion does begin – and don't push him – this type learns in record time provided parents are lavish with praise and express wonder at its efforts. Remember that the Leo is susceptible to all kinds of flattery, and it starts in the cot.

Watch your Cub puff up and flush with pride when you applaud those faltering first steps. Be prepared for absolute fury when tragedy strikes and he keels over on to his rear and is humiliated in front of all those present. He cannot bear to have witnesses to his fall from dignity. Speech-wise the Leo is usually precocious, mainly because this particular stage in development requires little physical exertion and also how else can the imperious Leo order the world around if all he can utter are a few incomprehensible grunts. Furthermore, you can bet that the first words to drop from that mouth will be a command of some description. Prepare yourself – this is just the beginning!

Toilet-training

Common sense will tell you always to ignore accidents in this direction, but with a Leonine child it is of paramount importance to do so. By accentuating or dramatizing his inadequacy in any way you will undermine his sensitive ego. Ideally it would be wise to begin toilet training perhaps a little later than usual, for by doing so you will minimize the mistakes and therefore the humiliation. Twenty months is a good age, and at this stage in development there is a relatively good chance that the proud Leo will be in complete control. Once more flattery will get you everywhere: compliments, plus overlooking mishaps, will lead to a dry child in record time despite the fact that toilet training was started later than usual.

Starting School

Again we have a similarity between the Leonine and the Arietian, but for different reasons. It is not the independent nature, nor the love of adventure, which makes school so attractive to the Leo as much as the prospective siblings that he will be able to win over to his court with sheer charm and force of his regal personality. It is totally impossible to ignore the little Cub; that commanding presence is obvious despite the diminutive stature. Observe the other children when he makes a dramatic entrance. You will sense a certain reverence. Therefore be as casual as possible on the first day at school. Cross your fingers and throw him in at the deep end! The Lion will not be in danger of drowning for more than a split second. By the time you pick up the child later, he or she will know all the other children by name. You can also be certain that they will already have hailed this Royal as a leader, unless, of course, there happens to be another Leo in the vicinity, in which case your Leo will enjoy deposing the King.

Should you feel that a mother's emotion may threaten the situation on this, his first day out in the big wide world, then get Dad to take the child to school while you attempt to accustom yourself to the idea that your little Cub is becoming independent, and will not appreciate a clinging mother.

THE LEO CHILD
Four to twelve years of age

Health

By the time your child has reached this age those back injuries may be on the increase, so do try to instil some respect for this part of the anatomy. Also, the danger from sunburn is still fairly acute, mainly because children will be children, and although you may have warned the child against staying in the sun for too long, you should not expect the Leo to take your advice seriously. The only thing to do is to examine the child on its return home and to watch out for any vomiting or shivers. Your Leo will be forever disgustingly healthy or always on the sick list. Hopefully your particular Cub will belong to the former.

Friends

Once more it is the group activities that will appeal to the Lion. You can be sure that he will always have his own little gang of which, it goes without saying, he will be in total command. Therefore any troubles these little angels get themselves into are sure to have been conceived by your little Cub. You can ignore that dazzling smile and protest of innocence. Generally speaking your Leo will be an extremely popular child and will cause you few problems. However, if for some reason he or she is spending most of the time sitting in front of the television you can bet that the reason for the neglect by his contemporaries is due to a boastful arrogance and an exaggerative nature. Young Leos have a habit of bossing other children around which, if it doesn't annoy the children, will infuriate other parents. Because of this you will probably need to apply a restraining hand. Don't scold the child harshly in front of his friends but try to instil a sense of justice. You can say, for instance, that he can take the lead today but that tomorrow it must be the turn of a friend. That is a fair way, and the Lion *must* be taught to respect it. This child is not the slightest big malicious, just a natural leader. Leos also have a strong urge to show off and it is hard to discourage it, especially if you have been unwise enough to let it get out of hand. Try to show that such exaggerated behaviour is undignified and you will notice a rapid change.

Leo is also a sign that loves to entertain. Leos are all natural hosts. Others will forever be brought home, but they will not be cooked or slaved for. Refreshments will be expected, but prepared and served by parents. There will, however, be a certain professionalism when it comes to handing the goodies around.

The Lion has flair and you will be surprised and pleased when you observe the masterly handling of these little get-togethers. Your Lion will be at the top of everyone's party list when invitations are extended. The Leo is a professional party-goer even when it is not his party, and this won't deter him from completely taking over. However, the Lion must not be allowed to become a dictator, and the section on discipline must be read and digested.

Interests and Games

The Leo has a natural love of theatre and drama and this should be developing and be coming to the fore now. Give him a chance and the Lion will be organizing all the children in the street into a regular concert party, and during the proceedings you can be sure that he will be a complete tyrant, one that will do credit to even the most volatile of Hollywood producers. Again, a few cautionary words about the feelings and wishes of others may be needed. Don't be too surprised should you be informed that friends are only too happy to do the Lion's every bidding. Later on you will probably discover, to your amazement, that this is true. None of us can ever resist a Leo, so why should friends be any different?

A word about sporting involvement: there isn't any! The Leo may be happy to be a spectator, but you shouldn't expect this character to exert himself. Furthermore the Lion will prove to be extremely ingenious when it comes to wriggling out of physical activities of any description.

The love of music may also have increased at this stage and you may find that you have a promising singer or dancer on your hands. The former should, ideally, join the school choir or music-group and the latter, provided you can afford it, given dancing-lessons. Any interest or game that can centre around theatrical life one way or the other will appeal. You may also observe a certain love-affair with power beginning to emerge and this will become only too apparent when the Leo participates in board-games. Monopoly in particular will set the adrenalin pulsating.

Accepting a New Baby

This need not be such a dramatic event providing the situation is handled calmly and wisely. Underneath all the Leo's arrogance and pride is a warm, generous and loving heart. Initially the prospect of yet another subordinate will excite the Cub. Later he or she will adopt a very protective attitude to the new offspring. Naturally you can expect the Lion to boss the new member of the family around, but just let anyone else try it! And that also goes for the parents! Should such a situation occur, your Lion will draw himself up to his full three feet six and challenge your authority. This all sounds quite ideal, but just try flattering the new infant while you have been thoughtless enough to humiliate your Leo in the infant's presence and he will rebel, treating both parents as enemies. Naturally enough there will be times when it is necessary to put that Lion in his place, but do it privately. If you want a peaceful life while your complex Cub is adapting to the new situation then pile on the flattery, especially when he insists. Before you know what is happening he will be taking over the new infant in the hope of more compliments from you. Don't make the mistake of bathing both of them together. Babies splash a lot, unless it is a Leo baby, and this is something your Cub will not appreciate. But do allow him to have the baby in his bed for a cuddle and perhaps for a bed-time story; this will help to promote togetherness. Treat the situation with ease and all the family will survive the birth of a new baby without conditions of warfare being declared in your own home.

Discipline

Discipline can be quite a headache, especially for the parent who prefers an easy quiet life. Too strict an attitude will crush the fiery spirit of the Leo, too much freedom and you will end up with a pompous, exaggerating and unbelievably arrogant child, one who will be thoroughly disliked by everyone.

Most Leos have delusions of grandeur, and some control must be introduced. Physical violence, even what you might consider to be a harmless smack on the bottom, is simply not the way. One does not strike the royal Leo unless one wishes to be firmly exiled from his affections and to be inciting rebellion. The Leo has to be shown that although he may believe the household was erected solely for his convenience this is simply not the case. Furthermore, others need to be considered and occasionally obeyed.

Don't flex your muscles of authority for the sake of it. Such an act would reduce you to his level, and although your Leo has not yet reached the age of twelve you have no excuse. A firm withdrawal of privilege will serve you far better, but only when he has been really naughty. No amount of ranting and raving on the Lion's part should deter you from this. Quiet inflexibility, immune to charm, is all that is required. For the rest of the time an appeal to his sense of justice or to his affectionate heart is all that is needed. Remember, when you tickle a cat under the chin you get maximum response, but impose your will with brute force and all you get is a nervous, neurotic animal.

Sex

Fortunately the Leo is the most naturally sexual and sensual of all the Zodiac signs, so no special advice is needed other than that given in the chapter at the end of this book.

There may be some instances where your Cub may display a pronounced interest for certain materials like fur or satin. Put it down to his natural sensuality. You would have to deliberately set out to inhibit or pervert the Big Cat as he or she is generally sexually well adjusted.

Homework and Study

Surprisingly Leos can work and learn at great speed when they want to. Nevertheless there are times when this character can be impossibly lazy, and when this occurs coaxing into good studying habits is called for. The best way of improving school reports is to make an appeal to vanity. This shouldn't be difficult as the Leo desperately wants to be superior to all contemporaries. When efforts are made, remember to reward them with praise. Don't go overboard: the Leo adores flattery and can never acquire enough. Make each compliment count, but only show your delight when it has been well and truly earned. This, together with occasional admiration for the achievements of his friends, will get him out of his regal inactivity and into his room! Frantic study will then be the order of the day.

Finding a Direction

If you are unfortunate enough to have a Leo who insists on sitting around listlessly, stimulation is clearly called for. After all, while the Leo is lolling around gathering dust he may at least be exercising that grey matter. This sign's fascination with power can now be encouraged providing you can persaude him to read a biography – but not just any biography. Paul Getty, for example, would be an ideal choice. The Lion should also be allowed to view certain television programmes devoted to the lives of great and powerful men. After a while, probably sooner than later, it will slowly dawn on the Leo's befuddled brain that these wealthy, powerful people did not get where they were, or are, by lazing around. Allow him to set his sights high, even though you consider them to be ridiculously so, for later on in maturity he will learn to recognize limitation. Who knows, with any luck he may not have to, for that lazy lout may turn into a president or magnate.

Remember that this type will take an interest in almost anything that smacks of power, and politics may be of great interest. Don't, therefore, be too surprised when he joins some radical political movement. Simply take an interest in these high-flown ideals, for at some later date it could well be your turn to puff up with pride.

THE LEO TEENAGER
Twelve to eighteen years of age

The Leonine's adolescence can be a rather turbulent period, for this type is emotionally up and down a hundred times each day. It can also be expensive, for the Leo needs rather more cash than the average run-of-the-mill teenager. The reasons for these are that the Leo teenager has a preference for expensive clothes and possessions, and that their natural generosity leads members of this sign to perhaps foolishly give away small change to their less fortunate chums. The wise parent will make the Leo understand fairly quickly that it can save some money, spend some and, if he must, give some away. The emphasis should be always on the former.

At least your Leo adolescent will seldom be lonely, but this type is often acutely prone to frustration. You'll learn to recognize this by the unexpected outbursts that shake the family home. This is the only way the Lion can relieve its tensions. The young Leo has enormous pride and is now at the stage when he is more than a little aware of the necessity of financial – and other – dependence on his parents. The situation will not be helped by the fact that he worships both parents. They must simply understand that it goes against the Leo's sensitive ego to be subjected to the orders, instructions and benevolence of others. Ways and means will be sought that enable spending-money to be earned, thus allowing independence to be retained. Parents may be subjected to a continual stream of dramas and histrionics, but the tendency to exaggerate problems will diminish if they are taken seriously. Try to make the Leo understand that he should concentrate his abundant energy to the solution of problems rather than the dramatizing of them.

Treat the Leo child like an adult and remember how you felt at that age. Love him even when he is at his most unlovable and he will grow into a Lion you can be proud of.

Dating

Both friendship and love will be dramatic, romantic and heart-breaking to this character, so try to be there without so much as an 'I told you so!' on your lips. The Lion loves people and will be a great party-goer and -giver, gregarious and perhaps promiscuous. But provided you have instructed your teenager sufficiently on contraception and venereal diseases, for instance, you can relax. You cannot restrain the Lion. That affectionate heart is made for contact with the opposite sex and if you attempt restraint the Lion will rebel and secretly go his or her own way despite your protestations.

The Lion needs freedom – he will take it in any case. Let him know that you trust and respect him and this will flatter his ego and he will then do his best not to let you down.

Alcohol

Although there will naturally be an exception, this is not the sign of the chronic alcoholic. The Leo does not turn to drink to escape the unpleasantness of life either. But do bear in mind that the Leo is a great socialite. He is social in everything, and being the perfect host he will want to serve drinks to friends so the occasional bottle of wine will do no harm.

It is also worth remembering that you cannot, in his presence, knock back the vodka while banning him from indulgence. Keep your own drinking out of his presence until you feel your particular Leo is old enough to partake with you. Don't imagine that for one moment you will be able to stop the Lion's social drinking, so don't drive it underground. Teach the rules of no driving and drinking, the importance of eating properly before drinking alcohol and the inadvisability of mixing drinks.

Handled sensibly, you'll discover that your Leo is particularly responsible in this direction.

Drugs

Once more you are a lucky parent, for drug-taking is not a Leo vice. Any occasional social smoking should not be over dramatized. Discuss it but don't get too angry. Remember that the Leo is going to have his or her own way in any case, if not openly then in secret. Once more an appeal to the ego will work wonders where threats will fail miserably. Hide any disapproval or panic and state sincerely that you are confident in him or her and understand that the occasional smoke of a soft drug does not necessarily lead to addiction. And, of course, tell him that you understand he is far too sensible and wise to finish up like some of his weaker contemporaries. This remark is enough, on its own, to insure that he will soon give it up – but don't expect an immediate abstinence, as this must be the Lion's own decision. In the meantime point out the legal aspects and state your personal preference for relaxation and enjoyment.

Now that you have acquainted him or her with the facts, let the Leo's decision rest. He or she is not going to be led astray, a fact you can be quite sure of – you are talking to the leader, not a follower.

SUGGESTED CAREERS

One thing is quite certain: your Lion will aim high in life. So don't bring him down by sneering at his dreams. As mentioned before, his acceptance of his limitations will follow later. But if he cannot aim high now, when can he? Besides, your Leo may well surprise you and turn out to be that world-famous impressario, inventor or businessman. However, just in case that should not prove to be the case here are some Leonine occupations that may attract.

Actor	Youth worker	Professional sportsman
Dancer	Managing director	Jeweller
Teacher	Commissionaire	

Any position carrying responsibility and a chance to show off. The Lion is ambitious, though not necessarily ruthless and, although he may be happy working for someone else, his employer will have to be someone he can respect. The work will also have to be congenial. If he ever insists that his boss is a fool then, if you bother to check out the allegations, you'll probably find out that he is speaking the truth.

VIRGO

THE SECOND EARTH SIGN

Symbol The Virgin

Colour Grey or navy blue

Metal Quicksilver

Planet Mercury

Motivation To criticize and perfect

Cool; unemotional; fussy about health and small details; has a practical mind; likes a quiet life

GENERAL CHARACTERISTICS

Dr Jekyll: positive

This type's main asset is a splendid power of discrimination. This Virgoan recognizes at a glance the value of other people and treats them accordingly. Rarely lavish with affection or praise it isn't easy for this type to love. It takes a tremendous amount to melt the heart. However, once committed, this type is loyal and faithful to the partner. Even then, emotion of any description is rarely shown on the surface. Feelings reveal themselves in day-to-day small, thoughtful actions rather than in any kind of extravagant gesture. The Virgoan is intelligent and critical of others, included himself. Basically shy, this is not the type to climb on a soapbox to make fiery speeches, nor will you find this individual making a spectacle of himself in public.

This type always knows how to behave and rarely if ever loses any composure or control. Certain astrologers have declared that this is a selfish sign, but the kind of selfishness that demands assistance and attention from others is the very last accusation that could be levelled against this type. Many of this sign dedicate themselves to work, very often for inadequate pay, finding more satisfaction in helping others.

Mr Hyde: negative

This character constantly searches for perfection but that doesn't mean that he or she is perfect. This type can be very trying – for example, such an individual has a dogged belief that no one can do things as orderly or as efficiently as he, and this type will also drive others mad with an insistence on promptness. When kept waiting there are no hysterics and anger from the Virgoan, instead a shrewish, nagging, fussy individual is the result. No point in the latecomer's standing up for himself – he won't have a chance. Others frequently admit they are in the wrong with this character in order to hopefully find some peace and quiet. This type of Virgoan also develops a mental block when it comes to admitting he is wrong, so if you are clever it is better to take the lead and the blame right at the beginning. That critical tongue will never let up. People are criticized for the way they speak, walk, act and dress. Not surprisingly this type rarely advances in any field of activity, as the ever-probing eye can always find flaws and impossibilities. Rarely does it find the possibilities and opportunities in any venture. Although Mr Hyde is particularly good at destroying ideas and situations, don't expect him to offer suitable alternatives.

This type is an original and genuine pain in the neck who sees himself as a saint. Will you tell him the honest truth? No! The wisest course is to give this type a very wide berth.

Is Your Child a Typical Virgo?

Answer the questions below honestly, score 1 for 'No', 2 for 'Sometimes' and 3 for 'Yes'. Turn to page 219 for the answers.

1. Is your child fussy with his food?
2. Is your child critical?
3. Does the child prefer a strict routine?
4. Does the child get upset even over the smallest thing?
5. Is your child shy?
6. Does the child need little sleep?
7. Does the child enjoy physical activity?
8. Does your child like to be clean and neat?
9. Would your child be offended if you attempted to feed him with grubby hands?
10. Does your child's mind work quickly?
11. Does your child find it difficult to mix with other children?
12. Does your child enjoy helping around the home?
13. Is your child mentally mature?
14. Does your child find sharing difficult?
15. Are there times when you suspect that your child disapproves of you?
16. Does the child gladly tidy away toys?
17. Does the child dislike meeting your friends?
18. Does your child rarely show pleasure?
19. Does your child like to be well dressed?
20. Is the child fascinated at the sight of his own blood?

THE VIRGO BABY
Up to four years of age

Even when this child is quite tiny his parents will notice how alert and quick yet at the same time more peaceful and tranquil he is than other infants. This will be a contradiction that will give you an idea of this little character's future personality. He is going to be one who can soothe and irritate in turn. A little later this person will be a great companion for his mother. Both sexes happily imitate whatever she is doing and sons will usually ignore any statements from their fathers that 'boys don't do such things'.

You may wonder why your Virgo baby does not appear to be as affectionate as some other children appear to be. Don't expect those born under this sign to show much emotion. However, this doesn't mean that emotion is not needed and large doses of love should be doled out every day. You'd better get used to the idea also that you have a critic in the family. Sometimes this will be humorous, but on other occasions it will lead you to pull your hair out with irritation and frustration. This type may be short on emotion but is usually long on realism and logic and the child will be totally sympathetic when his mother has an upset stomach or when father has a headache. However, although this child is far from perfect, and you will feel like committing murder when he refuses to wear some new item of clothing because it is wrinkled, for instance, most of the time – and this is your consolation – he is a joy to have around the house so try your best to remember this when the child is having one of his difficult days.

Health

Virgo rules the bowels and, to some extent, the skin, and health hazards are centred in these directions. Constipation will possibly be the first problem you will need to cope with. Breast-fed babies very rarely have hard stools but they may go for some days without having a motion and this is normal. It is also normal for babies to go red, grunt or strain when opening their bowels. Constipation in babies is when they frequently have very hard, dry stools. The problem is often helped by giving the baby more water. A child on strained foods may be helped by fruit purée, particularly prunes and apple. The older Virgoan child who is constipated will be helped by having plenty to drink and plenty of roughage in the diet, things like fresh fruit, wholemeal bread, coarse cereals and vegetables. Never give a weekly laxative. You can keep the bowels open by sensible diet alone, but if the problem persists then consult your doctor.

Rashes are another health hazard. Babies' skin is sensitive and rashes develop quite frequently. Sometimes they are simply the result of the child's getting too hot. Occasionally an allergy causes a rash and this can look like nettle-rash. In new-born babies small white milk-spots appear around the nose and cheeks. If you are at all worried you should always consult your doctor.

The Virgoan child frequently has an extremely sensitive stomach and can vomit almost at will, as you will no doubt have discovered. Such a sensitive system picks up infection extremely quickly, so hygiene needs to be scrupulous. Colic is also a common irritation. The baby will scream, sometimes for long periods, and draw his knees up to his chest. Anything you find that seems to help the baby during an attack is worth doing; some babies like to be cuddled or rocked, or even driven in a car, others seem to be better when allowed to suckle a bottle of warm milk. Gripe water can also sometimes help. Background noise can be soothing. If the colic seems exceptionally bad you should once again consult your doctor.

Food

Are you losing your hair, good looks and youth? Then they are probably the results of your attempts to feed and sustain your little angel. But what you probably don't realize is that he/she has already decided that it can quite adequately survive on little more than fresh air. Briefly, it takes three months for your Virgoan to condescendingly accept the breast or bottle, a year to get the occasional solid down a reluctant throat and thereafter it will be strawberry jam and chips all the way! And, if the changeover to cows' milk gives the baby colic then solids are going to make him throw up, or else you could discover that he/she is allergic to cereal. So tear up your baby books. Miss or master average will not apply here if your child is a typical Virgoan.

If he happens to like chips, cheese and strawberry jam, relax – it may not be a turn-on for you, but there is nourishment in this eccentric meal. Whatever you do don't make a fuss as babies and toddlers pick up on neuroses quickly. If food is refused, take it away. The Virgoan will ask when he is hungry enough, and besides most Western mothers overfeed their infants anyway. Also, do try to understand that a child who isn't mad about food is certainly going to be reluctant when it comes to feeding himself.

A few tips. Virgoans are frequently vegetarian, but love cheese, eggs and fruit. Make sure there is plenty around. It is not the end of the world if he does not happen to be a carnivore. Make your food attractive. You may doubt it, but eventually your Virgoan will join the human race.

Crying

The Virgo baby may make your life a misery at meal-times but at least this is no howler. Naturally, he or she will protest when wet, hungry or ill but Virgos are basically well-behaved and contented children. Having said that, this child is usually the possessor of a rather high-pitched cry so parents would be wise to pay attention before they are regaled by a little Mercury child in full throttle – not an attractive sound.

This type's most common reason for complaint is colic, which attacks the Virgoan quite regularly. Boredom comes second on the list. Your Virgoan will not demand constant attention or affection – he is fairly independent and unemotional – but don't expect him to lie there and simply look into space. The section on crying under Gemini deals with boredom adequately and should be referred to.

Teeth

Fortunately, the Virgoan is normal when it comes to teeth, so the section at the end of this book should be most helpful. Even so there will be little doubt in your mind when this child begins teething, a troublesome and trying phase, as he or she will obligingly break out in a rash on the cheeks and will appear flushed and hot. But it must be pointed out that the Virgoan is sensitive to skin problems, so don't imagine a rash on the chest or back is connected with teeth. Common sense will see you through that.

Bath-time

Your Virgoan infant will enjoy bath-time, not because of any great sympathy with water but because he loves to feel and smell clean. Bath-time is therefore a sensual experience and you should treat is as such. Purchase plenty of bath-powders, oils and put on clean night-wear after each bath. Never leave this little character in the bath for too long as his sensitive skin dries out in record time. Plenty of oil and perhaps a water softener is the answer.

Also watch out for allergies. If your child develops a rash after bathing you will need to investigate the soap, bubble-bath, or perhaps the cleanser you use to rinse out the bath after use or the detergent that you use to wash his or her clothes.

With care, bath-time can be a happy and rewarding experience for the Virgoan.

Interests and Games

Mercury, the planet of communication, rules this sign and Gemini too. Your child will therefore be fascinated by words and letters at an early age. Alphabet-bricks and rag-books are a wise buy. The more time you have to talk to him and help him communicate the better, and he will like it. While this type may watch television for short periods, he does have a limited attention span and expecting him to sit still for any length of time proves an impossibility.

This sign is also a medical one, and your little Virgo will, no doubt, enjoy playing doctors and nurses or with any toys pertaining to the medical profession. You will also have observed how obsessively the child likes to straighten or line up ashtrays, spoons, boxes and other objects. If he insists on arranging any household things in a certain tidy position he will be incensed with fury if you dare to alter the arrangement. What you are witnessing in these strange actions is his classifying, analysing brain working. Any toy which allows him to sift and classify will keep him amused for hours.

If your Virgo volunteers to wash some of his clothes, fetch a small bowl and an item of clothing and let him get on with it. This is his attempt at independence and hygiene and as such it should be encouraged.

Walking and Talking

The Virgoan has an extremely expressive face and words are often superfluous. One look at the big eyes and you will know immediately what is needed. As previously mentioned Virgo and Gemini are ruled by mobile and communicative Mercury, and as a result your child will walk and talk just as fast as he possibly can. Everything is done at great speed. The child will not totter for long and in no time at all he will be zooming around the house at high speed. You are also likely to despair when he tries mountaineering up the bookcase or stair banisters so lock valuables and dangers away. Not only is this child as agile as a monkey but just as inquisitive. If there is any Scorpio or Taurus in the child it will also be very determined. Such a combination is guaranteed to be rough on parents.

Speech-wise, your child will be just as agile inventing his own words and possibly his own language too! Initially this may hold back his natural development, but it is a phase that will soon pass. Why not try to introduce the child to one or two of the odder words in the English language? They will fascinate and perhaps put the child back on the right road.

Should your child insist on speaking gibberish, don't fret for this problem will soon straighten itself out when he realizes that others cannot understand him.

Toilet-training

The Virgoan child's behaviour is often eccentric when it comes to toilet-training and he will often acquire some way-out ideas where bodily functions are concerned. If you think that mealtimes are exasperating then just wait until toilet-training finally arrives. Your child may, of course, take to the potty like a cat to a satin cushion, for a while at least. Then quite suddenly, and for no apparent reason, he will wet himself wherever he happens to be. He may even decide to refrain from going at all and may hold himself back for as long as possible until a desperate cry emits from his lips and you both make a panicky dash for the potty! If you are lucky you'll make it!

One week the child will be disgusted by this necessity of life and the next he will be fascinated by it, wanting to examine what he has produced. This is his natural curiosity asserting itself and you should not be worried by it.

You could be in for a difficult time but allow the child to go through the various phases without fuss on your part, and when he successfully obliges on the potty then compliment and flatter him. Sooner or later the child will decide that he has better things to do than to waste half his time on this rather boring activity. When he does, the procedure will be dispensed with as quickly as possible, cleanly and without eccentricity – eventually!

Starting School

Once your Virgoan reaches the age of three he will need school, for that active head must be stimulated. At this point the child will have exhausted all the possibilities in your home. However, there is no point in over-emphasizing the fact that finally he can meet other little ones as this child will be unimpressed. The Virgoan isn't frightened of other people but just indifferent, so this is not the way to excite this type. The parent should rather stress the games and activities just waiting to be explored.

An emotional Virgoan is a rarity, so it is difficult to imagine any kind of emotional display on his first day alone at school unless it is a reflection of his mother's own feelings. Starting school for the first time should possibly be his father's task, for it is essential to keep this first parting casual.

Praise any painting or work that the child should bring home. This type often lacks confidence and now is as good a time as any to begin boosting that flagging ego. After all, if the child as much as suspects that he is not as bright as the others at school then he will not want to attend. Your child does not wish to lord it over the others, like a Leo; he simply wishes to be equal.

THE VIRGO CHILD

Four to twelve years of age

Health

Basically your child's problems will be similar to those he suffered as a baby, only more so. By this time you should now have a lengthy list of allergies, and you will now be adding to it fast. One skin complaint that may reveal itself is eczema. This is a fairly common Virgo complaint, usually starting with patches of dry scaly skin which become red, and they may weep. It may begin behind the knees or the elbows. Your doctor will advise on treatment and he will also inform you that children with eczema should not be vaccinated against smallpox until the eczema is cured. Eczema is not catching, nor is it caused by poor hygiene. Also at this stage there will be numerous little irritations in his rectum. Constipation may now have led to the beginnings of piles (haemorrhoids) and, unless you have been scrupulously clean and in some cases even when you have, the child may contract worms. Unwashed fruit is your greatest enemy here. Look for the symptoms . . . a child who itches around the anus and starts waking frequently in the night is likely to have threadworm. Go to your doctor or clinic for remedies.

Mostly, however, it is the skin complaints that will be the most worrying and, seemingly, never ending. Apart from allergies, worry can also lead to a rash in this child. The Virgo keeps his problems to himself unless he is encouraged to confide them to someone else. Now is a good time to begin winning his confidence, and don't lose sight of the fact that you are going to need it later if you are to minimize problems during adolescence.

The Virgoan's health is usually good, but he will be plagued by a series of irritating ailments. To make matters worse he is a born hypochondriac. You will suffer no problems when it comes to getting this child to swallow pills or potions. Your worry and attention will make your Virgoan feel important. You will need to ensure that he receives plenty of attention when he is well or this is just the child to imagine an ilness in an effort to attract your attention.

Friends

Your Virgoan is a discriminating individual so don't expect him to be surrounded by thousands of friends. He is selective and knows who and what he likes. This, together with the tendency to criticize others, can make the child feel lonely at times. However, when this type does finally find a friend, help to keep the relationship going by extending invitations. When a Virgoan finally takes to someone he will stick to the friend through thick and thin.

Parties, not surprisingly, are agony for this type. Being self-conscious, the Virgo is not a good mixer. Never force the Virgoan to attend a party if it is quite obviously bound to upset him. The Virgoan will still loathe large groups of people as an adult. This type will feel intimidated by parties, for he does not have the Leo's confidence nor the Gemini's gift for superficial talk. Neither should you worry if the one, single friend is worshipped. This character is a perfectionist and those close to him are quite special.

The Virgoan does not belong to the funny hat, whistle-blowing and jokey fraternity. Left to develop in his own good time he could emerge as a self-confident, selective and sophisticated individual so don't push him into being something he can never be.

Interests and Games

Virgo is an intellectural sign so you will find that your child will take to most of the board games, especially where he needs to exercise his brain. Introduce this type to Draughts and in no time at all you will wind up with a chess expert. The attraction to the medical profession will in some cases endure, while in others it may have developed along scientific lines and there may be an obsession with chemistry and chemistry sets. Reading-matter will revolve around science fiction and self instruction. Most Virgoans like to keep fit and this is apparent at a very early age. He or she will be the first person to suggest a sponsored walk or a cross-country hike . . . all very healthy. Also, both sexes are very fleet of foot and make excellent sprinters, usually breaking all school records and winning all the cups and prizes.

While on the subject of keep fit . . . it can only be a matter of time before your child becomes a health food freak. You will be subjected to statements like: 'Did you know seaweed has more vitamins than cabbage?' and 'One can contract tapeworms from eating pork!' If you didn't know these things your Virgoan will soon educate you, and you should prepare to be bombarded with these and other pieces of such information.

The Virgoan is a unusual child but you will adjust to him.

Accepting a New Baby

While your new infant is still immobile life should be tranquil. The Virgoan will nod approvingly while you feed and bath the new baby, as he is intelligent enough to know that new babies need to be cared for and that it is a time-consuming operation. The Virgoan will frequently offer assistance and you will be so efficient that you will almost feel confident enough to leave him in charge. Postpone your relief at this situation though, and wipe that smug expression from your face, for once the baby begins toddling the dramas will begin. The Virgoan is a tidy and organized soul and, furthermore, acutely self-centred and selfish. The first time your new infant damages one of the Virgoan's possessions you'll discover that the love affair is well and truly over. The Virgoan will want to play with baby's new toys but he will not share his own. The answer to this is to fit a strong lock to the toy cupboard and to hand over the key to your Virgoan. He can then pack away all his treasures and baby will not be able to get at them. After a while you may be able to persuade your Virgoan into sharing his older, perhaps stronger, toys, but do not insist should he refuse. It is too early and you will only create resentment. Occasionally this individual will floor you by displaying some unbelievable generosity and he is quite likely to bestow his most treasured possession on the baby. This is instigated by the sudden realization that perhaps it would be a good idea to have this interloper on his side, so the burst of self-sacrifice is not what it appeared to be! Of course show your delight, but it is not yet the time for self-congratulation. In fact it is unlikely that any real warmth will develop until your infant has refrained from throwing his porridge on to the floor and overturning his potty and has learned to talk. Once this occurs your Virgoan will slowly become a little parent.

Discipline

The typical Virgoan is an obedient child and discipline should not be a problem. This character is loaded down with common sense, so appeal to it. Explain clearly that it hurts when the cat's tail is pulled, just the same as it would should his finger be put on something hot. But refrain from going into complicated explanation until the child is older or confusion will reign. A good example is always the best lesson of all. You wish he were less selfish? Then let him observe the generosity of those around. Don't scold him as this will only make him hug all that is his closer to him.

As for the occasional smack . . . provided it is reserved for really naughty behaviour it won't do your unemotional Virgo any harm provided you kiss and make up before bed-time. Don't make it a habit, though. This is not a difficult child, although he could turn out to be something of a rebel later. If you wish to avoid this, then never insult his intelligence. He understands far more than you give him credit for.

Sex

The Virgoan has a reputation of being totally disinterested in sex. This is untrue and unfair. Regrettably though this is a sign that is easily sexually inhibited, and many Virgoans grow up feeling a little uncomfortable whenever the subject is brought out into the open and discussed. Nevertheless, those born under this sign are as sexual as any other and this must be appreciated, for what parents need to understand is that the Virgo is selective, not prudish.

However, you can relax in one respect, it is very unlikely that your Virgoan will turn into a sex maniac, so don't fret about corrupting his mind. If you are to instil a happy, open attitude to sex it is important to start early and answer honestly all the questions put to you. The Virgoan is bright and inquisitive and should you be embarrassed this will be sensed and will in turn touch off his own self-consciousness. The parents' reaction to the child is of paramount importance, so throw your inhibitions out of the window, read the section at the end of the book and you won't go far wrong.

Homework and Study

The typical Virgoan is not a problem when it comes to homework or study. In fact this is the sign of the swot provided that is a clear objective has been established. Like the Taurean, routine and method are adhered to and a parent is rarely faced with a Virgo child who prefers to watch television when he knows it is homework period. Children born under this sign are frequently teachers' pets. They love to give practical assistance and will stay after school hours to clean blackboards, tidy desks and replace books. This may not be well received by classmates but it does help to establish contact with the teacher. This child loves to please, especially when he knows those in authority are expecting him to do well. As a result, no particular problems need be expected in this direction.

Finding a Direction

As previously mentioned Virgo is a medical sign, so it is as well to explore this possibility of a direction in life before experimenting elsewhere. Buy, or borrow from the library, biographies of famous medics. Many exhibitions are periodically held portraying the history of medicine in one form or another. If your Virgoan is destined to be doctor, nurse or dentist, these displays should ignite some spark of interest. Should you be successful, then encourage the child all the way. Naturally friends in the profession can be of invaluable help later, so bear this in mind.

Mathematics also are associated with Virgo and any kind of game you can invent with figures will be eagerly appreciated. Buy him a ruler and measure tables, chairs, beds, everything in sight. He can write down his calculations and findings in a little book. If your Virgoan is stimulated he will get totally carried away and will then measure everything from his egg-cup to the family cat!

Most children of Virgo enjoy sifting and classifying. Rearranging bookshelves until satisfied is enjoyable to them and they will then offer you a record of the whereabouts of each book. However, should he seem bored with this idea then you may have a child obsessed with the body beautiful, in which case he or she may be enthralled with the value of various foods. Books to stimulate must then be made readily available. His interest may be revealed in an absorption for unusual cults such as yoga, or possibly even a sport. Discover, if you can, at an early age exactly what it is that stimulates and develops his interest. A busy active mind makes for clear ambitions and fulfilment and leaves little time for destructive behaviour.

THE VIRGO TEENAGER
Twelve to eighteen years of age

This is an extremely painful time for most Virgoans, for things couldn't be worse in a physical sense. Both sexes suffer agonies with their skin, for acne waits around every corner. Dental problems in the form of crooked, protruding or discoloured teeth mean that braces and treatment are often necessary. These physical imperfections coupled with the Virgoan's self-consciousness and hypochondria make for a miserable character.

The Virgoan plight is so acute that his or her family may find it amusing and indeed wrestle unsuccessfully with a chuckle or two especially when many multi-coloured pills are taken in a day not to mention the wonder products that are guaranteed to get rid of acne.

Recall your own problems in adolescence, try to remember how you suffered and how your parents seemed unable to understand. Take an interest in the potions and pills while suggesting that a reduction in the intake could be made. After all, doesn't it make better sense to take one pill or potion for the express purpose of tackling spots from the interior, while taking another to tackle them from the outside? This has to be explained practically. Suggest that too many pills make it impossible to judge which work and which do not. In this way you appeal to the analyst who will gladly experiment along your suggestions. A trip to the doctor might appeal to the hypochondriac, especially if the acne seems to have run rampant. Fathers should also bear in mind that shaving can be agony with just one spot, never mind a complete, overall eruption! An electric razor would be a thoughtful present in these circumstances.

Attempt to take your Virgoan as seriously as he takes himself and make certain that he knows you are there to listen and advise when needed. Otherwise leave him alone.

Dating

The Virgo is fully aware of the opposite sex but taking positive action is something else. This type is haunted by thoughts and fears of rejection and so he procrastinates, frequently missing several opportunities to ask a girl out before sufficient courage is gathered. That first date will probably be a first love. If you have been a wise parent your Virgo will confide in you when the relationship hits a stormy impasse. If not, the child will withdraw from you leaving you helpless on the sidelines. If you should be unlucky then try to show interest while keeping your opinions to yourself. The typical Virgo teenager will not fight or protest when you expect him or her home at a decent hour.

However, should your fifteen-year-old stay out all night then you can be sure that you have a Mr Hyde rebel on your hands and a firm stand will be needed. Give in on several unimportant issues without budging in this respect. After all, it is your house and if he or she doesn't like the rules you can suggest that at a later date he or she move. However, a devious parent will also give a quick lesson in home economics; this is likely to dissuade your shrewd Virgoan from premature independence. Fortunately the Virgoan rebel is rare and your particular teenager probably belongs in the obedient section of this sign.

Alcohol

Your Virgoan will make you irritated by his picture-straightening and nagging hypochondria but the typical member of this sign won't give you problems with alcohol. Many Virgoans are teetotal and those who do imbibe do so in moderation. However, in case your teenager has just arrived home drunk you need a few words of advice.

Check out his drinking companion. In a previous section concerning friends you will note the Virgo's devotion to one special friend. It is quite possible that this friend likes to get intoxicated quite regularly, in which case your Virgoan will likewise be employed. You will then need to point out two things to your erring Virgo. Firstly the cost – who is paying for this liquor? – and secondly that friendship is a two-way street. If he is drinking to please his friend perhaps the friend should occasionally abstain in order to prove his consideration. This may not call an instant halt to his drinking, but you should on no account make any attempt to break up the relationship. Your Virgoan is an intelligent individual who will suddenly realize how expensive and stupid such behaviour is. Generally, drinking alcohol is only a phase unless you push your Virgoan into it.

Drugs

Not only is the Virgo moderate and sensible with alcohol but the same attitude is adopted with drugs. They hold little or no attraction for him unless you wish to take into consideration the veritable chemist's shop he possesses in his room. But these are medicines to him for his many ailments, and you must understand this fact. Therefore, they do not count. Besides you won't find an upper, downer or any kind of escapist drug among the lot. While at this impressionable age it might be wise to suggest an occasional inventory. After all, some drugs, oops . . medicines . . need to be kept under certain conditions, otherwise they are either useless or dangerous after a stated time. Should you discover that your Virgoan is on some kind of upper such as amphetamine (speed) or bennies (benzedrine) then, apart from checking out his friends, discover what is worrying him. It is possible that if he is studying he may be taking them in order to stay awake to all hours to get in as much cramming as possible. If so you will need to remove such stress and make some adjustments so he becomes a healthy teenager, not a neurotic. This is the time for both of you to make attempts at re-establishing contact and reopening the lines of communication.

All this is unlikely to occur, though, for the Virgo is practical and sensible and prefers to keep both feet on the ground.

SUGGESTED CAREERS

Some suitable careers are listed below but because Virgo and Gemini are ruled by versatile Mercury those born under these signs may be sometimes spoiled for choice or they may be multiple talented. Don't be surprised if your Virgoan follows two careers or jobs and happily swings from one to the other. At some later date, in middle life, it is quite likely that your, say farming, Virgoan decides that it is time to enter the film business! Encourage his many interests, they are an essential part of the character. The only positive action the parents should take is to make an attempt at instilling in their teenager a desire to finish everything that he has started. Otherwise you will find this individual going in one direction, stopping half way and retreating, only to go off in another direction, a sure way of getting absolutely nowhere.

Your Virgoan could be suited for the following occupations:

Secretary	Inspector	Writer
Analytic scientist	Craftsman	Telephone operator
Statistician	Literary critic	Shop assistant
Gardener	Journalist	Doctor
Accountant	Commentator	Nurse
Teacher	Linguist	

Any career connected with health and hygiene

LIBRA

THE SECOND AIR SIGN

Symbol The Scales

Planet Venus

Colour Indigo blue

Metal Copper

Motivation Justice and management

Easy going; indecisive; quick to establish relations; charming; artistic; refined; reluctant to make commitments

GENERAL CHARACTERISTICS

Is Your Child a Typical Libra?

THE LIBRAN BABY

Health

Food

Crying

Teething

Bath-time

Interests and Games

Walking and Talking

Toilet-training

Starting School

THE LIBRAN CHILD

Health

Friends

Interests and Games

Accepting a New Baby

Discipline

Sex

Homework and Study

Finding a Direction

THE LIBRAN TEENAGER

Dating

Alcohol

Drugs

Suggested Careers

GENERAL CHARACTERISTICS

Dr Jekyll: positive

The strength of this character is the certain, sane, well-balanced element that runs through his whole nature. Such a Libran hates injustice and unfairness and anything ill proportioned or ugly in life. This also applies to exaggeration and all feelings that are morbid, depressive, hysterical or strained. This individual's normal, natural method of expression is in art and music in all its forms.

This is a delightful sign, for the Libran is loving and can fill his days with what are called the little things of life, that is to say those constant petty items of self-sacrifice of the kind no one notices, and they do so cheerfully. This type is many sided and often has difficulty in choosing a profession, making several false starts and then changing. In most cases the desire for perfection makes the Libran exceedingly painstaking, patient and particularly careful about detail, rarely doing anything twice.

The Libran is scrupulously honest in financial matters and in all spheres where ready tact, social charm and all round ability tells. Laziness and a certain indecision are the biggest faults, but these are not as accentuated in this type as they are in the following.

Mr Hyde: negative

The bad side of the Libran usually reveals itself in a tendency to be a Jack-of-all-trades. The parents of this type will despair over his start in life but to no avail. He tries this and that, rarely making a success out of anything he attempts. He foolishly tells himself that he is searching for perfection, so he splits hairs and procrastinates and progress is then painfully slow. Indecision creates acute agonies in those around him. Romantically speaking, this type has a brief memory where affections are concerned and this particular Mr Hyde will suffer from a broken heart for all of twenty-four hours! The tendency towards fickleness cannot be denied, and he trifles, especially in youth. The natural Libran's impulse is to size up every third or fourth member of the opposite sex as being his true soul mate. Love and friendship are hopelessly mixed up in his head, and should this individual be accused of indecision the effect is almost humorous. Tell him that every astrological textbook mentions the indecisions of the Libran and he will state: 'That is not accurate, it certainly doesn't apply to me, does it?' Fortunately even a bad Libran cannot be too awful, so even the Mr Hyde character manages to charm the fiercest foe.

Is Your Child a Typical Libran?

Answer the questions honestly. Score three for every 'Yes', two for every 'Sometimes' and one for every 'No'. Turn to page 220 for the answers.

1. Does your child take an interest when shopping for clothes?
2. Is your child a natural flirt?
3. Does the child notice when you have had your hair done?
4. Does he clam up when you lose your temper?
5. Is the child's work-pattern erratic?
6. Are the words 'It's not fair' frequently on his or her lips?
7. Is the child artistic?
8. Does the child find it hard to say no to other children?
9. Is decision-making difficult for the child?
10. Does the child love the company of others?
11. Does the child enjoy his food?
12. Does the child love animals?
13. Is the child sensitive to environment?
14. Does the child enjoy dressing up?
15. Is the child musical?
16. Is the child hurt when criticized?
17. Is your child lazy?
18. Does your child easily understand that he cannot always have his own way?
19. Does the child like pleasant smells?
20. Is your child extremely affectionate?

THE LIBRAN BABY
Up to four years of age

There is no denying the fact that the Libran baby looks as if he might just have escaped from Heaven. His or her mother will accustom herself to the fact that whenever she takes the baby out for walks, admiring crowds will cluster around the pram. Eventually she will become blasé about the situation and may even enter the child in the local baby show – he has a good chance of winning, too.

As the Libran child grows he or she loses nothing of his or her physical beauty. However, by the time he is toddling around one or two of the smallest faults being to emerge.

'Shall we go out, darling?' uttered by his mother will bring a thoughtful look to the child's features. 'Come on,' says mother 'when shall we go out?' Such questions are a mistake. This child is indecisive and mother has just posed two big problems. Firstly, shall we go out? and secondly when? Notice the hopeless confusion written all over the child's face. It is true that at a later stage the Libran must be taught to make decisions but just at this moment never give him a choice – it is the worst thing you can do to this type. Besides, this can have advantages at this tender age, for while your Libran is trying to decide just what to do, like painting his father's best suit blue or green, you will have had time to step in and avert disaster!

The Libran child needs peace, quiet and rest in large doses and yet another problem from this may be the Libran laziness. You'll notice that your child will play hard for long periods but then must rest. There is nothing wrong with him – so don't rush to the doctors. All the little character is doing is gathering himself for the next onslaught.

Health

The Libran is the original bouncing baby we see portrayed on baby products, pink, dimpled and chubby. This individual is not only a charmer, but a healthy one. However, this sign rules the kidneys and while problems at such an early age are unlikely there is no harm in bearing this fact in mind. Lots of water will keep those organs healthy and give him a good start in life. Bladder infections are probably the biggest health hazard and, whenever your Libran's urine becomes highly coloured and strongly pungent, probably accompanied by nappy rash, then it is time to visit the doctor. Like all air signs this baby is fairly nervous and highly strung and very susceptible to colour and sound. If you doubt this fact then the next time you redecorate the nursery make it a soft blue or pink. Patterns and bright or dull colours upset this baby and repainting in soft colours it is quite possible that you can turn a whining infant into a sleeping beauty.

Food

It is a fact that there is something sensual about the consumption of food. This applies to us all, but to the Libran it is an unmistakable truth and one he learns early. There'll be no problems at meal-times while your baby is still on the breast or bottle. He adores this first delight in life – just observe the utter contentment spread across his chubby face as he suckles! You'll need to ensure that service is good however, for this sign, although not impatient, will successfully strike guilt into your heart if you are late. The baby will feel betrayed – all that good faith and what do you do? Let him down!

Later, the love affair with meal-times does not diminish. But the presentation of the meal is of the utmost importance. The Libran child will assess the meal's potential by its appearance and smell. If it looks boring or unattractive you can expect a full-scale war. Nevertheless, with a little effort this child will present no problems at all, being ever ready to experiment with new foods and new experiences.

Food is a joy to this child and, in many instances, solids can be introduced at approximately three months. However, your baby will leave you in no doubt as to when liquids are no longer enough. So play it by Libran instruction and instinct.

Food problems do not exist, even with the passage of time, unless you consider the Libran's natural and excellent good taste a drawback. It is quite possible that parents may not have the time or money to rustle up a quick chicken a la king and strawberry soufflé although, if she can, she can be absolutely certain that here is an appreciative consumer.

Crying

A new Libran baby given friendly cuddles and words during the day is less likely to give trouble at night. There is a fact that needs to be accepted, though: Libra is the sign of the cat-napper and your infant is quite likely to wake up, chat a little, cry a little and then go back to sleep. Pop your head in at the crying stage and he will soon drift back to sleep. Naturally all babies, including Librans, cry when they are wet, dirty or ill, but in this instance attention takes top priority. All those born under this sign are social and dislike their own company; they don't actually want anything but they simply need to know that someone else is around. This is sufficient. Don't hush friends and neighbours because baby is sleeping. He loves the everyday sounds of people talking, moving around, and so on. It makes this child feel secure.

As previously mentioned, a soft colour in the nursery also helps as it soothes and relaxes. Music can also be guaranteed to calm the savage breast and when baby is fretful you'll find that a lullaby will work wonders.

The Libran baby is not the Zodiac brat and is usually so delightful that no one can ignore him or her.

Teething

Should you be unfortunately confronted with a screaming Libra infant, then try to recall his usual genial, contented and charming self. This will help you to appreciate that something must really be wrong. It could well be the beginnings of those nasty, hard teeth. Generally speaking this is a well-mannered child who doesn't like to make an unseeming display. You can therefore imagine just what he is feeling. Lots and lots of love and some teething gell will do a lot to placate the baby and an occasional lullaby will also be much appreciated.

Usually the Libran cuts teeth like he does everything else – with style. Parents may not even be aware of their existence until visibility makes it impossible for them to be ignored. A runny nose, an over-powering odour of the urine will be symptoms to watch for if there are problems, and for further advice see the end of the book.

Bath-time

The Libran baby rarely enjoys bath-time until he is old enough to sit up. Until then he feels rather insecure floating around in all that water. In this particular instance you should not place your child in the full-size bath. A small baby-bath will be much less of an ordeal. Later, the pleasant smells and warmth associated with this ritual will eventually win him over, to the extent where your child will actually look forward to the event. Also, if you have other children, this character will enjoy sharing their bath-time. Pleasure is always doubled for the Libran when it is shared with another. This will, of course, afford opportunities for fun and games. Floating home-made boats and squeezing sponges over one another will delight the child. The freedom of splashing about together is also enjoyed, but for the sake of your home this should be kept within the bounds of reason.

Interests and Games

Some children are quite content to play alone and never seem to need the participation of others, their parents included. This doesn't apply to the Libran, though. He needs a partner, firstly with whom to share experiences, secondly with whom to initiate games. Quite often this character does not know where or when to begin when he is left to his own devices and as a result he may give up and do nothing. Bear this in mind.

This particular child is easy to bring up. The only exception to this could be the constant need for stimulation. Wherever possible the child will enjoy the company of others. He may only sit and watch them, but sometimes this is sufficient. Later, when he is more confident, the Libran will offer his toys as a sign of friendship, and will be mortified if the hand of friendship is rejected. Naturally, then, you will need to devote much time to playing and stimulating this individual.

The Libran is particularly good at balancing, so toys and objects than can be used for this purpose will please him. Puzzles will help to educate this type, who cannot naturally make a decision, so start educating him at a fairly early age. For example: does this piece fit, or is it that one? Initially this child may not enjoy the experience, in which case abandon it immediately he shows disgust or unrest. Ressurect the puzzle at intervals. This is good training for this type. Those born under this sign are extremely colour-conscious and your child will learn them long before he can count. Any pastel-coloured toy will be enjoyed and painting also pleases. This is a fairly lazy infant, so the more you stimulate him at this age the better. To leave such a child alone for too long is his idea of purgatory.

Walking and Talking

As frequently mentioned, the Libran is not the most energetic of children, and that incredible smile can be guaranteed to send other people scurrying to do his bidding. Because of this the Libran infant will wonder why he should bother to stir himself. In actuality there is no point in pushing him. You cannot teach a child to walk and it will occur when he is good and ready. Initially your baby will begin to put weight on his feet and bounce up and down. Later, when the crawling stage is reached, he will start to pull himself up on the furniture. However, this child may well be late in learning to walk and if so accept it and be prepared to be patient.

Speech on the other hand develops fairly early. To the Libran it is a more useful and less energetic activity. The socialite is strongly emphasized in him and, after all, one cannot be sociable when one only has a series of grunts and groans in the vocabulary. Such a child is extremely expressive and face- and body-talk are often substituted effectively when he is frustrated in expressing himself verbally. One way or the other those messages will come across loud and strong. Be on the alert for them.

Toilet-training

Toilet-training is an accomplishment that is never achieved overnight nor until your child is ready. To the typical Libran this is a rather unpleasant business, so don't make matters worse by starting too early – before eighteen months – or by conveying anger or disappointment when he fails. It is quite possible that your Libran may seem to take to sitting on the potty for long periods of time. This may seem to denote that your child knows exactly what you want and that it has something to do with those wet nappies. Regrettably, and you must consider this, your child just may not know what he can do about it. Because of this he will sit on the potty and hope for the best. Should this occur your child just isn't ready, so postpone your toilet-training efforts for the time being.

One of the easiest ways to train this little character is by example, of course. As previously mentioned this type enjoys sharing an experience, so when a parent sits on the lavatory baby should sit on the potty in front of him or her. This will make the child understand that using the lavatory is a natural part of life. Later, of course, at school this fact will finally sink home. But by instilling toilet-training at home you may have a dry child earlier than you would otherwise have had. Just let this child move on to any new stage at his own pace, and avoid hampering or restricting his natural progress in any way.

Starting School

During the days leading up to the important first day at school, parents need to convey the fun and company the Libran child will find at school. This child adores people of all ages and is not in the least bit worried or fretful at the thought of meeting strangers. He knows how to charm a snail out of its shell and is therefore full of confidence. Providing your Libran is also secure in your love then this stage should be taken in his stride. The fact is that the experience may affect the parent more than the child, and remember that the Libran will be quick to pick up any apprehension.

Ideally, when entering the school, the child's parent should introduce the Libran to the best-looking member of the opposite sex then stand back while he or she turns on the charm sufficiently to illuminate the entire school.

THE LIBRAN CHILD

Four to twelve years of age

Health

The Libran's sensitivity to colour and sound is by now fully developed, so whatever you do never force him to witness disharmony, especially between parents. The Libran loathes tension, loaded atmospheres or outbursts. They are sufficient on their own to instigate a series of obscure illnesses. Psychosomatic, yes, but real to this Libran child nevertheless. Therefore, if your child seems to constantly suffer from stomach pains or headaches, better make an effort to discover what it is that is causing such distress. Also, continue your vigil against possible kidney trouble in the future, and be on your guard if your infant ever complains of backache and investigate it at once. Gallons of water or lemon barley will do much to keep those Libran kidneys healthy, plus the fact that constant drinking may well become a habit and serve to avert later problems.

Friends

The Libran experiences no problem in making friends, unless his parents are anti-social or over houseproud. Your home will ring with the sound of your Libran's friends just as soon as he is capable of asking them home. Naturally, this is a two-way street and your infant will be out visiting just as often as he is entertaining. This will mean a lot of fetching and carrying those infants not yet capable of using buses or trains. Don't restrict this social butterfly or he will grow into a morose or lazy teenager. The Libran girl is fashion conscious and any money spent on her wardrobe will delight her. The cry of, 'I've nothing to wear!' will assault your ears from the age of three. Your Libran boy will also be loathe to go anywhere incorrectly attired. Appearance is of great importance to both sexes, and you may just as well get used to it now. This type will never argue with anyone and he continues to make friends in record time, so much so that if you are not careful socializing will take precedence over all else.

Interests and Games

Dressing up is probably the best-loved game for all Librans and any old clothes should be put aside for this purpose. Parents should buy a strong hefty lock for their wardrobes for it is quite likely that the Libran child will decide that *old* clothes are simply not what he or she had in mind.

Music and painting are two other interests that stimulate this type and tuition in either may well prove to be beneficial and rewarding. The absorption in what is fashionable and what is not may lead either sex into spending hours in drawing and designing outfits. This in turn may lead to a fascination for sewing, especially if mother uses a sewing machine.

Bear in mind that this is an air sign and many boys born under it are fascinated by aeronautics. This can be developed along many different lines, from reading about to designing aircraft to modelling. It is up to you to discover which aspect of this hobby is likely to appeal to your own particular Libran son or daughter.

This is not a sporting sign and the Libran becomes adept at inventing excuses for avoiding hockey, netball, football, or any other school games. Father's being a football fanatic may amuse the Libran boy but it is unlikely to inspire or activate him. You'll need to change direction if you are hoping to have reared an olympic athlete. This is essentially a gentle and artistic sign. Boys are not effeminate, although the sign is of a feminine nature, but simply the types who grow into women's men, the kind of men who understand and adore women. Never force any child where he or she does not want to go. The Libran hates unpleasantness and may unwisely oblige you simply to keep the peace, but forcing him into anything is a dangerous threat to his individuality and true self.

Accepting a New Baby

Once more you are lucky with your Libran, for if he is to date an only child the prospect of a companion will be welcomed with excitement. You may, however, need to explain in advance that it will be a while before the new baby can really be a playmate, or the Libran could be bitterly disappointed with a baby who simply lies around without so much as a hello. Fortunately, this character is not short of friends or a hectic social life and he will be kept very active until the baby becomes a little more interesting.

Don't fall into the understandable trap of pushing the Libra child out to see his friends when you are busy with the baby. Invitations must be extended, for in this manner you will provide him with an opportunity to parade the new baby to his friends. Neither must you expect much practical help. The sight of soiled nappies will revolt the Libran's aesthetic soul, so keep them out of sight and gratefully accept any help that is offered.

As soon as the baby becomes more of a person your Libran will become more and more devoted to him and eventually you will be proud of the obvious and unselfish love displayed between the two; no one can resist a Libran. Proceed carefully during those first critical months and your fears and doubts will finally be stilled.

Discipline

Violence, both physical and verbal, should never be used unless you wish to bring up a neurotic Libran. Once those precious scales of justice are off balance so will your child be. Two things are essential when disciplining this type – a strong sense of justice, and the ability to uninhibitedly explain how his actions can harm others, something this type never does willingly. He will loathe to consider that he has been unfair or cruel to another person and this is the key to disciplining this character.

Never withold affection or send him to bed unhappy. Problems must be sorted out openly, firmly and free from drama. This type does not deliberately misbehave. Bringing up a Libran is a joy, so no problems should be insurmountable.

Sex

The Libran must always strike an even balance with those golden scales and this alienates the typical Libran to any kind of deviation or perversion, so by following the advice at the end of the book you should be able to rear a sexually well-adjusted Libran.

Initially you may believe that you have given birth to one of the world's greatest lovers, and, to an extent, this is true. Few other signs can surpass the Libran's natural expertise with the opposite sex and it starts from the word go. In spite of this, the Libran is not a mad sexual beast. It is the flirting and the chasing that appeals so much, as you will discover at a later date.

Relax – your little angel will not be leading a full sex life by the time he or she is twelve! Despite symptoms to the contrary, flirtation and sex at this stage are not associated.

Homework and Study

A word that spells effort to the Libran is homework. Put this eight-letter word together with the Libran and the end product is incompatibility. When listening to the varied excuses for not doing homework you may have to stifle some admiration for in this respect your child is extremely inventive and will assault you with various forms of elaborate, confused tales that can usually be thought up in two seconds! The root cause of this procrastination lies in the fact that study, for the most part, needs to be tackled alone. Therefore, to a degree, you are powerless to assist the child. However, kindly intervention on your part, plus some understanding, may help to make study more palatable, especially if a friend can be introduced into the proceedings.

The more interest you take in his homework the higher his grades are going to be. This responsibility should ideally be shared between both parents, and see if brothers and sisters, if any, can be persuaded to help and encourage. The more the merrier for the Libran.

Finding a Direction

The most important aspect of the Libran's life is his relationship with others, partnerships in particular. Provided you can give your child a good insight into how to live with, please and generally handle others, you will have laid the foundation-stone to both his personal and professional lives. This individual cannot function properly without others and he is usually acutely aware of this fact; an unpopular Libran is therefore a pathetic sight.

You cannot give this child a book and realistically expect him to be stimulated, but take some time and read it with him and he will be eager for more. Naturally this is time consuming but either you share and stimulate with the child or you accept the fact that you will be later confronted with a lazy drifter, one who will sway this way and that depending upon the direction of the wind.

To alleviate some of the pressure to which your Libran child may feel subjected enrol him in as many clubs as possible. Just as long as he is with others he will be happy and free from apathy and stagnation.

Generally speaking, the more time parents can spend sharing this child's interests the better. The subject of activity isn't that important, though a preference for the arts is likely. However, a full life is the healthiest and happiest for this child, and the one that will help you to raise a well-balanced adult.

Television is a particularly destructive influence upon your Libran. Television has its value when used correctly, but the Libran cannot be relied upon to be selective, and if he is allowed to have a free choice in this direction you will observe your child slowly turning into a mentally constipated vegetable. It is not that this individual actually becomes involved in the action; he gets hypnotized and so doesn't become involved with the world around. It is a kind of no-man's-Libra-land, and you can forget getting any kind of sense out of him until that switch is firmly off. Obviously, then, such a habit should not be formed in the first place. Anything is better for this child than a slow process of turning him into a mindless wonder. Ideally avoid turning the television on in his presence.

Minimize the time the Libran spends sitting around and he will soon find the energy and enthusiasm for his own particular role in life.

THE LIBRAN TEENAGER

Twelve to eighteen years of age

The characteristic charm, grace and popularity of this sign eases the Libran into adulthood so smoothly that you are only occasionally reminded of your offspring's maturity. One of the first things to remember is that while your teenager may appear supremely confident, this is just a great big show. He will occasionally give himself away when he is greeted with stifled amusement or derogatory remarks about some latest get-up. He will not explode or rebel, but he will look very, very hurt. Both sexes are fashion-conscious and are certain to make some momentous mistakes with their clothes while they are learning. Give advice when asked and leave fashion magazines around which may give some practical help. Friendly advice on the opposite sex or tuition on the social graces is not required. In fact, he is probably better informed than his parents on these two points. However, advice can be given if requested, otherwise keep silent. An open and enlightened attitude to his generation is all you need to help your Libran through these slightly sticky patches. It is true that he may want to join a rock band and she is a frustrated song writer. But why not, especially if you can persuade them to follow these interests in their spare time. Don't ever lose sight of the fact that the Libran is just the sign that may produce a second Bob Dylan or Joni Mitchell. Besides, if your Libran is totally talentless, you can be quite sure that he or she will be the first to recognize the fact.

Dating

This side of the Libran's life will prove to be his parents' rejuvenater, for all the parents' own many heartbreaks and mistakes made as teenagers will rush back into their minds. Parents too will learn how to instantaneously fabricate some outrageous excuse when a demanding boyfriend or girlfriend rings and the Libran teenager simply refuses to come to the telephone. In fact, parents may become so enmeshed in his love-life that they may lose sight of the fact that they are parents, and become more of a friend or pal. This is splendid, but a friend or pal cannot in all seriousness begin to lay down the law when it comes to the hour the child is expected home, and so on. You, as a parent, would be wise to allow a natural friendliness develop, but try to keep a certain objectivity and give occasional subtle reminders of your status. Certainly, your teenager should be treated as an adult, but this is a character devoid of any kind of track record in life and, until some experience has been gained, it is necessary for you to gently hold the reins.

Alcohol

The Libran possesses an over-developed love for the so-called luxuries and comforts of life, and this generally includes a love of good wine. His taste can usually be relied upon to save the Libran from becoming an alcoholic. After all, to be realistic, vintage wines and good spirits are just not within the range of the average teenager's budget, especially on a regular basis. Though it will be more readily available to your female Libran when she is taken out to dinner, her expensive habits will be too costly for most of her beaus and this in itself is a deterrent.

Parents should not attempt to lecture on the problems of alcohol as this will make it seem more desirable. Rather, instil the rules of alcohol, such as no drinking and driving or drinking on an empty stomach, and so on. You can be quite certain that this type of teenager is not a secret drinker, not unless he is keeping an extremely good vintage wine for himself!

Drugs

Drug-addiction regrettably is frequently associated with members of this sign, especially drugs of the hallucinatory variety. It isn't that difficult to understand why. The world is full of violence and ugliness for the Libran, two things he finds particularly distasteful. The Piscean will react to this by putting his head in the sand, the Sagittarian and Aquarian attempt to alter the world by entrenching themselves in politics, while others of the zodiac simply shrug and state that this is the way of the world. The Libran does not feel free to take any of these routes; he inclines to make attempts to locate a more beautiful world, the one within his head. Hence the desire for hallucination. This naturally does not apply to *all* Librans as some find their beautiful inner world in music, painting or love. However, denied full satisfaction such as this, and with perhaps the added misery of a broken home or the inability to find some direction, for instance, the Libran can resort to relief and solace in drugs.

Much, of course, also depends on his circles of friendship and his ability to fit in. If he is constantly aware of being on the outside, your Libran may try anything if he considers it may result in acceptance. Bear in mind that this is not a solitary animal. Despite the fact that your Libran may experiment at some point, this does not mean you should panic provided we are discussing a well-balanced member of this sign.

SUGGESTED CAREERS

Don't mention the word job or occupation in the presence of this character! Vocation, yes, or even profession, but choose your words very carefully. The Libran is quite likely to decide that it is necessary for him to fly to Paris and starve in a garret, join a rock group or nurse lepers in the jungle. Refrain from convulsing or laughing. You are dealing with a romantic, one who should be taken seriously. Of all the millions of Librans who must have considered choices rather similar to these, only a very minute percentage actually possess the skill or practical application to see such ideals through to their conclusion. Listed below are some professions that may well attract Librans.

Beautician	Model	Property valuer
Dress-designer	Diplomat	High-wire performer
Hairdresser	Welfare worker	Juggler
Milliner	Receptionist	Lawyer
Furrier		

Any artisitic work will attract this type. Professional partnership is also recommended and favoured. Dress-designing, dress-making, art dealing, the record business or a business concerned with musical instruments will also appeal. This sign makes an admirable front man for Librans possess the ability to make clients feel happy and at ease.

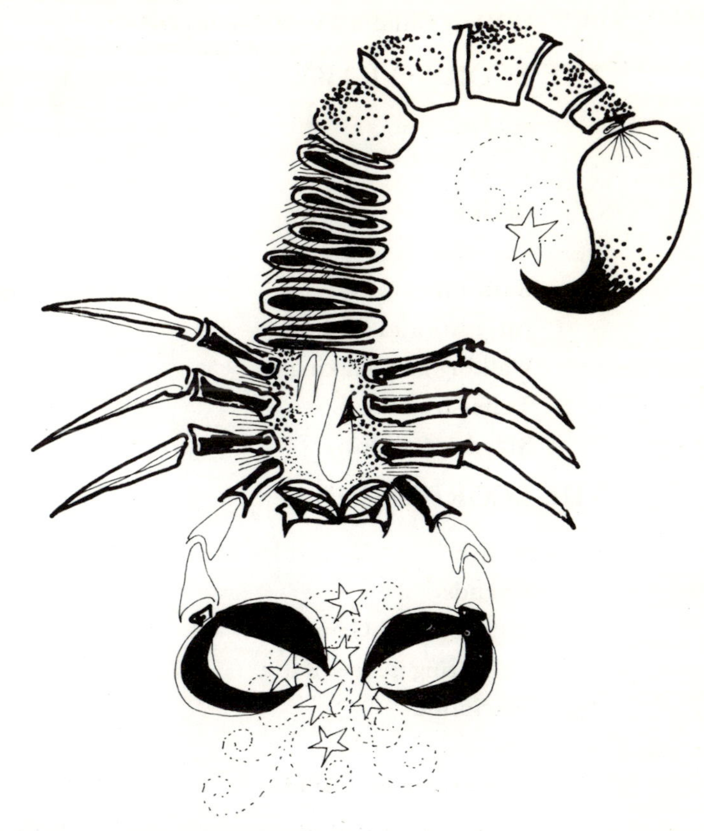

SCORPIO

THE SECOND WATER SIGN

Symbol The Scorpion

Colour Deep red

Metal Steel

Planet Pluto

Motivation To govern or inspect

Intense; steadfast; domineering; secretive in personal matters; ruthless

GENERAL CHARACTERISTICS

- Is Your Child a Typical Scorpio?

THE SCORPIO BABY

- Health
- Food
- Crying
- Teething
- Bath-time
- Interests and Games
- Walking and Talking
- Toilet-training
- Starting School

THE SCORPIO CHILD

- Health
- Friends
- Interests and Games
- Accepting a New Baby
- Discipline
- Sex
- Homework and Study
- Finding a Direction

THE SCORPIO TEENAGER

- Dating
- Alcohol
- Drugs
- Suggested Careers

GENERAL CHARACTERISTICS

Dr Jekyll: positive

The Scorpion's world is one of power, and this individual's highest achievement is the manifestation of that power in the most tremendous of tasks, namely complete self-mastery.

Those born under this sign attempt to destroy egotism, to dominate desire and expel everything that can retard moral, mental and physical regeneration. This drives him to attain complete control over the will, intellect, passions, emotions and even bodily activity. This, then, is the Scorpion ambition. And very frequently, in spite of many false starts and shortcomings, they make considerable progress on the way to realizing them. Scorpios are also, generally, psychic but often fail to realize it. They make such exceptionally good use of their senses that they attribute their achievements to rapid diagnosis. It is true that no one can penetrate and assess another individual as efficiently as a Scorpion. The intense virility of this type naturally makes it somewhat difficult for the female of the species, as she has problems in accepting the limitations and restrictions imposed by her sex. In both love and friendship the Scorpion is tense and exclusive and therefore prone to many sudden attractions and repulsions. They loathe sentimentality and emotional behaviour in other people; this is usually due to the fact that they find difficulty in expressing their inner thoughts and feelings even when they desire to do so, and this happens rarely for they are naturally laconic by nature. However, when Scorpios are deeply moved, feelings surge forward and on these occasions they are apt to say far more than might have been warranted.

Mr Hyde: negative

This particular character has his own unfathomable reasons for being exceptionally cruel on occasions. This reveals itself in an exhibition of sadistic wit – other people are then described as, perhaps, obese, stupid or failures. Rarely are these remarks made in private but usually in the presence of a large gathering; try putting this type in his place and he will erupt and burn like a volcano. In this case, run for cover before the lava begins to pour forth. In this particular instance the inner passions of this type are completely uncontrollable and jealousies are usually beyond the bounds of reason to other people. He will be over-bearing, domineering, sarcastic and sometimes frigid and no other sign can hate with such fierce passion. Dislikes, slights and injuries are nurtured for positively decades and then, without warning, the Scorpio strikes in retaliation while the poor victim is bemused and totally unable to understand the attack. It is also impossible for this character to take a back seat and, to retain the limelight, resort to unfair or unjust criticism in an effort to attract attention. The negative Scorpio is secretly delighted when he uncovers a weaker or more fallible being, and he will generally proceed quite ruthlessly to express the other's faults to those around.

These obvious shortcomings find their origins in the Scorpion's sting, although this type can unconsciously turn it upon himself and become self-destructive while attempting to destroy others.

Is Your Child a Typical Scorpio?

Answer the questions honestly. Score three for every 'Yes', two for every 'Sometimes' and one for every 'No'. Turn to page 220 for the answers.

1 Is your child jealous?
2 Is he difficult to shift once his mind has been made up?
3 Does your child have a tremendous thirst?
4 Is your child possessive?
5 Does your child bear grudges?
6 Is it difficult for your child to express love?
7 Is your child revengeful?
8 Can your child be uncontrollably violent?
9 Is your child suspicious of strangers?
10 Can your child be destructive?
11 Do you believe that your child is psychic?
12 Do others have difficulty in understanding him?
13 Is it difficult for your child to mix with other young people?
14 Does your child have a vivid imagination?
15 Is your child annoyed when you show affection to another person?
16 Does your child take a dislike to someone for no good reason?
17 Does he dislike changes in routine?
18 Is your child uncomfortable with animals?
19 Is your child intensely loyal?
20 Does your child treat you as if you were his own, personal slave?

THE SCORPIO BABY
Up to four years of age

If you have just brought home a Scorpio infant, you will need to ensure you make a quiet corner away from the child where you can read a book, eat your food, and so on, somewhere that is perfectly safe from your baby or toddler. The demands come in thick and fast from a very early age, so don't imagine that you can escape for your presence is required *immediately* and for an indefinite period. It doesn't matter that your tiny Scorpion may only weigh five pounds; this little character is an extremely strong type, one who has a will-power to match his little muscles. Poor Father – you seriously believe that you'll soon show this youngster who is boss? You'll discover that you'll have to think again. Your little Scorpio positively relishes a fight – not only that, but he intends to triumph. Compromise will not be found in the Scorpio vocabulary. He may pretend to submit, but don't be fooled. That infant is simply biding his time, waiting for an opportunity when the fight can be resumed at a more favourable time. There will be moments when your Scorpion toddler will turn and penetrate you with its eyes, looking so fierce that your knees will begin to knock! Gather courage, and refuse to be put off. Glare back, kindly but firmly. It may be difficult to acquire the perfect kind of glare, but keep practising. Grin through clenched teeth and give your orders with emphatic conviction. Your triumphs may only be temporary, but it is a step in the right direction. As long as you are firm you will gain your child's grudging respect. . . until he is older, then you'll need to earn it.

Health

Scorpio rules the reproductive organs and, lets face it, they are located in an area of the body that gets a lot of hard wear during babyhood! Not surprisingly nappy rashes occur quite frequently. However, prevention is better than cure so change those nappies frequently and always wash the baby's bottom with warm water at each change. Dry him well and apply nappy cream before putting on a fresh nappy. Thorough washing and rinsing is also important.

A few words on recognition of the rash. Nappy rash makes the skin look red, sore or spotty. If you see it appear, change the nappies more often than usual and follow the above routine. If after four changes there is still no improvement, use a one-way liner instead of cream. Failing this, put a mattress on the floor, cover it with waterproof material and let baby lie on this with his bottom exposed to the elements! Naturally, the room needs to be warm. If the rash still persists the wisest course is to consult your doctor. *Never* experiment with other creams or potions.

The Scorpio child also tends to suffer from an above average number of eye infections, conjuctivitis or 'pink eye' being the most common. It is called pink eye because it tends to make the eyes look rather red. Often the eyelids are rather gummed down in the mornings by a sticky discharge. Clean them thoroughly with cotton-wool soaked in water that has been boiled and allowed to cool. Then wipe from the inner corner of the eye to the outer. Conjunctivitis can be spread by using the same towels or face-flannels as the sufferer, so make sure that each member of the family keeps to his own. If the discharge persists after a day or two, once again consult your doctor.

Apart from these complaints the Scorpion baby is usually strong and healthy.

Food

The Scorpion is not a fastidious eater, but he certainly leaves parents in no doubt as to his preferences and, should your little tyrant decide to come out against cereal, for instance, then it is a foolhardy parent who attempts to coax or, worse still, force this child into changing his mind. One look at that red face, those intense eyes and the firmly closed mouth should be sufficient to deter the most courageous of adults – if not, numerous bowlsful, used as missiles with you as the target, should be! Take the coward's way out and surrender! You'll have to sooner or later, so you may as well make it sooner before you give your child a mental block in connection with meal-times.

If the child's parents are also born under this sign, then war is guaranteed to be declared. However, bear in mind that once unpleasantness is associated with food your life is going to be purgatory. The Scorpion infant is not difficult to sustain provided that food is presented in a relaxed atmosphere. Furthermore, this type is insatiable with favourite foods. Here you can relax, for he won't starve. Even the most inexperienced parent cannot fail to understand the messages sent out regularly and clearly by this little character. Therefore, should the bottle prove unsatisfactory after three months, he won't hesitate to inform you that something more substantial is required, and this baby knows what is good for him. Therefore be guided by his intuition before hc begins to pile on the pressure.

Crying

You cannot have failed to understand by now that when the Scorpion wants anything he wants it *now*, not in five minutes. And don't expect him to ask politely. This little dictator does not begin by cooing gently, working up through a whine to a piercing scream. *He* is the most important person in your house, probably in the world, and he can effectively pierce your eardrums at fifty feet. However, be prompt with nappy changes, food, etc., and he will eventually decide that you are fairly efficient and can be relied upon to do your duty and as a result there will be no reason for him to exert himself in any way.

Apart from the usual needs your Scorpion is particularly susceptible to thirst. You would be wise to bear in mind that he is also prone to nappy rashes, and regrettably while you pour it in one end he is letting it out at the other! Change this character as soon as he is wet and avoid those tears.

This character is also very possessive, and on those occasions when he shrieks and you are unable to detect any good reason for distress you can be fairly sure that he is feeling neglected. This type needs to be constantly reassured of your presence. Purchase a baby seat and cart him around with you while you busy yourself around the home. He does not demand constant cuddling, but the mere sight of you and the sound of your voice will soothe a jealous heart. The Scorpion baby is an exhausting child but at least while his sting is turned on others it will not be turned inwards to himself, a fact to be dwelt upon.

Teeth

Your typical Scorpion baby will never quietly and obligingly cut his teeth without your knowledge. The first symptoms to watch for will be a nappy rash accompanied by a loud shriek. And it is going to be one or the other or both until all the teeth are through. Wise parents will share the burden of attention, especially at night, for when lack of sleep leads to a neurotic mother she quite obviously will not be able to cope with this character. Take it in turns to ease the pressure, it is the only way. Should the situation become intolerable, visit your doctor for assistance as he may be able to prescribe some medicine to help the baby sleep. For further advice see the section at the end of the book.

Bath-time

Bathing the baby is one of those occasions when you will be delighted with your Scorpion baby, for Scorpio is a water sign and Scorpions take to it like veterans. It may even be possible to teach this particular child to swim at a very early age. Observe all the safety precautions and you will not have a moment's worry in this direction.

However, do bear in mind that while a splashing six-month-old baby cannot create too much of a mess a six-year-old can flood the bathroom with an incessant assault of waves and puddles. Allow the baby to have fun, but you will be sorry if you permit this ritual to get totally out of control at an early age.

Games

Regardless of his or her sex, your Scorpion will delight in a romp with his parents. This sign is a fighter, a fact that will no doubt come home to you on being at the receiving end of one or two nasty whacks, usually from a tightly balled fist! This may be great fun and good for your infant, but bear in mind that he will get bigger, and bigger, and stronger – and the baby shouldn't actually expect to beat up his parents at a later date. Play and romp, but don't be slow to let the child know when you are hurt. This piece of advice is for your own good, as you will discover at a later date if you ignore it now! By now you should have begun to realize that this is quite an aggressive child and such tendencies and energy needs to be channelled. A toy drum is an excellent substitute for a human punch-bag, and you will need to get rid of that excess vitality before you can get the child to any mental preoccupation.

Scorpion boys are fascinated with anything to do with soldiers, guns, and so on, and stories of daring exploits positively enthral. The Scorpion girl will most likely be a bit of a tomboy, but she will also adore dressing up in nurse's uniform complete with medical bag for treating her teddy's cuts and bruises!

Because Scorpio is a sign of toughness a wise parent will encourage the sensitive and more loving instincts at an early age. Cuddly toys will help, and a game of mothers and fathers and playing house will keep your Scorpion quiet for hours.

Walking and Talking

When it comes to the physical act of walking and talking the Scorpion child is unenthusiastic but not downright lazy either. We are therefore discussing an average baby. However, you can expect this little character to dispense with the act of crawling, mainly as a result of his innate dignity.

At about fourteen months the baby will begin to pull himself up on to those fat but wobbly legs. Soon, before you know what has happened, he will be running around under your feet. Here is a helpful tip – the Scorpion possesses fierce pride, so when he falls over he is going to be anything but pleased about making a fool of himself in front of others. The wise parent will pretend not to have noticed and should never rush over to help him. It is necessary, with this type, to overlook inefficiency; in this way he will learn much quicker.

Speech-wise, your Scorpion may be fairly precocious. After all, he can hardly organize the household with an incoherent babble so prepare to be verbally asaulted with orders at a very early age! If you are wise you will emphasize and teach that there is a right and a wrong way to ask for something. This is, perhaps, more important than concentrating purely on vocabulary and structure or the child will naturally fall into a manner of speech that will be brusque and offensive to outsiders.

Toilet-training

When a Scorpion's got to relieve himself, he doesn't wait. And if your child is too immature to control himself, and therefore be trained, then you may as well save yourself the aggravation of attempting the impossible.

At around eighteen months he *may* be ready to cooperate. But displays of frustration or annoyance on your part at his incompetence will delay toilet-training him for yet another year. The baby could even throw his potty downstairs and refuse to entertain the idea of ever sitting on it again. You may think him strange but he may also appreciate some privacy when he is learning to use the potty, so don't plonk him on it in the presence of your friends. Never forget his self-respect and pride, no matter how young he may be. Refrain from making this stage of development stressful. Keep it casual, choose the right age to start and he will soon cooperate and be dry in record time.

Starting School

The procedure explained in the Starting School section for Cancer will also apply to Scorpions, not because the Scorpio is as sensitive or as nervous as the Crab but because he is very possessive, fiercely possessive with his mother, and only when he is absolutely convinced that she will return will he accept being left alone at school.

However, once he is willing to remain at school there will be no looking back, for at school there is a whole classroom of children just waiting for someone to come along and dominate them and he is just the person for the job! The Scorpion is also competitive and in a matter of weeks he will find it an absolute necessity to excel and prove his worth. Providing you can survive the first seven to ten days, you will have absolutely nothing to worry about. Therefore, show understanding and patience at this stage.

THE SCORPIO CHILD
Four to twelve years of age

Health

During this age-group your son's sensitive reproductive system should give little cause for concern. However, a Scorpion daughter may just begin menstruation before the age of twelve, in which case there may be some complication until her body has accustomed itself to the changes that take place between childhood and womanhood. Listen to any complaints of aches and pains and, if they continue or are regular, then a trip to the doctor is needed. Accidents with heat or sharp objects may also come in a continual stream with both sexes, and parents need to carefully observe all safety precautions with fires, hot saucepans, knives, and so on.

Scorpio is a sign which often has difficulty in expelling natural toxics from the body. It is advisable to bear this in mind should your child develop any so-called obscure illnesses that appear to baffle the experts. However, generally speaking this is a healthy sign and one look at that well-muscled body and you will realize that it is going to take a very powerful bug to make even the vaguest impression.

Friends

Your Scorpion is exclusive in friendship, as with everything, and he knows exactly whom he likes and dislikes and no amount of coaxing or reasoning will change that opinionated mind. He may possess one or two devoted friends, but even these will need to tread carefully for as soon as the Scorpion decides that he has been badly let down, and this can be either real or imaginary, he will not be reconciled with them. The Scorpio is a demanding friend and those he deigns to befriend must be fiercely loyal and live up to his high expectations of them. Parents should attempt to explain the fallibility of the human race. If he can be made to understand early enough that none of us is perfect then he may just grow into a slightly less intolerant child, but don't rely on this. It may help if you gently point out his own faults. Do tread carefully, though, for the Scorpion loves to uncover weaknesses in others but doesn't take too kindly when others follow his example.

Anything serious or secretive appeals to the Scorpion, so small bands of friends are sure to be formed and organized into a secret society. And you as an adult must make no attempt to enter the group. However, any den or secret place you allow them to use for their meetings will be much appreciated. He will not form a witches' coven but his group will be no doubt deciding on a fitting punishment for the teacher's pet, or another such world-shattering issue.

Your Scorpion is a mystical and unusual child, so let him grow and develop in his own way.

Interests and Games

Apart from secret societies both sexes are attracted to detectives and cops and robbers, and books, toys and board-games with this theme should delight Scorpions. Don't make the mistake of assuming that it is the violent aspect that appeals to them. On the contrary, it is the joy of uncovering a mystery. Sherlock Holmes must surely have been born under this sign, for he is a perfect example of a Scorpion in action.

As this child grows, his absorption with the unknown may lead him into science fiction, the occult or research science. Watch out for the first signs of this and, when you recognize them, encourage the child. Alternatively, as with the Virgoan, this can be a medical sign, although the approaches to the subject differ. The Virgoan likes to treat and cure whereas the Scorpion prefers to delve and discover the causes of illness. While young this fascination will be channelled into medical games and playing doctors and nurses will be a favourite. The Scorpion also often excels in water sports. In fact he will refuse to take part in anything unless he has a more than good chance of winning. Clearly, then, this is not a good loser. Therefore, never pressurize the child into activities where he will be made to feel ineffectual; it is more than that Scorpion pride can take.

Accepting a New Baby

Do not imagine for one moment that it is going to be easy to introduce a rival to your Scorpio child. You should not then expect your jealous, possessive Scorpion to react favourably to a competitor. There is no way you can force, coax or demand that your Scorpion accept a new baby. This can only happen in time, and lots and lots of it.

Do show plenty of love, especially when he displays difficulty in expressing his own feelings. The Scorpion is full of hidden emotions; they heave, bubble and strain at the leash but rarely pour forth in a steady stream.

Don't ask the Scorpio for assistance with the new baby. He will eventually volunteer, but it takes time.

Don't cuddle the new infant too much when Scorpio is lurking in the vicinity. Don't dump junior in Scorpio's lap, or he might just give the baby a shove and up-end him on to the floor.

The Scorpio should not be punished too severely should you catch him prodding or pinching the new infant. This is a situation that requires a loving talk and a clear explanation on how easy it is to hurt the baby.

Don't work out your frustrations with the baby on your Scorpion. Time and love are your healers, although you could try an appeal to his pride, with remarks such as, 'Mrs Smith thinks that her baby is prettier than ours, what do you think?' Your Scorpion will never admit that his family is inferior in any way to another. Such a ploy may even stimulate the protective instinct. If so, you are on the way to a well integrated family.

Don't push your Scorpion. When he finally accepts the new addition he will be part of a tight, exclusive set of love-objects as this is the way a Scorpion thinks of his family. And your Scorpion's loyalty to his brother or sister will make you sigh with relief when you realize that the waiting and the effort were worth it.

Discipline

Discipline is another difficult aspect of the Scorpion childhood. In all instances the Scorpion harbours a violent streak, so physical assault of any description is strictly out unless you want to teach him how to utilize his powerful frame, in which case you will be the first for a smack. Restrain your temper, teach consideration for others, appeal to his sense of reason and, when desperate after a particularly naughty act, confiscate his privileges for a while.

Raise your Scorpion to understand that you are a friend of justice, one who does not punish without good reason. You may have to give way on small issues, but stand firm on the important ones. This way, the Scorpion will grow to respect you, and this is not to be confused with fear. While you hold on to that respect, peace will be retained; should you lose it you may have problems.

Sex

No doubt you will have read in astrology books of the Scorpion's sexuality. They have quite a reputation! As a parent to this sign you need to ensure that this sexuality is freely expressed, or it may later become perverted or sublimated into ruthless ambition. Follow the advice at the end of this book and this will enable you to eliminate inhibition from the beginning. Show your child that you are quite happy to answer all his questions and that he is free to ask them. Convince him that such discussions are as natural and as normal as conversations regarding school or what to have for dinner. Your Scorpion may initially be reluctant to come out openly with queries, and it is up to you to put him at his ease.

Furthermore, bear in mind that this sign rules the genitals, and infections to this area may occur rather more easily than would normally be the case. Make sure that he knows about venereal disease and hygiene. Sensible parents will have no special problems with their Scorpions but those who are coy or inhibited are going to have a particularly difficult time with this aspect of the Scorpion's life. They may even damage his natural development. So dust out the cobwebs from that cluttered brain and honestly help your child to grow into a well-adjusted sexual adult.

Homework and Study

Determination is always a well-developed part of the Scorpio personality and providing he is ambitious, sufficiently stimulated and intelligent no problems are envisaged with homework. This type does not expect an easy life and he quickly grasps the fact that life is what he decides to make it.

Naturally this is a two-way street, for your Scorpion may be equally determined not to do homework or study. In this case, flatly point out how well this or that friend is doing, keeping it casual, as this character dislikes being overtaken by anyone, including much-loved friends. He will not drop behind and feverish activity will follow any revelation which suggests that this may occur.

Bear in mind that a Scorpio can always achieve what he wishes and make certain that he does, regularly appealing to his pride.

Finding a Direction

The ever-present interest in the mysterious or unknown can, at about ten or eleven, be stimulated by books dealing with astronomy, crime, or the discoveries made by eminent scientists, and anything unknown or unsolved will galvanize your Scorpion's ambitions. From then on it is encouragement all the way. If his all-consuming passion is meaningless to you his admiration will be aroused by your admitted ignorance and any attempt you make to rectify this. He cannot help but follow your splendid example! Your efforts to learn with him will bridge any gaps in the communication lines and lead to a peaceful existence when adolescence strikes. Make this child proud of you and he will never let you down and will strive to make a success of his life not only for his sake but also for yours.

As always, the Scorpion is in no doubt as to which direction he will ideally follow in life, hopeful you will approve, for it would be impossible to change that stubborn mind once it has settled on an objective. With help and encouragement this child can go far. The chapter on suggested careers at the end of this sign's section will provide some indication of what to expect.

THE SCORPIO TEENAGER
Twelve to eighteen years of age

Adolescence is particularly tough on the Scorpio because he is a strong, dominating and opinionated character and at this stage in his life he is dependent on others and forced to consider their feelings and opinions. This is enough when his parents are understanding and loving but purgatory if they are not. A parent with a sense of humour is the greatest asset a Scorpion can possess. Those born under this sign who learn to laugh at life, and occasionally at themselves, will be far happier than their more serious brothers and sisters.

However, it is important to laugh *with* the Scorpion and not at him. When your Scorpion son arrives for breakfast with a face covered with tiny pieces of blood-stained tissue-paper, indicating a difficult time with the razor, or when your Scorpio daughter, having spent hours labouring over eye make-up, forgets and rubs her eyes so she looks like a panda, control your laughter and instead tell your son or daughter stories of the kind of fool you made of yourself at their age. This way the entire family can enjoy a joke at your expense, but then you are, one hopes, a little more mature and less sensitive than your Scorpion teenager.

Also, tensions can be eased if your Scorpion is encouraged to be independent. Don't prevent him from obtaining a spare-time job. His pockets will jingle with the sweat of his *own* brow. Furthermore, any decisions regarding this teenager or his future must be discussed in his presence and his opinions and feelings duly considered.

Remember your own arguments and misunderstandings with your parents during these years. How did you feel? Weren't you occasionally guilty of the sulks or depression? The only difference is that you *thought* that you were right and the Scorpion *knows* he is right! The most infuriating thing is that he usually is right.

Dating

The Scorpion teenager is magnetic, compelling and physically mature, and very often this type attracts older members of the opposite sex. Parents will need to close their mouths when a seventeen-year-old son walks in with a twenty-five-year-old woman or when introduced to a distinguished forty-year-old man a daughter is infatuated with. Can the children handle such wordly and mature people? The answer is – very likely. But if not, your teenager has to learn some time, and there are worse ways of growing up. Besides, have confidence. Your Scorpion is well informed, so trust him or her. And anyway, you should know, more than anyone else, that no one can make your offspring do what he or she doesn't want to do. Besides, an older beau will be on your side when it comes to keeping that teenager out too late, although it might be as well to bear in mind that there is nothing you can't do after twelve midnight that you can do before. Apart from the older lover syndrome the Scorpion will not play the field. Remember back to his childhood – how your Scorpion only played with a selected few? This procedure is now repeated in his or her love-life – it is one obsessive romance at a time. Your teenager's years during adolescence are going to be made up of romantic tears. This type learns the hard way where the opposite sex are concerned, so get a supply of tissues, you are in for a wet bumpy ride!

Alcohol

The Scorpion is going to learn all about alcohol whether you like it or not. This is a water sign and Scorpions are strongly attracted to all forms of liquid especially when they are depressed or tense. Because of this, try to alleviate all pressures you may believe are weighing him down whenever possible. There is no point in your preaching about the evils of alcohol and nor should you go to the other extreme. Your good example is the safest route. If you use alcohol sensibly yourself then your Scorpion is likely to be moderate in his own intake.

However, should you catch your Scorpion teenager secretly drinking and you can honestly say that you have allowed him to drink with the family, you should keep cool. Talk to him and try to find out what, if anything, is worrying him. Much obviously depends upon your relationship with the Scorpio. If your communication lines are open then your Scorpion's drinking habits shouldn't trouble you unduly.

Drugs

You may have one or two twinges of worry regarding alcohol and this sign, but the typical Scorpion is not drawn excessively to drugs. It is difficult to explain why not, for normally a person drowning his troubles in drink would do the same with drugs. Scorpions, though, actually enjoy the mechanics of drinking: deciding which drink to have, pouring and mixing it and, of course, the slow enjoyment that comes from the sensual action of sipping the drink. The socializing that goes with drinking may also appeal. Merely popping a pill or smoking a joint does not satisfy this need. However, the occasional smoke may be the exception. The idea of sharing a joint, however, is not the Scorpion's idea of fun and heavier drugs will never appeal. To sum up – it is unlikely that you will have much to worry about with drugs, but do keep your eyes and ears open, for parents should not be the last to know.

SUGGESTED CAREERS

The Scorpion does not drift. He may make mistakes, but he is always positive. His vocation or profession may well be located among the Scorpion occupations listed below and if it is you can be sure, although you may not approve, that your Scorpion knows exactly what he is doing.

Psychiatrist	Undertaker	Spiritualist
Psychologist	Pathologist	Insurance broker
Detective	Pharmacist	Businessman
Butcher	Medium	Armed forces
Policeman		

Anything professional that taxes his abilities to their fullest extent will appeal to the Scorpio. Nothing is difficult for the Scorpion if it involves research rather than speculation. A hard worker, he will gear his intensity happily to an academic career. He will regularly undertake long periods of study, often in specialist branches of medicine.

SAGITTARIUS

THE THIRD FIRE SIGN

Symbol The Centaur

Colour Light blue

Metal Tin

Planet Jupiter

Motivation To counsel and guide

Active; outgoing; freedom-loving; generous with friends; at times careless; broad-minded; often lacks discipline; opportunistic

GENERAL CHARACTERISTICS

Dr Jekyll: positive

One of the most prominent characteristics of this sign is an extraordinary power of mental activity. It brings reason to bear upon everything that comes under observation. It also becomes extremely active when attempting to get to the bottom of things in general, facing the facts of life, reducing problems to their simplest terms. The Sagittarian curiosity is insatiable.

The Sagittarian is intensely interested in everything and is often successful in interesting others. This is an extremely social animal who loves to be in touch with his fellow men, taking an eager interest in their welfare. This type is not content to sit upon the sidelines announcing to the world exactly where it is going wrong; he wishes to actively change things.

Strangely enough, bearing this in mind, Sagittarians are often detached from their relations. If they happen to find members of their immediate family congenial, all is well and good; they add them to their list of friends and treat them as such. If not, they will point out their faults and foibles with unfailing frankness. One can never keep a Sagittarian quiet when he is attempting to point out the truth to others. In love and friendship the same frankness and outspoken sincerity that characterizes the many friendships of this type are also to be found in connection with love-affairs, but in this field of activity there is more chance of their general breeziness blowing up the clouds and not dispelling them. A loved-one may ask about previous relationships, only to be treated to the most intimate details and sorely regretting having ever asked the question in the first place.

However, the Centaur's keen sense of freedom means that he will rarely ever get to the intense involvement stage with anyone. On the whole, independence is valued and admirers come in multiples.

Mr Hyde: negative

The Mr Hyde tendencies naturally take a more accentuated and less desirable form. Marriage is frankly decried by both sexes as an intolerable burden, a tie and a bore. Men safeguard their personal liberty by cultivating a blunt and boorish discourtesy with women who aren't their equals, and by permitting themselves to relax into easy-going familiarity only with those they are not expected to marry. Women often allow their unconventionality to generate into free and easy ways with men, especially if they have an inclination to sport, imitating the tricks and mannerisms of their male comrades in ways and speech. Both sexes tend to become inherently selfish and inconsiderate in spite of a certain rough kindness of manner. Because this type lives in the present he is consequently apt to lack loyalty and sentiment, qualities that demand memory of the past for their development.

They rarely allow their emotions to carry them away and are seldom inclined to be vicious. They are careless of reputations, both for themselves and others. There is, however, a curious child-like transparency about these people, probably resulting from the absence of complex emotions such as jealousy and vindictiveness, which makes them easy to understand and which ensures speedy detection if they attempt to go off their own straightforward line and dabble in deceit. Sagittarian theft is invariably exposed, and the comparatively harmless lies in which this type indulge are very rarely believed. They cannot lie and cheat successfully and will wisely never make the attempt.

Is Your Child a Typical Sagittarian?

Answer the questions honestly. Score three for every 'Yes', two for every 'Sometimes' and one for every 'No'. Turn to page 221 for the answers.

1 Is your child hyperactive?

2 Is it easy for you to tell when he is lying?

3 Does the child push you away when you are physically loving?

4 Is the child totally free from inhibition?

5 Does the child speak rapidly?

6 Is your child clumsy?

7 Does the child love a change in routine?

8 Is the child sociable?

9 Is the child independent?

10 Does your child love the great outdoors?

11 Is his concentration poor?

12 Are his physical movements rapid?

13 Does the child have some crazy ideas?

14 Is the child friendly with everybody?

15 Does your child hate to be dressed up?

16 Is the child an opportunist?

17 Does the child love climbing?

18 Does your child occasionally embarrass you with his truth-telling?

19 Does your child loathe to be physically restricted?

20 Does your child have difficulty sleeping?

THE SAGITTARIAN BABY

Up to four years of age

That Sagittarian baby of yours may at present need your love and be completely dependent upon you. Make the most of it for as soon as he is big enough he will be the most independent soul in your family. Now, however, the Sagittarian waves his emotions and feelings at everyone to come in his direction, and when others do not respond he is acutely disappointed. This is a playful child, one who loves to clown. You will soon discover that the silliest things will amuse him. All Sagittarians love company and even as infants they show their funny nature and desire for friendship. Your little darling will cry when he is left alone, but when he is brought into a room where grown-ups are talking you'll find that he will sleep contentedly. This is due to the reassuring sound of human voices.

At this stage in his life the Sagittarian needs the security of human sights and sounds, and if they are denied him he will withdraw and take on a substitute, maybe a torn, dirty piece of rag or an old scruffy toy without any ears or eyes. Such an object, however, will represent security but bear in mind that the baby would much rather have you.

Health

Sagittarius rules the liver, and though it is most unlikely that you'll have any problems with your baby in this area, any constant vomiting accompanied by a yellowing of the complexion should be reported to your doctor immediately. As soon as your child gets up and about you will discover just how clumsy the Sagittarian can be. Cuts and bruises will be so common that you will almost arrive at the stage where you will ignore them. Generally when a toddler bumps himself all that is needed is a kiss to make it better. But if the skin is broken, wash your hands and clean the cut with soap and water and a little antiseptic. Only use a dressing or plaster if it seems necessary, for children heal quickly. Also, a particularly good idea is to have your child regularly immunized against tetanus, the very serious illness that can follow cuts and grazes. If your child ever bangs his head and seems to lose consciousness for a few moments and then comes round, but is listless a short time after, see your doctor and report everything that happened.

It may be, of course, that accidents will be slightly more serious, but fractures can and do occur in small children. Still growing bones are often softer than adults' and they bend and break more easily. The signs of a broken bone are usually pain on movement and a tender swelling near the fracture. There may also be a certain amount of bruising and the limb may move in an odd or unusual manner. Keep the child as still as possible and contact the doctor or hospital immediately.

Food

The Sagittarian is not an eccentric eater and there are rarely problems with over-eating or fastidious behaviour. To your child eating is a necessary but not an over-interesting part of everyday life. However, there are certain to be some foods that he or she refuses for reasons known only to the Sagittarian mind. Remember that this is an individual and he is perfectly entitled to his likes and dislikes. If the Sagittarian child refuses his food there is no point in your insisting that he eat his greens because they are good for him or, for that matter, not to eat too much sugar because it is bad for him. This is pure nonsense to the Sagittarian and it offends his sense of logic. Such statements are only permissible when followed by an explanation. You'd be wise to purchase a book that explains in detail the value of food – you are going to need it!

You will also quickly discover that your Sagittarian dislikes any ritual that entails sitting down inactively three times every day. He will accept the necessity for it, but why not do something else at the same time so it won't be such a waste of time for him. The art of conversation could well be developed and expanded at meal-times. Therefore, you would be wise to refrain from ignoring the intellect while replenishing the body. Armed with this information the parents of a Sagittarian should have a relatively easy time when sustaining the infant.

Crying

It is useful to remember that Sagittarians are given over to depression. Fortunately they throw it off quickly, and their natural bouyancy saves them from self-pity. Usually given a little cuddle at the right time this baby, or adult, will learn to smile once more. Of course, as with all babies, your Sagittarian will become distraught when he is wet, hungry or ill. There will, however, be occasions when this infant bursts into floods of tears for no apparent reason. In reality this distress is due to some restriction like confinement in the playpen, high chair or cot. Bear in mind that this baby has a well-developed sense of freedom, and restraint is tantamount to cruelty. Let him sit in an ordinary chair as soon as he can and avoid a playpen except in emergencies.

Never put your child into the cot until you are convinced that he is tired. Allow this infant as much freedom as is realistically possible and your Sagittarian will remain the sunny child he is at present for a long time to come.

Teething

It will not be difficult to recognize the teething of the Sagittarian baby. Under normal circumstances this type is a natural, happy and content child, then almost overnight this baby becomes a red-faced tyrant. His temperature soars and his snuffles seem to be a permanent feature. He puts everything into his mouth, and later rejects it in fury when relief is not forthcoming. Love and attention will obviously help, but distraction may be the more worthwhile.

The little Centaur is mentally active, so try to keep him fully occupied during these fraught periods. Teething gell may help at night but if he insists on yelling night after night, visit your doctor. Too many parents believe that the medical profession cannot possibly be interested in such trivia, but the chances are that your doctor will be most sympathetic and may prescribe something to help.

Remember that the Sagittarian does not behave badly unless he has a good reason, so it should be relatively easy for you to imagine the pain he is in. See the section at the end of the book for further advice.

Bath-time

The Sagittarian and bathing are simply not compatible. Just because his Scorpio or Cancerian brother takes to the water like a playful pup, don't expect the same reaction from this fire sign. The end product of fire and water is steam, and your bathroom will be thick with it unless caution is your key word. While your Sagittarian baby is still tiny he will be nothing short of terrified of bath-time, so reduce their number from an unnecessary seven per week to, say, four. Encourage confidence by refusing to perform this ritual at any other time than when you are relaxed and able to take your time over it, for this baby will sense your nervousness or irritation. Check that the water is the correct temperature before immersing him. Never run the bath taps while he is in the bath as the sound is confusing and frightening to a Sagittarian baby. Most important of all, convey your confidence by holding him firmly and lovingly.

Provided you observe these simple rules the Sagittarian baby may gradually grow to accept bath-time as part of his daily routine. But please don't ever expect him to look forward to it with anticipation. Later, even the simple action of washing will be too much trouble. The Sagittarian child is the original 'Pig-pen'. He will need regular inspections to make sure that he has rinsed away that week-old tide-mark. Even preaching simple hygiene, such as washing hands, can be hard work. Cleanliness must begin early and in the home, as your Sagittarian honestly cannot distinguish between clean and dirty, tidy and untidy. You will have quite a battle ahead, but it is important to begin on the right footing.

Interests and Games

The Sagittarian's sense of logic plays an important part in playtime. Fitting shapes into a picture or box with holes will fascinate the child, as will all puzzles. Although this type may love the occasional fluffy toy he needs less soft animals than other babies. Regretfully for your ear-drums, he also adores noise, but do think twice before purchasing musical instruments, especially if your nerves are bad. Watch him in action with a spoon and a plate: deafening.

You should not expect him to sit quietly and play, as he needs action and adventure and if you don't supply them he will find them around the home somewhere. It is most essential that you remember to lock away dangerous objects or medicines, as this is the original mountaineer. Physical exertion is most important and the more he channels off in the playground or park the quieter your home-life will be. Daily outings, then, are important. Bed-time stories need to be tales of daring knights, dragons and ladies in distress awaiting rescue. Hopefully you are the energetic and enthusiastic type of parent and, if so, your Sagittarian couldn't ask for a better upbringing; if not, be warned, as you are going to find your Sagittarian very hard work.

Walking and Talking

As previously mentioned, Sagittarians are physically very active animals, so it is certain that he will be an early walker. Watch him at six months treading air in a search for the ground when you lift him. Even so, do not make the mistake of driving him into walking. The chances are that once he does find mobility you'll wish he had stayed put for just a little longer. The world is an adventure-playground to the Sagittarian and it does not take him long to work out that many fascinating objects are always just that little bit out of reach. Mobility then is greatly coveted and nothing will be safe when he starts moving. Locks should be efficient where treasures or dangers are concerned. Do observe all the safety precautions regarding fires, light-sockets, wall-plugs, stairs, and so on. The Sagittarian is also not slow to talk, but babies rarely develop in two directions at the same time, and until the novelty of walking has disappeared do not expect him to attempt to improve or hasten mental development.

Once he does begin to talk, reach for your encyclopaedia. Those first words of his are sure to contain a question, to be followed later by another, then later by another. . . . Once he reaches this stage your little Sagittarian's day will begin with a question and he will fall asleep with another on his lips. Why does daddy cuddle you so much? Why can't I stay up until late? Why does the light go off when you turn the switch? Why is spinach good for you? Later, when he grows up a little, these questions will be exchanged for others like: 'Why do I have to come in at ten o'clock when you say you trust me?' 'What does it matter what the neighbours think? In fact, why do you care more about what they think than you do about me?' Practice a few answers while he is still in nappies or you will be unprepared later.

Toilet-training

Your Sagittarian will probably be late in taking to the potty for several reasons. Sitting down is simply a waste of time to him and he is not that neurotic or worried by the occasional wet nappy, pants or floor. You cannot force the issue so do not bother to try. Control does not begin until the child is approximately eighteen months old and this fact, together with the Sagittarian's natural reluctance, means that you will rarely make any progress in this direction before the baby is two, and possibly much later if you make toilet-training an upsetting ritual. The Sagittarian adores flattery, so pile it on when he obliges you and hide your disappointment when he fails. Let this character be your guide and he will be dry just as soon as he is good and ready.

Starting School

The parents' experiences here should not be at all unpleasant. The advice and procedure located under the Aries section applies to Sagittarians equally. This is the easiest child to introduce to the outside world. There is so much he wishes to explore and discover that school is an adventure and not something to dread. The Sagittarian is independent and he may actually enjoy short periods of time away from home and parents. The more possessive and clinging the child's mother is, the more he will anticipate his periods of escape. Such an attitude continues throughout his life, so keep your tears out of sight and walk with confidence. That bundle of energy cannot wait to start this all-important part of growing up.

THE SAGITTARIAN CHILD

Four to twelve years of age

Health

That notorious Sagittarian clumsiness should by this age be well to the fore of your child's character, and accidents will come thick and fast. Do remove obvious obstacles and try to anticipate some of his more energetic movements. A Sagittarian free from cuts and bruises is such a rarity that he should possibly be put on display! Accept this accident prone side to the character, stock up the medicine cabinet and be watchful. There is little more you can do. To wrap a Sagittarian in cotton-wool or to restrict him in any way whatsoever would lead to neurosis, and once this happens you can be sure that you will really have problems.

Now that your Centaur has matured a little his liver may begin to reveal its sensitivity. Attempt to curb self-indulgence and excesses wherever possible. Naturally you cannot always be with your child, especially when he is attending parties and the like. Nevertheless, if your child should constantly seem to be ill after eating particular foods, then don't wait . . . visit the doctor and put your mind at ease by catching the trouble before it becomes too serious.

Friends

The Sagittarian has a booming social life. Furthermore, success in sporting activities often lends weight to his or her popularity. This type is a natural leader, and friends can be changeable and he is invariably falling out and making up with them, especially during moments when his leadership is challenged.

You will be unable to keep up with the to-ing and fro-ing of friendships and perhaps you should not attempt to do so. Allow him to bring friends home whenever possible but do not be surprised if it gradually dawns upon you that in general he prefers to be out and about. The Sagittarian is rarely alone, making friends easily. Other children are attracted to this cheerful, optimistic, enthusiastic and mischievous soul. A lone Sagittarian is hard to imagine and would in any case be a sad individual.

Interests and Games

Sport, sport and more sport, almost to the exclusion of everything else, is typical of the Sagittarian and the outdoor life holds strong appeal. Girl guides or boy scouts will suit this type admirably. The camaraderie, sports, camping, etc., are all Sagittarian activities. You'll also notice that when you attempt to persuade your Sagittarian to sit still and read he becomes unbearably restless. Not surprisingly then that those born under this sign often have problems with reading and spelling. To counter this, buy some easily readable books on their pastimes. It may help to stimulate their interest in reading and improve spelling. It may be the case that you feel your particular Sagittarian is sports mad. If so, try to create an interest in drama or music. Those born under this sign have a natural empathy with theatricals and you may be successful in coaxing him off the tennis-court, for a while at least! Basically the Sagittarian needs plenty of activity, and this should have been made abundantly clear by now, so do not stifle the natural exuberance and love of life.

Accepting a New Baby

It is quite likely that your Sagittarian will hardly notice the change in domestic arrangements when a new baby is born. He may have a new brother or sister, but don't expect him to help or to suffer agonies of jealousy as both are totally alien to his personality. The new addition will be of no interest at all to the Sagittarian until the baby at least begins to resemble an older child and can run, jump, talk and fight. When this does occur your Sagittarian will take the leadership, hold out his grubby hand of friendship and proceed to give lessons on fun, mischief and adventure. The younger child will follow his big brother or sister around with eyes round with admiration and wonder. The two will then probably become inseparable. Whatever you do, don't pressurize or push the new addition on to the Sagittarian. Bide your time, patiently, and your problems may occasionally arise singly but never in multiples.

Discipline

There is no point in your standing in front of your Sagittarian waving your authority, for he will simply stand there waving back in open defiance! However, if you are fair and try to be as honest as he then he will learn to respect the rules. But you will have to be firm when you know you are right and give way when you are wrong, giving good solid reasons for both.

If you, as a parent, possess a well-developed sense of justice and find it relatively easy to distinguish between right and wrong then you will have few, if any, problems in disciplining your Sagittarian child. However, should you be naturally short-tempered and aggressive, and believe that children should be made to toe the line even if it takes a smack, or if you are a highly nervous individual, then you have a heap of trouble ahead.

Disciplining a Sagittarian is as hard as you choose to make it, as this is always a reasonable and logical child. Certainly, he is a mischief-maker and downright imperfect but he recognizes and admits it when he is in the wrong. All that is required of parents is for them to explain the possible repercussions of bad behaviour. Generally, this is sufficient. But if he really has behaved atrociously, or refused to listen, then resort to the withdrawal of privilege.

Handled wrongly this child can become sulky, arrogant and uncontrollable. Smacking him is the worst possible example to set. Always be just and fair and he will grow up to respect you and, later, will bring his problems to you because he knows he can rely on an unbiased, wise and objective opinion.

Sex

If you are inhibited or easily embarrassed, either you or your Sagittarian can expect trouble, for it is essential that you bring him up confident in the knowledge that his parents will satisfy his sexual curiosity without discomfort or shame. The Sagittarian is naturally well balanced, open and honest in his approach to everything in life, so avoid complicating this excellent character or reducing him to self-consciousness or, worse still, making him feel ashamed of his body. By the time this type is twelve or thereabouts he should be aware of and be prepared for all the changes that occur during puberty. Your child should understand how and why both male and female bodies function. This includes conception, birth, menstruation, orgasm and masturbation. Once he or she is past twelve it will be time to acquaint him or her with the facts about venereal diseases, contraception and homosexuality. Obviously, this is only meant as a rough guide, but sex education should begin as soon as the Sagittarian learns to speak, for that is about the time the first questions will be asked!

Homework and Study

When the sun shines or friends call it is not going to be an easy task persuading your Sagittarian to sit and tackle any kind of study. Adrenalin and adventure flow rapidly through his veins; inactivity does not. Parents can make an attempt at making him understand that he is letting them down. This might work if it is not dramatized or overdone. This type does not willingly like to be unfair to anyone. However, an appeal to his natural competitive nature and love of challenge may serve parents better. Explain to him that of course you realize maths are beyond him and you don't expect him to do as well as some of his friends. He'll feel that anything those fools can do he can do better and, as for maths, if he really wanted to he could succeed standing on his head. It is simply that he doesn't want to – or does he? Never coax, threaten or bully the child unless you wish to start a bloodless rebellion and once the Sagittarian rebels he will be beyond your control or influence.

Finding a Direction

If you carefully examine the figure of the Centaur you will observe an object clasped with loving care – a bow and arrow. It is not there to make the Sagittarian look impressive; your Archer is searching for a target. An objective to him is as important as life itself and if he cannot locate one then his parents will need to gently nudge several into his sights. Until he is finally stimulated the Sagittarian will not take aim or fire.

This type needs three things. Firstly sport, to work off excess energy; secondly, the great outdoors, for relaxation and decision-making; and thirdly, study or work in which he can immerse his well-developed brain. The more ambitious he is the better. This is an optimistic sign and if he cannot dream now, when can he? Don't undermine those daydreams, they may not be so very outlandish. Pay attention when your child expresses a desire to be a president or prime minister – it may surprise you to see him make it one day.

The Sagittarian is quick to notice how imperfect the world is and he will want to do something constructive about it. Encourage him to watch news programmes or documentaries and to read books on politics. If you want your Sagittarian to succeed then sit down and plan with him. Help him to understand just how he can achieve his objectives. Should he, for instance, be interested in the law then discover what qualifications are required and lay them before your child. Once the way ahead is clear he will not object to excessively hard work or effort but once the direction is obscured he sits and rots. Applaud all his efforts, nurture his enthusiasm and your Sagittarian will go from strength to strength.

THE SAGITTARIAN TEENAGER

Twelve to eighteen years of age

Even the most sophisticated Sagittarian practices the somewhat unfortunate knack of saying or doing the wrong thing at the wrong time. It is a characteristic associated with and one greatly accentuated by puberty. The genius for *faux pas* is probably due to the tendency to speak and move without sufficient thought. Red faces will be a common feature in you house until your Sagittarian has acquired a little more experience. All you can do is to take preventive action. Never allow the Sagittarian child to overhear anything you do not wish to be broadcast around the neighbourhood or to anyone otherwise, at some point, he will tell someone whatever it is you want kept a secret. His intentions are the best in the world. You must understand, for instance, that he is genuinely proud of his mother and wants the world to know; he cannot understand, though, why she should be so upset simply because he happens to give her age away.

Life tends to get a little complicated with a Sagittarian under the roof. Apart from the fact that he needs barring from social occasions unless his parents are totally secret free, you'll despair at his untidiness and his reluctance to enter the bathroom. The Sagittarian is one of those scruffy, unhygienic people who is as happy as a pig in mud about the situation. Understand that these awkward phases will die a natural death. Lay on the heavy hand and the Sagittarian becomes a rebel with a cause. This type needs as much freedom as possible in which to develop as an individual. The process involves the constant adoption and rejection of different ways of life and attitude. Interfere and he will become immersed in one of these undesirable stages. But he is not impossible, despite your thoughts to the contrary. Tell him that he cannot stay out too late because it worries you, for this or that reason, and he will understand. But expect him to wash or cut his hair because you don't like the length or the odour, and he will sneer, 'So what. What kind of reason is that supposed to be?' Be firm where it is necessary, otherwise give him freedom, freedom to attend some protest-march for instance, even if it becomes necessary to bail him out of the police station. He is, after all, expressing an opinion. Sooner or later it will sink in that there are other ways and an interest in politics may be born. Love and understand your Sagittarian, dirty, clean, short-haired, long-haired or bald, and he will finally become a well-adjusted adult. But don't expect him to ever cease in his experiments with life for these are an integral part of him. Be constantly broad-minded, just and fair and you will see your Sagittarian safely through the most difficult part of life.

Dating

The discovery of the opposite sex could at least solve one of your problems, for it may prove to be a short cut to improving your Sagittarian's untidiness and reluctance to wash. If you are really lucky the love of his life may just have a highly developed sense of smell, in which case, overnight he will become a reformed character. However, don't rely on this, for the Sagittarian tends to play the field rather than devoting himself to one member of the opposite sex. Generally, dating would not be seen as such by an outsider. This individual looks for a friend rather than a lover. The Sagittarian male will become friendly with a girl at the football or cricket club and will attend matches with her, but moonlight and roses will not enter his unromantic head. The Sagittarian female latches on to some character who shares her political views or interests in drama and she exchanges ideas and thoughts with him. Each Sagittarian will be shocked when the friend declares undying love and he or she will sprint out of the relationship at record speed! Parents will not need to fret about a threatened teenage marriage, that is the last thing on the Sagittarian mind. This attitude will not change when your teenager eventually loses his or her virginity. The boy or girl friend is still a friend only now they have something else in common. Gradually your Archer will begin to show a preference for lots of relationships, for in this way that precious sense of freedom is less threatened, but if you have sexually educated your teenager, especially in contraception and venereal disease, then you will have no heartaches.

Alcohol

One would imagine that this scatty character would be the first to turn to the bottle, if for no other reason that to experiment. Up to a point this is true and he may arrive home at a fairly early age rather the worse for drink. But this is a brief phase. He will not take long to work out that alcohol interferes with his sporting capabilities, spoiling his performance and training, and that it befuddles the brain which he prefers to keep clear and logical. When under the influence he will become aware of saying and doing things that he later regrets and will also find alcohol too expensive. Therefore, be indifferent to any experiments, avoid the lectures on what may or may not happen to him, or you will incite a rebellion. Do not encourage him, remain calm and he could eventually be teetotal, in which case it may be your own drinking habits that come in for scrutiny and criticism.

Drugs

The Sagittarian approach to drugs is almost identical to his attitude to alcohol. Do not expect him to ignore their existence; they are there and at some point the Sagittarian will decide it is time to experiment. Before you have an apoplectic fit — think. How many interests and experiments has he carried out since he learned to walk and talk? Hundreds? Thousands? And how many have survived and developed? Six? Seven? Wait before lecturing him on drug abuse, especially as there is the slight possibility that he might only be taking them to shock you. Do not give him this satisfaction. Indifferent is the way to be.

After a short period of time you will discover that drugs have been rejected for the identical reasons as alcohol was. Besides, if he should be taking them to ease stress, you will not be achieving anything by piling on more pressure. Be patient – after a period of, for example, six months, talk to him more calmly about this new development. Discover if he does in fact have a problem. If so, it is time it was solved. When this has been satisfactorily carried out, the drugs will soon fade out of his life.

Bear in mind that no matter how superficially chaotic or crazy your child is, underneath there is a sensible, logical adult and it is to him you must always appeal.

SUGGESTED CAREERS

The Sagittarian takes a while before deciding which field of work appeals to him. Probably half a dozen attract him, so encourage him to study while he procrastinates. At some point a bolt of lightning will strike and then it will be all systems go. If he suggests any of the following careers he will be on the right track to fulfilment.

Teacher	Interpreter	Publisher
Professor	Horse-trainer	Writer
Lecturer	Traveller	Librarian
Philosopher	Explorer	Bookseller
Lawyer	Sportsman	
Barrister	Jockey	

COMPATIBILITY TABLES

Aries with Aries	Generally speaking there is no room for two Aries in a relationship. Fierce competition expected until dominant personality has triumphed.
Aries with Taurus	The Bull is practical, shrewd, determined and stubborn. He/she is confused by the impulsive, impatient and headstrong Ram. Compromise difficult but not impossible.
Aries with Gemini	Both are full of brilliant ideas and dislike the mundane. This is common ground on which to work. Chaos predicted.
Aries with Cancer	The Crab is shrewd, sensitive and domesticated, the Ram is none of these. Someone could get hurt . . . namely the Crab.
Aries with Leo	This can be a fiery, warm relationship with great absorption in each other. Egos may clash on occasions but otherwise an excellent combination.

Aries with Virgo

The Ram is full of action, Virgo is a thinker. Mutual hobbies may bring them together, but without such sharing life will be difficult.

Aries with Libra

These are opposites, so they may find a happy compromise. But the Ram loves a fight while the Libran prefers to walk away.

Aries with Scorpio

The Aries is strong enough to ignore any attempt by the Scorpio to take over, but the Ram's ability to give way will be sorely tempted and he/she will often do the opposite to the Scorpio's wishes just to be awkward.

Aries with Sagittarius

Both love the outdoors, activity and doing things together. A good relationship.

Aries with Capricorn

With hard work it may be possible for them to accept the faults seen in one another, but in general the disadvantages outweigh the advantages.

Aries with Aquarius

The Aquarian can hurt unintentionally by detached, unresponsive moods. Otherwise a good relationship.

Aries with Pisces

The Fish is lovable, flexible and imaginative, and will love to be included in the Arietian's plans. A good relationship with the Ram in charge.

Taurus with Taurus

Where you find two Bulls you find two happy, jolly and overweight souls. Due to similarities in character, both vices and virtues, the relationship is either excellent or a total disaster.

Taurus with Gemini	The Gemini's chameleon-like moods baffle the Bull. The Taurean's love of order and routine bore the Twin. Sparks are going to fly.
Taurus with Cancer	This relationship improves with the passing of time. Any tendency to bully on the Bull's part leads to the building of a wall of resentment. Hard work is needed for this relationship to work.
Taurus with Leo	The Leo wishes to be the centre of attraction and needs to dominate. The Bull cannot understand why and will not concede. Constant battles expected.
Taurus with Virgo	Both are practical and good with finances. The Bull likes attention, the Virgo is happy to give it. A good relationship.
Taurus with Libra	Both strive to develop the higher mind and all aspects of the arts – the only meeting ground so utilize it. This is all there is.
Taurus with Scorpio	These are opposites so there may be some balance, but this is a brittle relationship.
Taurus with Sagittarius	The Sagittarian can teach the Bull to widen his interests but the Taurean's loathing of change will be the biggest stumbling-block. A shaky relationship.
Taurus with Capricorn	The Goat is affected by outside stresses. The Bull can sense such tension and discuss it, thereby easing the burden. An excellent relationship.

Taurus with Aquarius

The Aquarian is unconventional and does not recognize superiors unless they have earned his or her respect. The Bull is conventional and usually obedient. An incompatible combination.

Taurus with Pisces

The Fish is adaptable and, to a point, willing to do the Bull's slightest bidding. But when the latter's stubbornness surfaces the Piscean quietly swims away, either mentally, physically or both. Mutual interests may help. A touchy relationship.

Gemini with Gemini

Both share characteristics. Ideas and interests are hard to keep up with. But . . . is anything ever concluded? A good relationship but hopefully one Geminian has some strength of purpose.

Gemini with Cancer

When the Gemini finally decides to rest, he/she may appreciate the quiet Crab. But when the Gemini is in a mood for action the Crab will bore. An up and down relationship.

Gemini with Leo

The Leo respects the Geminian's desire for individual freedom, but in return will demand constant praise and admiration which he/she may occasionally get . . . occasionally. A fairly good relationship.

Gemini with Virgo

Two active minds here, so intellectual rapport is assured. But that Virgoan tendency to nag, criticize and become bogged down in trivia will not be understood. A lively but hard-going relationship.

Gemini with Libra

The need for personal freedom is shared, as are the needs for an active social life and desire for constant change. An excellent relationship.

Gemini with Scorpio

The Scorpion rarely explains his or her feelings, the Gemini never stops. The two have little in common. A tense relationship.

Gemini with Sagittarius

Opposites, so a balance may be established. Mutual respect given, so with give and take peace can be retained.

Gemini with Capricorn

Two characters more dissimilar would be hard to find, but personalities can be made to complement each other. The relationship depends on the amount of work each is prepared to undertake.

Gemini with Aquarius

These two will agree on a constant change of friends and interests. Characters are complimentary. A good relationship.

Gemini with Pisces

Pisces has two sides, as does Gemini. Sometimes the two compatible ones surface, sometimes the two incompatible. An up and down relationship.

Cancer with Cancer

The intricate feelings of both could cause trouble, the occasions when desires coincide could be rare. Each will expect the other to adapt. A shaky relationship.

Cancer with Leo	The Leo likes to be the dominant force and can see no reason to give in just because the Crab is sensitive. A relationship filled with drama.
Cancer with Virgo	Complimentary characters, but petty quarrels could mar the harmony. An uneasy relationship.
Cancer with Libra	Although dissimilar, the Libran enjoys working at partnerships so there will be times when this one will work.
Cancer with Scorpio	The Crab admires the Scorpio's strength and is happy to be dominated. A good relationship.
Cancer with Sagittarius	If this relationship is to work, both need to enjoy fighting. Rows come in plenty. A wearing relationship.
Cancer with Capricorn	Opposites, therefore a balance may be achieved. The Crab is tenacious, the Goat determined. It is hoped these tendencies will be used constructively.
Cancer with Aquarius	The Crab is proud of his or her intuition, the Aquarian proud of his or her logic. A compromise is needed.
Cancer with Pisces	Both are imaginative, instinctive and intuitive. An understanding relationship should grow.

Leo with Leo	Identical personalities can work, but not when both are proud, dominating and attention seekers. Some moments of harmony, but trouble is never far off.
Leo with Virgo	The Virgo understands the Lion's need for the limelight but does not regard it as important and utilizes energies elsewhere. A tense relationship.
Leo with Libra	Basically compatible until the Lion wants to fight, for Librans will not indulge in confrontation of any description. A good but somewhat frustrating relationship.
Leo with Scorpio	The Lion's ego is too sensitive for the Scorpio tongue. A battling relationship.
Leo with Sagittarius	In this relationship the Leo has someone to give all of that warmth to, for the Sagittarian recognizes the value of this and gives in return. A good relationship.
Leo with Capricorn	Priorities differ and constant bickering is the result.
Leo with Aquarius	The Lion will believe that the Aquarian must be warm under that aloofness, but will be sadly disappointed.
Leo with Pisces	The Leo has constant fodder for the ego here until the Fish rebels. But compromise may be possible.
Virgo with Virgo	A mutual outlook on life will form a bond here, though peace will be regularly shattered by petty squabbles and fault-finding.

Virgo with Libra	The Libran is everything the Virgo would secretly like to be. The latter will try to emulate being ever ready to perfect himself/herself, but the slightest thing will throw this relationship off balance.
Virgo with Scorpio	The Virgo will be happy to be dominated, providing he or she feels the Scorpio is worthy of this, if not, expect all hell to break loose.
Virgo with Sagittarius	Virgo would also like to be more outgoing like Sagittarius, but the latter's tact will lead to jealousy. A fraught relationship.
Virgo with Capricorn	Both are sensible, practical and realistic, so this should be an easy-going relationship.
Virgo with Aquarius	Both are independent, but because of dissimilar characters they are in danger of drifting apart.
Virgo with Pisces	These are opposites who will have a struggle to find a compromise. The Fish likes to dream, the Virgoan is realistic. A difficult relationship.
Libra with Libra	Both share mutual characters. They will have fun but don't expect them to achieve much together. A decision-maker is needed.
Libra with Scorpio	An exhausting relationship. Both tend to burst with vitality and are over-demanding with loved-ones. Apart from this they have little in common.

Libra with Sagittarius	Both enjoy constant motion outside the home and may drift apart.
Libra with Capricorn	The Libran cannot understand the Goat's sober attitude to life. Develop mutual interests.
Libra with Aquarius	Two naturally compatible characters. A close relationship should develop.
Libra with Pisces	The Libran is kind but loses patience with the Fish's insecurities. An up and down bond.
Scorpio with Scorpio	These two have much in common, but who is boss? If this is established without a fight, then all will be well. But two strong fighters like this can only lead to trouble.
Scorpio with Sagittarius	The Scorpio may like the Sagittarius but will never understand him or her. Compromise is needed.
Scorpio with Capricorn	Both are determined, and if this determination can be channelled into mutual interests then the relationship may work, but it will not be easy.
Scorpio with Aquarius	Neither like to be thwarted, both are opinionated. Trouble in store. Peacemaker please?
Scorpio with Pisces	The Fish needs a strong character to lean on, and here he or she is. An excellent relationship.
Sagittarius with Sagittarius	Both love activity outside the home. If they ever meet they should get on.

Sagittarius with Capricorn	How can the optimistic Sagittarian and the pessimistic Goat be expected to reach compromise? Only with painful difficulty.
Sagittarius with Aquarius	Both love the outside world and have a million interests. If the latter coincide then a bond may form of great strength.
Sagittarius with Pisces	Strong fire (Sagittarius) and weak water (Pisces). Only result is steam. Much give and take needed.
Capricorn with Capricorn	Mutual characteristics make for understanding, but the going gets heavy when mutual depression strikes.
Capricorn with Aquarius	These two are very different, but if love is strong enough a bridge across differences may be built.
Capricorn with Pisces	The Goat likes responsibility, the Fish does not. This can be the basis of a good relationship.
Aquarius with Aquarius	Mutual characteristics and interests aid this relationship. But watch out when self-opinionated moods descend.
Aquarius with Pisces	The Water-bearer cannot understand such emotion and sentiment. The Fish in turn will decide the Aquarian is unfeeling. Compromise hard to find, unless a love of the arts is shared.
Pisces with Pisces	A loving, devoted and touching relationship. But don't expect decisions, this is an impossibility for both.

GOLDEN RULES FOR PARENTS

1. Never make promises unless you are sure you can keep them. This will lead to a lack of trust as well as disappointment.
2. Never lie to your child. They will later do the same to you. It will then be goodbye to mutual trust and respect.
3. Remember, a child should not do as you want him to out of fear. This simply indicates a parent too ignorant or lazy to try anything other than aggression.
4. Be his or her friend, but not contemporary. The latter is impossible and embarrassing for all concerned.
5. Never be too busy to listen, even if your talk must out of necessity be postponed until later in the day. Never let it be permanently delayed.
6. Remember that the child is an individual, not a little you or your partner. Your child has a right to his or her opinion and it doesn't have to be the same as yours.
7. Don't make a big deal out of sexual education. Teach it naturally and progressively over the years.
8. Don't patronize or laugh at your teenager.
9. Emotional and mental care are more important than a clean vest.
10. Respect their privacy. Never enter their rooms without knocking, or poke around in their belongings.
11. Teach them to respect you as an individual with a right to your own privacy and opinions.
12. Make as few big changes in their young lives as possible.
13. Let them know that you are always available when wanted. This creates security.
14. Never interfere. The child won't listen if he hasn't asked for your intervention.

15 Give the child responsibility at a young age. It helps to make him or her feel important and grown up and gets them used to it.

16 Never force a direction in life. You may want your daughter to be a ballerina, but a 12-stone 10-year-old just isn't going to make it! And besides . . . does she want to?

17 Give love and make all sacrifices without thought of getting something in return. Remember . . . your child will have to do the same for his or her own children one day. Those who give love freely get it without asking.

18 Show affection and control any embarrassment.

19 Sexual equality is important for both sons and daughters.

20 Equal domestic responsibility for both sons and daughters.

PSYCHIATRIST AND PSYCHOLOGIST

There are certain circumstances, which have been mentioned in each preceding chapter, in which a psychiatrist is advisable. In general, however, I tend to believe that such a move would make a child feel like something of a freak. He or she may even decide, in turn, that perhaps he or she should start to act like one! The exceptions to this have been covered.

From may own experience, and the experiences of others known to me, I know there is a role to be played by the psychologist. But only a minimal one. Psychologists have their role to play, especially when it comes to assessing your child. You don't have to wait until he goes through a difficult stage in life and ideally at the age of ten or eleven a visit to one of these eminent gentlemen is extremely helpful.

You may well discover that although your childs' chronological age is eleven, he may have an emotional age of eight. His chronological age may again be eleven, but its reading age may only be nine. And so on. Once you know these things in your child's development you can, of course, act accordingly and be more sympathetic. After all, if your child is still stumbling over five-letter words at the age of eleven, you may feel worried, not to mention neurotic. This is turn leads to pressure and tension applied to the child, whereas if you have discovered that the child has a reading ability of only an eight-year-old this information can prove to be an invaluable shot in the arm for your patience!

Further information that can be gleaned and put to use is the knowledge that your child is possibly creative, mathematically minded or mechanically so. This will give you good indications in which direction to encourage the child. There is, of course, one pitfall, as always. Naturally enough your psychologist will assess your child's intelligence. You may discover that the dummy you have reared has, in actual fact, the IQ of a genius. The child you believed to be well above average could turn out to have the IQ of a well-tended cabbage! The value of IQ tests is much debated and argued, and rightly so. After all, there is little point in knowing that your child has an IQ of 150 if he or she has little inclination or energy to use it. It is nice to bear in mind, but it shouldn't influence you in any way.

In my own opinion, the combination of one visit to a psychologist for assessment and another to an astrologer for character can do more good for your understanding of your offspring than a hundred visits to any psychiatrist. However, the parent should guard against becoming hooked on the psychologist's plush office and comforting presence. It will be all too easy to decide that little John or Mary needs at least one visit at least once a month. This is, I believe, taking things too far. One trip, two at the outside, should be sufficient.

SEX

This subject has been covered fully by many books. In fact, there are times when one seriously begins to doubt that the human race ever thinks of anything else!

Therefore, I have decided to treat this subject as briefly as possible.

Steering a middle way on this most important subject can sometimes prove difficult for many parents. They feel uncomfortable or embarrassed when discussing emotional and sexual needs. Others are so zealous that they tend to pump sex education into their children from the age of two onwards. I'm quite sure that these children are sick to death of the subject by the time they are 13. Or they are in such a state of expectation by the time they reach puberty that they are bound to be disappointed in their first experiments.

This is a natural side to life and should be treated as such. As a general rule the under-eights should be treated to a straightforward answer to every sexual question, without too much elaboration. From eight to twelve, when asked a question one could take the opportunity to fill in any information that was earlier neglected, such as masturbation. It is most important that this once taboo subject be treated with all honesty and without embarrassment. After all, the genitals are only a part of the body, like any other part. We all touch them whether we like to admit it or not! One should dispel all the old ideas. Simply explain the facts and leave it at that.

From 12 onwards it is necessary for your child to complete his or her sex education. But remember, copulation is only part of it. Sticking to the purely physical, it is important to explain homosexuality, rape, venereal disease and of course contraception.

I'm sure that eventually your offspring will discover the various positions, so I won't go into them, so to speak! And the possible deviations. However, all questions connected with either should be answered.

All too often sexual manuals lay down the facts and statistics for us all but neglect to mention the emotional needs of each individual. One cannot lay down strict rules and regulations to this side of human relationships. However, it is up to each parent to explain the importance of. a loving, caring relationship. Conversely, it is equally important to teach the difference between love and sex. Your child needs to understand that simply because sexual arousal is present it doesn't necessarily mean that one has fallen in love.

As always it is a case of steering a middle course. It is wrong to romanticize to the point of extreme, and it is equally wrong to reduce everything down to basics.

If you have made a good job of communication with your child, and hopefully this book will have been some use, you should not experience any problems when it comes to discussing the sexual side to life.

HEALTH

It is suggested that a doctor be summoned urgently for your child for any of the following reasons:

1 If there is any serious accident such as uncontrollable bleeding, a severe burn, scald or blow on the head, or if you suspect that your child has swallowed something like poison or a solid object such as a safety pin, etc.

2 If your child appears to have any difficulty breathing.

3 If your child shows symptoms of having a fit.

4 If the child has diarrhoea (watery stools) together with vomiting.

5 If the child has *any* severe pain anywhere.

6 If your baby shows no interest in feeds and lies unnaturally limp and quiet.

7 *If you cannot get hold of your own doctor in any emergency, take the child as quickly as possible to the nearest casualty hospital department.*

If you think that your child has swallowed something that could be poisonous, here's what you should do:

1 *Keep calm.* Poisoning is seldom a matter of seconds or even minutes.

2 *Do not* try to make the child vomit.

3 Telephone your doctor or take the child to the nearest hospital and explain fully your suspicions.

INFECTIOUS ILLNESSES

Chicken Pox

The child may be fretful for some time before any spots appear.

The spots are separate with a head to them and they itch, blister, then the scabs fall off after drying. Try not to scratch the scabs or pick them off for fear of scarring. Calamine lotion is safe and soothing. Chicken pox is infectious for two days before the spots appear until at least a week from the onset. It might give an adult shingles. It comes out 10-21 days from contact with an infectious person.

German Measles (Rubella)*

The child may be mildly off-colour with cold symptoms and swollen glands behind the ears. A rash then develops, red like small pinheads. This may be slight and short lived. The child should avoid women who may be in the first four months of pregnancy. The illness is infectious from its onset to the end of the rash and it comes out 2-3 weeks after contact.

Measles*

The symptoms are a cold, cough, runny nose, water or pink eyes and a raised temperature. Spots appear which run into each other in a red rash, usually starting on the forehead and chest. The child should avoid bright lights if the eyes are affected and convulsions or earache should be reported to your doctor. The illness is infectious from the onset of the cold until one week after the rash. Measles comes out 10-15 days after contact with an infectious person.

Mumps

There may be a raised temperature. The child will be off-colour with general aches and pains. This is followed by a painful swelling under the jaw on one or both sides and it hurts to open the mouth. The child should be kept away from all males over 11 years who haven't had this illness. Mumps are infectious three weeks from the onset and it comes out 14-21 days after contact.

Scarlet Fever

The child will have a sore throat, headaches, raised temperature and vomiting. A bright red rash follows one to three days later. The illness is infectious up to two weeks after its onset. It comes out 2-4 days after contact.

Whooping Cough (Pertussis)*

There is a cough or cold for several days, then spasms of coughing and vomiting. The cough is distressing to hear. The illness is infectious for five weeks after the onset of the characteristic 'whooping' cough. It comes out 7-14 days after contact.

* *Protection is available against these diseases*

TEETHING

Many babies cut their teeth with no trouble at all, some make hard work of it. Still others pick up infections at the same time they are cutting their teeth. If gums look inflamed, don't press solids or a cup, let baby have plenty to drink in the bottle. Teething gell is helpful and can give temporary relief. There is no point in worrying whether your baby is early or late in teething – there are no special rules. If teething is accompanied by raised temperature, diarrhoea, convulsions or any other unusual sign, your child has probably developed an infection and you should consult your doctor.

There are twenty teeth in the first set of baby teeth, but while the bottom front teeth usually appear first, again your baby will have his or her own way of doing things. The first generally appear sometime in the first year, sometimes as early as four months, but often a lot later. All are usually through by the time the child is two and a half.

The first trip to the dentist is advised when the child is two, even if it is only to quickly open and shut the mouth. The important thing is for the child to get used to the atmosphere and the strange face.

QUIZ ANSWERS

When reading the below do bear in mind that nobody is all good (Dr Jekyll) nor all bad (Mr Hyde). Most of us are a mixture of both. Once you have completed the quiz you will have a better idea of just how much vice or virtue your child possesses, and how negative or positive he or she may be. If he, or she, is not typical of the birth sign, you should read the Introduction in order to find out why.

CAPRICORN

1–30

That little angel of yours could not possibly be a hundred per-cent Capricorn. He or she is far too extrovert and relaxed and fun-loving. You are far more likely to find this "Goat" described under the chapters devoted to Sagittarius or Aquarius.

31–50

This score indicates that you have a Capricorn of the Dr Jekyll variety. This means that your child has inherited most of the nicer qualities associated with this sign without too many of the unpleasant ones. However, this type will tend to be a little serious and reserved, so see what you can do to help develop a sense of humour. It will help in later lite.

51–60

This score indicates that there is more of Mr Hyde in your child's personality. Therefore the faults associated with this sign will be very much to the fore of his or her character. Later on this child could have a melancholic or depressive effect on those around. Try to keep this little Hyde busy and maybe he will forget to shoulder the problems of the world.

AQUARIUS

1–30

This particular score proves that your child is not a true Aquarian. He is far too emotional and sensitive. It is quite likely that several of the child's planets are in Pisces, so read that section. Don't try to make the child fit the typical Aquarian image.

31–50

This is the score of the typical Dr Jekyll Aquarian, which means that the better qualities of this sign apply to your child. However, although there may be one or two of the more unpleasant traits, in general the section on Mr Hyde will not apply. Later, too little warmth could be a flaw in the personality so try to encourage warmth.

51–60

This is the score of the true Mr Hyde Aquarian. This little person has most of the faults associated with the sign, but fortunately even a bad Aquarian isn't that awful. Parents may be able to learn something about this individual's weaknesses by reading carefully through the section on Mr Hyde.

PISCES

1–30

This child possesses too much common sense, logic and realism to be a true Pisean. Your answers seem to indicate that there is a great deal of Aquarius lurking there somewhere. Read that chapter and you could learn quite a lot.

31–50

This score would suggest that you possess a true member of this sign, one of the Dr Jekyll variety. Fortunately this means that he or she possesses most of the virtues of the sign and not many of the vices. Nevertheless, he or she is likely to be too easily influenced by others. Try to teach self-reliance and decision.

51–60

This is the score of a true Piscean of the Mr Hyde variety. This makes your child overly sensitive and possibly a rather weak individual. That vivid imagination is going to lead him or her into a series of problems unless you can teach this character to put those feet firmly on the ground in every way possible.

ARIES

1–30

Although your child may have some Arietian tendencies, they are certainly well hidden. Read the chapter devoted to Pisces; it may be more helpful.

31–50

This is the score of the higher Arietian, the Dr Jekyll. Your child is lucky enough to have most of the virtues of this sign and few of the vices. This little Ram is a strong person and knows exactly what he or she wants from life and can obtain it without hurting others. Perhaps he or she should focus a little more attention to the private side to life rather than to the professional and chasing ambitions.

51–60

This is the score of a true blue Arietian, for both good and evil. It might be a good idea to read the section on Mr Hyde. Most of the pitfalls in this child's character are written in this section. This may help you to recognize and accept them and also to do something about them. This child's strong 'me first' attitude could eventually lead to loneliness.

TAURUS

1–30

There is obviously some Taurean in your child but hardly enough to qualify for this sign. He or she is far too adaptable and gregarious. If you read Aries you may find a better character analysis there.

31–50

This is the score of the typical Taurean. This is the type who will like life to be relatively uncluttered and uncomplicated. He or she may possess one or two of the nastier characteristics described, but for the most part this is the score of a Jekyll.

51–60

All of the Taurean chapter should apply to this child, including the section devoted to Mr Hyde. You'll have to teach this child to control a stubborn streak, for in this way improvement is possible which may lead to a happier life than he or she would otherwise find.

GEMINI

1–30

Gemini appears to have left little trace on your child. He or she is far too conservative and stable. This would seem to indicate the presence of an earth sign. Try reading either Virgo or Taurus, but don't try to make the child fit the characteristics for they should be quite obvious.

31–50

This is the typical Dr Jekyll Gemini, which means that although your child may at times be considered a little highly strung he or she is in fact versatile and adaptable. It may be impossible to improve this Gemini, unless you can help him or her to conquer bad concentration, and teach it to delve a little deeper into the many things that come under his or her wandering gaze.

51–60

This is a drifter. A jack-of-all-trades will be the phrase constantly used when referring to your child. This is a typical Gemini for both good and bad and the parent would be well advised to read the section devoted to the Mr Hyde character. Attempt to iron out one or two of the faults before this particular Gemini gets too old.

CANCER

1–30

Your child is far too resilient, independent and uninhibited to be a true Cancer. No doubt one or two of the characteristics may fit nicely, but basically there is a stronger influence. Try reading the Gemini chapter; it may be more useful.

31–50

It sounds as if your child is a typical Cancer, of the Dr Jekyll variety! Unfortunately this sign is a sensitive one and life must seem hard at times to your little Crab. Try to encourage wide horizons and a more resilient attitude to life. Above all else, give lots of love.

51–60

This is also the score of the Cancer, but your little Crab would seem to be more of the Mr Hyde variety. This type will need careful guidance, otherwise he could develop unhealthy mental attitudes. Persecution complexes will be easily assumed and will need to be controlled. Keep the child's head constantly active and you may be able to steer him away from the more morbid moods that would otherwise threaten.

LEO

1–30

This is not the score of the Leonine child although you would be well advised to cultivate some of this sign's warmth and generosity. I suspect you'll find more about your particular Cub under the section devoted to Virgo.

31–50

This is the score of the true Leo (Dr Jekyll) with all the generosity and depth of feeling given to this sign. You'll need to accept the fact that this Leo will always be a leader rather than a follower and encourage consideration for others.

51–60

This score belongs to the Mr Hyde Leo, which means that the big heart of this sign is mostly interested in his own desires. You'll need to teach financial common sense and the value of other human beings. However, even a bad Leo cannot be all bad, so take heart!

VIRGO

1–30

This is definitely not the score of the typical Virgoan. The child is too relaxed, gregarious and carefree. I suggest that you read the sign of Leo or Libra. But don't try to make these sections fit; your child should slot in with ease.

31–50

This is the score of a true Virgoan, basically of the Dr Jekyll type. Although he or she may have many fine qualities it is possible that the child will miss out on a lot of fun unless you can teach relaxation and the ability to take life less seriously. If your Virgoan can learn to accept others for what they are without wishing to make changes in them, then his life will be much happier.

51–60

This is the score of the Mr Hyde Virgo. And isn't he a difficult child to live with? This type will lose many friends and lovers if he or she cannot learn to overcome his or her critical streak on occasions. Read the Mr Hyde section once more and try to see where you can help this rather difficult personality.

LIBRA

1–30

This score is representative of a person too logical, down to earth and conservative to be truly Libran. Try reading the sections on Virgo or Taurus, even Capricorn. Do not make your child fit any of these sections but be truthful and you may find them very useful.

31–50

This score places the child in the Dr Jekyll group of Librans, giving the child many of the good points of the Libran and bypassing many of its faults. However, the biggest flaw in the child's personality is sure to be his overwhelming tendency to go along with other people's ideas for fear of hurting their feelings. Try to encourage this child to have the courage of his or her convictions.

51–60

Unfortunately this is the score of Mr Hyde Libra. Here the child will possess many of the faults of this sign and only a little of the virtues. You may find that the child tries to live his or her life totally in a world of fantasy and make-believe. Although this child will have many of the faults of Libra he will still have much of the charm given to this sign and should be quite a happy individual. Try to correct the weaknesses specified in the Mr Hyde section and the child should benefit greatly.

SCORPIO

1–30

Your Scorpion will undoubtedly possess one or two of these Scorpio tendencies, but generally speaking he is far too adaptable, independent and easy-going to be a true member of this sign. I suggest you might recognize him more effectively under Libra or possibly Sagittarius.

31–50

Life can be difficult for a true Scorpion, which this child is. However, in his case the general characteristics associated with this sign are softened, making him more of a Mr Hyde than a Dr Jekyll. However, jealousy could be a weak spot, one that may cause plenty of suffering in life, although this too may soften with maturity.

51–60

This is the score of the Mr Hyde Scorpio which is not altogether fortunate. Those with too many of the negative traits can be rather difficult to live with. Their critical and suspicious outlook will make them unpopular. If this control is not exercised they may finish up lonely and bitter. Do help your child to make allowances for the weaknesses of others. After all . . . none of us is perfect, and that certainly includes himself.

SAGITTARIUS

1–30

Your child is much too affectionate and stubborn to be a true Sagittarian. His or her whole attitude to life would seem to fit more readily into the sign of Scorpio or possibly Capricorn. I suggest you read these sections to find our more about your child.

31–50

Sagittarians tend to have the type of personality that draws others to them. This child is more of a Dr Jekyll than a Mr Hyde and this means that he possesses more of the good points than the bad of this sign. However, a sense of loyalty is liable to be absent from the make-up and this is a weak point that parents should try to improve.

51–60

This score belongs to Mr Hyde. Your child is probably gay and charming, but is likely to be a bit of a disaster where other people are concerned. He or she will need to be taught sincerity, loyalty and to be more steadfast. Read the section of Mr Hyde once more; it may help you to get your child over these weaknesses.